A HISTORY OF THE CONCEPT OF GOD

A HISTORY OF THE CONCEPT OF GOD

A PROCESS APPROACH

DANIEL A. DOMBROWSKI

Published by State University of New York Press, Albany

Production, Ryan Morris
Marketing, Anne M. Valentine

Library of Congress Cataloging in Publication Data

Dombrowski, Daniel A.
  A history of the concept of God : a process approach / Daniel A. Dombrowski.
    pages cm
  Includes bibliographical references and index.
  ISBN 978-1-4384-5937-0 (hc : alk. paper)—978-1-4384-5936-3 (pb : alk. paper)
  ISBN 978-1-4384-5938-7 (e-book)
  1. God—History of doctrines. 1. Title.
  BT98.D566 2016
  211.09—dc23

2015008207

10 9 8 7 6 5 4 3 2 1

Contents

Introduction

Literary critics are much more likely than philosophers, theologians, or religious studies scholars to talk about "genre" or a particular type of writing that admits of many different instances. No one objects when a new novel is written or when a new murder mystery appears. A rich genre has appeared relatively recently in philosophy of religion, systematic theology, or religious studies that is worthy of note and that admits of several additional instantiations: the history of God.

At least three works illustrate the type of writing I have in mind. First is the *New York Times* bestseller by Karen Armstrong, *A History of God: The 4,000 Year Quest of Judaism, Christianity, and Islam* (1993). This book was followed by the richly illustrated and sprawling work by John Bowker, *God: A Brief History* (2002), and the concise work by Paul Capetz also titled *God: A Brief History* (2003), where the subtitle makes much more sense. I love all three works, but for quite different reasons, as I will show. Much more needs to be said in this genre however. Some books appear to be in this genre, but are not. One book, *The Evolution of God*, appears to be in it, but it deals only tangentially with the history of the concept of God and is more concerned with the evolution of religious belief and the question of why people have believed in God at all (see Wright 2009).

The present work makes a scholarly contribution in this genre from the perspective of neoclassical or process theism. Although the authors of the above works mention process thinkers such as Alfred North Whitehead, Charles Hartshorne, Pierre Teilhard de Chardin, Daniel Day Williams, and John Cobb, there is no explicit treatment of the history of the concept of God as interpreted by process thinkers. In fact, although all three authors tantalize the reader by implying some sort of admiration for neoclassical or process theism, they nonetheless interpret the history of the concept of God in ways that are very much at odds with neoclassical or process theism. That is, despite the considerable strengths of these three books, they are all overly influenced by the tradition of classical theism. This book is an attempt to supplement the works of Armstrong, Bowker, and Capetz from a neoclassical or process point of view.

The book deals primarily with the concept of God and not necessarily with the existence of God. When I do discuss the existence of God, it is to illuminate some aspect of the concept of God. The hope is that the subject matter of the book will be of interest to those who are curious about this concept, whether they be theist, agnostic, or atheist.

A sense of urgency lies behind this book. As I see things, philosophical theism is at a crisis stage wherein two competing forces are at work: continued defenses of classical or traditional theism (described in detail in part 1) that are, on my interpretation, doomed to failure, on the one hand, and equally unpersuasive defenses of religious skepticism, whether atheistic or agnostic, on the other. Neoclassical or process theists try to drive a wedge between these two forces and are thereby likely to receive ire from both sides. Classical theists tend to be intellectual conservatives who are distrustful of any neoclassical or process innovation in the concept of God and religious skeptics tend to view neoclassical or process theism as a warmed over leftover from a bygone era. Although it will sound hyperbolic to religious skeptics to put the issue in the following manner, I think that Hartshorne does not in the least exaggerate when he claims that: "The theistic question . . . is not one more question, even the most important one. It is, on the fundamental level, and when all its implications are taken into account, the sole question" (Hartshorne 1962, 131). Or again, "philosophy's most important function . . . is to clarify the religious question" (Hartshorne 1965, 24). In due course I will try to deliver on these promissory notes.

This book resists both of the types of opposition mentioned and indicates the historical roots of the contemporary impasse. To put my thesis succinctly, if philosophical theism is to have a viable future (which is by no means guaranteed given the popularity of both the old and the new atheisms), it must retrace its steps in the past to see where it went wrong. If this judgment also seems hyperbolic, it is nonetheless important to note that Whitehead shared it decades ago, and he is reported to have said that the classical concept of God that has historically supported Christianity (as well as Judaism and Islam) is "one of the great disasters of the human race" (Whitehead 2001, 171). One could have legitimately expected so much more from it.

To cite just one preliminary example, if God is truly *omni*potent, as classical theists in the Abrahamic religions (Judaism, Christianity, Islam) attest, then there is no avoiding the conclusion that a mother who gives birth to an infant with an intensely painful deformity can be told (or, more accurately, should be told) that such a tragedy is either sent by, or at least permitted by, God. We can do better, I think. Indeed, we have to do better if philosophical theism is to flourish in that thinking people increasingly notice that the emperor of classical theism has no clothes.

The history offered herein is obviously not intended to be comprehensive so as to cover everything that has been said about the concept of God. Like Armstrong, Bowker, and Capetz, I offer a selective history, but my principles of selection differ from theirs. The major tension in the book involves the similarities and differences between classical theism and neoclassical or process theism. These three authors tend to assume that the legacy of the ancient Greeks for philosophical theism is the idea that, because God is (by definition) perfect, God could not change because to change would indicate a need to transition out of a less than perfect condition.

Granted, this caricature of the influence of Greek philosophy on philosophical theism captures part of the story that I will tell, but this story is much more complex than has been told to date. Whitehead is famous for his quip that "the safest general characterization of the European philosophical tradition is that it consists of a series of footnotes to Plato" (Whitehead [1929] 1978, 39). In no area is this claim more accurate than in the concept of God. A key part of this book is Plato's role in inadvertently influencing both classical theism and its neoclassical or process alternative in all three Abrahamic religions; hence the present history of the concept of God is broadly ecumenical.

Part 1, "Classical Theism," details exactly what I mean by "classical theism" as it developed chronologically in nine philosophers in various periods in the histories of the Abrahamic religions. Part 2, "Ancient Greek Philosophy," retraces the first part so as to examine three ancient Greek philosophers, Plato, Aristotle, and Plotinus, to show the historical origins of both the insights and the mistakes of classical theists. Part 3, "Neoclassical or Process Theism," examines chronologically various neoclassical or process theists from religions in the modern period through the mid-twentieth century, at which point I stop so that the history offered does not spill over into contemporary thought, defined roughly as that which has occupied philosophers and theologians and religious studies scholars in the late twentieth and early twenty-first centuries. Part 4, "Henri Bergson and Alfred North Whitehead," examines the thought of Bergson and Whitehead, who are, along with Hartshorne, the greatest neoclassical or process theists.

The thinkers in parts 3 and 4 offer the most defensible concept of God and the one that is most likely to lead to progress in philosophy of religion and theology in the future. Once again, like the works by Armstrong, Bowker, and Capetz, this work is a selective history, but my selectivity is such that I concentrate on the debate between classical theism and neoclassical or process theism.

In order to manage readers' expectations, I should mention four areas that this book does not concern. First, I do not address in any detail versions of the concept of God that are strictly temporal or strictly finite. This means that I will not be treating the concept of God as found in very interesting thinkers such as William James, Samuel Alexander, Edgar Brightman, Henry Nelson Wieman, and others. Second, I do not say much about pantheistic versions of the concept of God, and hence I do not devote much time to discuss influential pantheistic thinkers such as the Stoics, Baruch Spinoza, Sankara, and others. My assumption is that the debate between classical theism and neoclassical or process theism is a crucial one that involves most of the thinkers who have contributed most significantly to the development of the concept of God and who have influenced most heavily the concept of God operative in the Abrahamic religions. Third, I avoid certain theists (such as G. W. F. Hegel) who seem impossible to classify, appearing at times to be classical theists and at other times seeming to be process theists or pantheists (see Lucas 1986). And fourth, I do not treat the concept of God as it has developed in South Asian thinkers in Hinduism or thinkers in various East Asian religions. As with finite theism, pantheism, and Hegel, my reticence is primarily due to space limitations. That is, the debate between classical theists and neoclassical or process theists, as well as the historical background to this debate found in ancient Greek philosophy, is enough to warrant a whole book.

Regarding the concept of God in South Asian and East Asian thinkers, however, my reticence is also due to a lack of competence on my part. This should not be interpreted to mean that I think the thinkers I have omitted are not worthy of consideration. To the contrary: I suspect that an analysis of the history of the concept of God would be enhanced significantly by a consideration of both classical South Asian and East Asian thinkers (such as Ramanuja and others) as well as by a consideration of several more recent South Asian and East Asian thinkers in the early to middecades of the twentieth century (such as Radhadrishnan and others). The focused nature of this history in no way denies the deep links among several religious traditions worldwide, such as in the analogies among Whitehead's creativity, the necessary existence of God in Hartshorne, and Buddhist *sunyatta* or the unborn and ungenerated.

Throughout the work I am heavily indebted to Hartshorne and his implicit history of the concept of God, which surprisingly comes closest to explicit statement in an anthology he edited with William Reese, *Philosophers Speak of God* (Hartshorne 2000; this work was originally published in 1953 by the University of Chicago Press). I think this is truly a great book. In fact, the present book can be seen as an updated version of *Philosophers Speak of God* for the purposes of the largely neglected contribution it could make to the contemporary history of God genre. Like Hartshorne, I think that "process theism" is better labeled "neoclassical theism" to highlight the ideas that it is both "neo" and "classical," with the former term indicating the obvious innovation found in the concept of God process theists defend and the latter term indicating the fact that such innovation is paradoxically or oxymoronically rooted in ancient and medieval sources. The etymology of the word "radical" captures well both the forwardlooking innovation of process theism as well as its rootedness in the past in that the Latin *radix* originally meant "root."

Josiah Royce put the point I am trying to make well when he said: "Whenever I have most carefully revised my . . . standards, I am always able to see . . . that at best I have been finding out, in some new light, the true meaning that was latent in old traditions. . . . Revision does not mean mere destruction. . . . Let us bury the natural body of tradition. What we want is its glorified body and its immortal soul" (Royce 1908, 11). I must emphasize, however, that the history offered herein is not a piece of antiquarian lore; I move forward in light of the historically sedimented concept of God that is part of the inheritance of the Abrahamic religions. That is, the neoclassical theism I defend is as much "neo" as it is "classical" (see Pundt 1989, 8). Only by first going backward can we find a longterm, meaningful way forward regarding the concept of God. Furthermore, I do not examine any thinkers who are still living in that one somewhat useful operational way to distinguish between thinkers who are historical and those who are contemporary is to say that only the latter are alive. As the title of this book indicates, I am interested in the history of the concept of God up to the midtwentieth century. Many other books have already picked up where I end.

One recent work aims to update Hartshorne's *Philosophers Speak of God*, a valuable anthology edited by Jeanine Diller and Asa Kasher titled *Models of God and Alternative Ultimate Realities* (2013). But the dissimilarities are greater than the similarities between the two books, as I see things, for three reasons: (1) there is no overall perspective in the Diller and Kasher volume, as there is in the Hartshorne volume wherein neoclassical theism is defended; (2) the Hartshorne book is primarily historical, whereas only a portion of the articles in the Diller and Kasher volume deals with the history of the concept of God; and (3) a much greater portion of the Diller and Kasher volume deals with gods rather than God, nontheistic versions of ultimate realities, and world religions outside of the Abrahamic traditions. The Diller and Kasher volume has genuine virtues, but it is different in aim from the Hartshorne book. In any event, I engage, both positively and negatively, with the authors in the Diller and Kasher volume when it is instructive to do so.

For example, an article by Donald Viney in the Diller and Kasher anthology is truly magisterial. On his view, classical theism is "relativized" when it is seen that there are alternative versions of theism that are available for reflective scholars. Furthermore, this has implications for agnosticism and atheism, as Viney argues: "The question 'Does God exist?' is at best *vague* (if one hasn't a clear vision of the alternatives) and at worst *loaded* (if one actually privileges one concept of God or one mode of theological discourse). If there are many forms of theism, it follows that there are many forms of atheism—as many as there are forms of theism to deny. . . . Theology may then prove to be as dynamic as the God in whom Charles Hartshorne believed" (Viney 2013b, 77). It also holds that there are many forms of agnosticism, as many as there are forms of theism and atheism with which to withhold assent.

Viney alerts us to many of the themes to be developed in the present history: that it is a caricature of neoclassical or process theism to say that it points to an imperfect God; that it is a mistake to equate theism with supernaturalism; that the question "Does God exist?" presupposes the question "What do you mean by 'God'?"; and that one ignores the neoclassical or process Copernican shift in the concept of God at one's peril (Viney 2013b).

One other introductory point is needed. In addition to being a work in defense of neoclassical or process theism, this book is also an exercise in perfect being theology or perfect being philosophy of religion. This is the view that what should drive discourse regarding God is clarification of the concept of a perfect being. Of course the most famous exercise in this type of thinking is St. Anselm's ontological argument, which is arguably the most discussed argument in the history of philosophy over the past 1,000 years (see Dombrowski 2006). Indeed, Anselm can be seen as the founder of perfect being theology or philosophy of religion. I take it that "perfect" and "greatest conceivable" and "best possible" and "most worshipful," and so forth, have a family resemblance to each other and any differences among these and related locutions need not bother us here. The key point is that if there is a God, this divinity would be the perfect being of perfect being theology or philosophy of religion. As Katherin Rogers puts the point, "the reasons for believing that God must be a best possible or perfect being are closely related to the reasons for believing that there is a God at all" (Rogers 2000, 4).

However, there are competing versions of what "perfect being" means. In fact, two dominate this history of the concept of God: the classical or traditional theistic concept of a perfect being as static, as found in Anselm, Rogers, and many others, on the one hand, and the neoclassical or process concept of a perfect being as dynamic, on the other. This debate helps shape the history of the concept of God I offer. From what I have said already, however, it can be legitimately inferred that I feel a certain kinship to perfect being thinkers even if they are classical or traditional theists in that perfect being theology or philosophy of religion is more likely to enable us to make progress regarding the concept of God than other types of theology or philosophy of religion, such as those who concentrate on orthodoxy ("correct" doctrine) or orthopraxy ("correct" practice).

Part 1

Classical Theism

At the outset I would like to make clear that by "classical theism" I refer to a view of God in philosophy and theology, not to biblical or scriptural theism. (Throughout the book I explore the question whether classical theism or neoclassical theism does a better job of preserving the best insights regarding the concept of God found in the Bible.) This view involves at least the following five features:

1. Omnipotence (including the related claim that God created the world out of absolute nothingness).
2. Omniscience (in the sense of God knowing, with absolute assurance and in minute detail, everything that will happen in the future).
3. Omnibenevolence.
4. Eternity (in the sense not of God existing throughout all of time, but rather of God existing outside of time altogether).
5. Monopolarity (to be described momentarily).

Part 1 examines, in chronological order, nine important classical theists who exhibit these five characteristics in their concept of God. I start with the first classical theist, Philo, and end with Immanuel Kant. In addition to explicating the concept of God found in these thinkers, I critique classical theism so that readers get a sense of exactly what the problems are with the classical theistic concept of God. Once again, I offer a selective history that not only does not examine every classical theist, but it also does not even examine the bulk of the work in the classical theists considered. However, with the above five features as guides, I explore the crucial philosophical features of some key classical theists both to understand their concept of God and to pave the way toward a more defensible stance.

1

Philo

(30 BCE–50 CE)

Given the five features outlined in the previous introduction, it makes sense to claim that the first classical theist was Philo, who was a Jew in the first centuries of both eras who philosophized in Alexandria in Egypt. Philo is noteworthy because he was apparently the first thinker to philosophize about God, so as to reach the conclusion that the concept of God involved the above five features, including belief in divine omnipotence, even if Philo did not quite subscribe to creation *ex nihilo* (see May 1994), *and* to assume (perhaps erroneously) that this concept of God was an abstract version of the God found in the Bible.

Philo defends a version of the argument from design for the existence of God in which the regularity and order of the workings of nature are evidence of the existence of a divine creator. Although Philo has a very strong apophatic sense (from the Greek *apophatikos* for negativity) of what cannot be said about God, he is like most negative theologians in being profuse in what he does say kataphatically (from the Greek *kataphatikos* for positivity): God is unchangeable, outside of time, creator of time, uncreated, utterly simple, unified, self-sufficient, immovable, omniscient, necessarily existent, passionless, not in space, cause of all, and omnipresent. Quite a list for someone who thinks that we cannot know God! The lesson here is that we ought not to take at face value the alleged humility of apophatic thinkers regarding what they claim not to say about God (Hartshorne 2000, 77–81; also see Philo's "On the Unchangeableness of God" and other works, vol. 3).

One way to organize Philo's (and other classical theists') litany of divine attributes is in terms of the concept of monopolarity. Let us assume for the moment that God exists. What attributes does God

possess? Imagine two columns of attributes in polar contrast to each
other:

one	many
being	becoming
activity	passivity
permanence	change
necessity	contingency
self-sufficient	dependent
actual	potential
absolute	relative
abstract	concrete

Philo's classical theism tends toward oversimplification. It is compar-
atively easy to say, "God is strong rather than weak, so in all relations
God is active, not passive." In each case, classical theists such as Philo
decide which member of the contrasting pair is good (on the left), then
attributes it to God, while wholly denying the contrasting term (on the
right). This leads to what Hartshorne calls the monopolar prejudice
(Hartshorne 2000, 1–25).

Importantly, monopolarity is common to both classical theism and
pantheism, with the major difference between the two being the fact
that classical theists admit the reality of plurality, potentiality, and
becoming as a secondary form of existence "outside" God (on the right),
whereas in pantheism reality is identified with God. Common to both
classical theism and pantheism is the idea that the categorical contrasts
listed above are invidious. The dilemma these two positions face is that
either deity is only one constituent of the whole (classical theism) or
else the alleged inferior pole in each contrast (on the right) is illusory
(pantheism).

This dilemma is artificial, however, produced by the assumption that
excellence is found by separating and purifying one pole (on the left)
and denigrating the other (on the right). That this is not the case can
be seen by analyzing some of the attributes in the right column. Classical theists are convinced that God's eternity does not mean that God
endures through all time. Rather, on the classical theistic view, God is
outside of time altogether, and is not, indeed cannot be, receptive to
temporal change. Many classical theists follow Aristotle (who, as we

will see, is the greatest predecessor to classical theism) in identifying God as unmoved. Yet both activity and passivity can be either good or bad. Good passivity is likely to be called sensitivity, responsiveness, adaptability, sympathy, and the like. Insufficiently subtle or defective passivity is called wooden inflexibility, mulish stubbornness, inadaptability, unresponsiveness, and the like. Passivity per se refers to the way in which an individual's activity takes account of, and renders itself appropriate to, the activities of others. To deny God passivity altogether is to deny God those aspects of passivity that are excellences. Or, put another way, to altogether deny God the ability to change does avoid fickleness, but at the expense of the ability to lovingly react to the sufferings of others.

The terms on the left side also have both good and bad aspects. Oneness can mean wholeness, but also it can mean monotony or triviality. Actuality can mean definiteness or it can mean nonrelatedness to others. What happens to divine love when God is claimed to be pure actuality? God ends up loving the world, but is not intrinsically related to it, whatever sort of love that may be. Self-sufficiency can, at times, be selfishness.

Hence in each pair of polar contrasts we should diagram the divine attributes not the way the classical theist does so:

(good) permanence   (bad) change

But rather in the following manner:

being   becoming
(good)   (good)
(bad)   (bad)

The task when thinking of God is to attribute to God all excellences (left and right sides) and not to attribute to God any inferiorities (right and left sides). In short, excellent-inferior, knowledge-ignorance, or good-evil are invidious contrasts, and hence they ought not to be predicated of God, who, by definition, is the greatest conceivable. But one-many, being-becoming, activity-passivity, permanence-change, and the like are non-invidious contrasts. Evil is not a category, and hence it cannot be attributed to God. It is not a category because it is not universal; and it is not universal because subhuman reality cannot commit it; even if it can be its victims. That is, both animals and God may very well feel evil but they cannot commit it, God because of the supreme goodness of the divine nature, animals because of their ignorance of moral principles.

Within each pole of a noninvidious contrast (for example, permanence-change) are not only invidious or injurious elements (inferior permanence or inferior change), but also noninvidious, good elements (excellent permanence or excellent change). The neoclassical, dipolar, process theist does not believe in two gods, one unified and the other plural. Rather, the process theist believes that what are often thought to be contradictories are really mutually interdependent correlatives, as Hartshorne indicates: "The good as we know it is unity-in-variety or variety-in-unity; if the variety overbalances, we have chaos or discord; if the unity, we have monotony or triviality" (Hartshorne 2000, 3).

Supreme excellence, to be truly so, must somehow be able to integrate all the complexity there is in the world into itself as one spiritual whole. The word "must" indicates divine necessity, along with God's essence, which is to necessarily exist. The word "complexity" indicates the contingency that affects God through decisions creatures make. In the classical theistic view, however, God is identified solely with the stony immobility of the absolute, implying nonrelatedness to the world. God's abstract nature, God's being, may in a way escape from the temporal flux, but a living God is related to the world of becoming, which entails a divine becoming as well if the world in some way is internally related to God. The classical theist's alternative to this view suggests that all relationships to God are external to divinity, once again threatening not only God's love, but also God's nobility. A dog's being behind a particular rock affects the dog in certain ways; thus this relation is an internal relation to the dog, but it does not affect the rock, whose relationship with the dog is external to the rock's nature. Does this not show the superiority of canine consciousness, which is aware of the rock, to rocklike existence, which is unaware of the dog? Is it not therefore peculiar that God has been described solely in rocklike terms: pure actuality, permanence, having only external relations, unmoved, being and not becoming?

One may wonder at this point why classical theism has been so popular among philosophical theists when it has so many defects. There are at least four reasons. First, it is simpler to accept monopolarity than dipolarity. That is, it is simpler to accept one and reject the other of contrasting (or better, correlative, noninvidious) categories than to show how each, in its own appropriate fashion, applies to an aspect of the divine nature. Yet the simplicity of calling God "the absolute" can come back to haunt the classical theist if absoluteness precludes relativity in the sense of internal relatedness to the world.

Second, if the decision to accept monopolarity has been made, identifying God as the absolute is easier than identifying God as the most relative. Yet this does not deny divine relatedness, nor does it deny that God, who loves all, would therefore have to be related to all, or, to use a roughly synonymous word, be relative to all. God may well be the most relative of all as well as the most absolute of all, in the senses that, and to the extent that, both of these are excellences. Of course, God is absolute and relative in different aspects of the divine nature.

Third, there are emotional considerations favoring divine permanence, as found in the longing to escape the risks and uncertainties of life (see Plato's *Seventh Letter* 325d–326b). Yet even if these considerations obtain, they should not blind us to other emotional considerations, like those that give us the solace that comes from knowing that the outcome of our sufferings and volitions makes a difference in the divine life, which, if it is all-loving, would not be unmoved by the sufferings of creatures.

And fourth, monopolarity is seen as more easily compatible with monotheism. But the innocent monotheistic contrast between the one and the many deals with God as an individual, not with the dogmatic claim that the divine individual cannot have parts or aspects of relatedness with the world.

In short, the divine being becomes, or the divine becoming is. God's being and becoming form a single reality, and there is no reason that we must leave the two poles in a paradoxical state. As Hartshorne puts the point: "There is no law of logic against attributing contrasting predicates to the same individual, provided they apply to diverse aspects of this individual" (Hartshorne 2000, 14–15). The remedy for "ontolatry," the worship of being, is not the contrary pole, "gignolatry," the worship of becoming: "God is neither being as contrasted to becoming nor becoming as contrasted to being; but categorically supreme becoming in which there is a factor of categorically supreme being, as contrasted to inferior becoming, in which there is inferior being" (Hartshorne

2000, 24). In neoclassical or process theism the divine becoming is more ultimate than the divine being only for the reason that it is more inclusive, as we will see.

Thus, the theism that I am defending against the classical theism Philo initiated has several features:

1. It is a *dipolar* theism because excellences are found on both sides of the aforementioned contrasting categories (that is, they are correlative and noninvidious).
2. It is a *neoclassical* theism because it relies on the belief that classical theists (especially Anselm, as we will see momentarily) were on the correct track when they described God as the supremely excellent, all-worshipful, greatest conceivable being, but classical theists did an insufficient job of thinking through the logic of perfection.
3. It is a *process* theism because it sees the need for God to become in order for God to be called perfect, but not at the expense of God's always (that is, permanently) being greater than all others.
4. It is a theism that can be called *pan-en-theism*, which literally means "all is *in* God," say through divine omniscience. God is neither completely removed from the world (that is, unmoved by it), as in classical theism, nor completely identified with the world, as in pantheism (the belief that "all *is* God").

Rather, God is:

1. world-inclusive, in the sense that God cares for the whole world, and all feelings in the world, especially suffering feelings, are felt by God; and
2. transcendent in the sense that God is greater than any other being, especially because of God's necessary existence and God's preeminent love.

We should therefore reject the conception of God as an unmoved mover not knowing the moving world (Aristotelian theism); as the unmoved mover inconsistently knowing the moving world (classical theism); or as the unmoved mover knowing an ultimately unmoving, or at least noncontingent, world (pantheism).

Classical theists such as Philo may raise two objections that ought to be considered. To the objection that if God changed God would not be perfect, for if God were perfect there would be no need to change, there is this reply: In order to be supremely excellent, God must at any particular time be the greatest conceivable being, the all-worshipful being. At a later time, however, or in a situation where some creature that previously did not suffer now suffers, God has new opportunities to exhibit divine, supreme excellence. That is, God's perfection does not merely allow God to change, but requires God to change. This does not mean that at the earlier time God was less than perfect in that at that earlier point the later suffering did not yet exist.

The other objection might be that God is neither one nor many, neither actual nor potential, and so forth, because no human concept whatsoever applies to God literally or univocally, but at most analogically. A classical theist such as Philo might say, perhaps, that God is more unitary than unity, more actual than actuality, as these are humanly known. Yet one wonders how classical theists, once they have admitted the insufficiency of human conceptions, can legitimately give a favored status to one side (the left side) of conceptual contrasts at the expense of the other. Why, if God is simpler than the one, is God not also more complex, in terms of relatedness to diverse actual occasions, than the many? Analogical predication and negative theology can just as easily fall victim to the monopolar prejudice as univocal predication. "To be agent and patient is in truth incomparably better than being either alone" (Hartshorne 1983, 54). This is preeminently the case with God, and an intelligent human being is vastly more of an agent and patient than a nonhuman animal, which is more of both than a plant or especially a stone. Stones can neither talk nor listen, nor can they decide for others or appreciate others' decisions.

One wonders how Philo and other classical theists can reconcile the self-sufficiency of deity in Aristotle (to be discussed later) with the providential concern and omnibenevolence of the biblical God. One denies and the other asserts a real relatedness between God and the world. Philo initiates this logical contradiction, as the great Philo scholar Harry Wolfson realized (see Wolfson 1948). Philo's and other classical theists' easy acceptance of this contradiction seems to be due to the fact that the sense of God's power is seen as stronger than the sense of God's love, and hence there was no intensely felt need to develop a concept of God that really secured a place for omnibenevolence. And the highest sort of power has historically been seen in classical theism as pure activity immune to any influence (Hartshorne 2000, 76–77).

Monopolarity works at both a human and a divine level in Philo in that fickleness is seen (but why?) as a worse character trait than selfish rigidity. By contrast, suggesting that the higher the being in question, the higher the level of responsiveness to others, makes sense. If knowledge requires a certain sort of patiency with respect to the object known, then beings with lesser knowledge have lesser patiency status, whereas the greatest conceivable being would be receptive to all. That is, it is not merely pushing others around that is admirable. How odd it is to privilege impassibility when our very brains are the most responsive portions of ourselves as organisms. On the contrasting dipolar view of neoclassical or process theists, God is supremely passive and complex as well as supremely active and integrated, in the senses that and to the extent that each of these attributes is admirable (Hartshorne 2000, 81).

• One can start to see the neoclassical or process critique of classical theistic omnipotence at this point. Preeminent power would have to involve preeminent "re-sponsiveness," on this view, rather than aloof "inde-sponsiveness," if this odd word be permitted in order to make my point. Admittedly, divine rule cannot be overthrown, but this is not because the dipolar God is impassive. God *always changes* and both words are needed. Philo is the first classical theist in that he begins the long tradition of metaphysical abuse of scripture. Saying in biblical fashion that God is one is to show disagreement with polytheism, but this does not necessarily commit one to the claim that there is no internal complexity (say in terms of responding to the multiplicity of sentient beings in the world) in the one God. Supporting the idea that God is timeless on biblical grounds is difficult, to say the least. The idea that change necessarily implies change for the worse is indefensible both on rational and biblical grounds. God's legitimate "changelessness" can be better understood in terms of God's always existing, indeed of God's always changing, and of God's steadfastness and dependability. The God who always is, as revealed to Moses in the tetragrammaton (the mysterious yet famous four letter response at Exodus 3:14 when Moses asks for the name of God: YHWH), is one who is alive and breathes (Hartshorne 2000, 81–84; also Bowker 2002, 178).

Importantly, the problems I see in classical theism are not due, as they are often alleged, to the heavy influence of the Greeks on the classical theistic concept of God (even if they are due to the way in which classical theists appropriate the Greeks for their own purposes). For example, philosophical theism was helpful to Philo in escaping from polytheism. This was an ongoing project for the ancient Hebrews since they started out as polytheists (believers in many gods), gradually moved to henotheism (the belief that there is one god who is superior to all the other gods), and then gradually and fitfully moved to monotheism (the belief that there is one God). Thinking categorically (rather than in mythopoetic terms) about God facilitated these transitions. Experts even doubt that Philo had a firm grasp of spoken Hebrew, although he was clearly a master of Greek. But this is not the source of his problems regarding the concept of God, as I see things. We will consider the idea that divine dynamism is part of (albeit a largely neglected part of) the ancient Greek legacy. Philo himself flirts with this dynamism when he contrasts God's essence (*ousia*) with God's powers (*dynameis*) or energies (*energeiai*). Yet he remains a staunch defender of what I call monopolar theism (see Capetz 2003, 12; Armstrong 1993, 68–70, 115).

The Hartshornian judgment that Philo was the first classical theist and the view that his influence was enormous (even if largely unrecognized), rely to a great extent on Wolfson's scholarship, whom Hartshorne sees as one of the greatest historians of philosophy. No doubt some will see Hartshorne's and Wolfson's glorification of Philo as hyperbolic, but the bold (in the Popperian sense) and challenging thesis they present to us is nonetheless hard to refute: Finding a significant statement about the concept of God in medieval philosophy or in the Protestant reformers (except regarding specifically Christian topics such as the Incarnation or the Trinity) that is not found in Philo is difficult. But we have seen that this does not mean Philo's concept of God is unproblematic, a concept that involves a forced marriage between the Greek concept of changeless being and the loving God of the Bible or religious experience. In fact, the identification of God with a principle of fixity does an injustice not only to the God of the Bible, but it is also a corruption of Plato's philosophy. One cannot help but wonder about how intellectual history might have been significantly different if Plato's simplified view and the concept of God he initiated had been informed by the more complex (and, I allege, more accurate) view presented in Plato's dialogues. We should beware not only of views of God that entirely lack intellectual content, but also of views of God based on bits of philosophy that have no relation whatsoever to religious insight or experience. An example of the latter is Philo's (and Thomas Aquinas's and others') view that the relationship between God and the world is real to the latter but not to the former (Hartshorne 1962, 122–123; 1965, 31, 145; 1967, 28; 1970, 38; 1972, 63; 1983, 7, 67; 1984a, 115; 1990, 31).

Claiming that Philo was not only the first classical theist, but also that he was the first medieval philosopher makes sense. Both Hartshorne and Wolfson tend to see medieval philosophy as that period in the discipline between ancient thinkers who lacked access to scripture and those modern thinkers who had access to scripture but who did not acknowledge its authority. That is, medieval philosophers are those who both have access to scripture and who see it as authoritative. (In this regard it may very well be Spinoza rather than Descartes who is the first great truly modern philosopher.) Seen in this light there is not as much of a gap between Philo and Augustine as might be supposed, given the fact that they adhered to different religions (Hartshorne 1983, 67). Both were monopolar theists who exhibited the five characteristics of classical theism mentioned earlier.

2
St. Augustine
(354–430)

Classical theism is not a religion, but a philosophical or theological concept of God that has heavily influenced thinkers in the Abrahamic religions. Consider the North African Augustine's classical theism in the fourth and fifth centuries. In a famous part of his *Confessions* (1998, Books 10–11), God's steadfastness is clearly interpreted in terms of divine eternity in the sense that God exists outside of time altogether and hence is immune to any sort of change. In fact, God created time and change, according to Augustine. Like Philo, Greek philosophy heavily influenced Augustine, and he was convinced of the trustworthiness of the Hebrew Scriptures; to these he added the Christian New Testament. And like Philo, questioning monopolarity and the ideas that God was wholly immutable and nontemporal did not occur to Augustine, which is surprising because of Augustine's nuanced treatment of time as psychological and not merely physical (Hartshorne 2000, 85; also see Kenney 2013a).

Why Augustine might think that there had to be a being who embraced all of the past, present, and future within a single glance is at least understandable. But if there were such a being, this would signal the ultimate victory of the ancient Greek philosopher Parmenides: a block universe where everything in the future would be known with absolute assurance and in minute detail by God. Augustine seems to realize this when, in his later writings, he drifts away from his earlier defense of human free will in *On the Free Choice of the Will* [*De Libero Arbitrio*] (2010) and toward determinism. Unfortunately, Augustine did not think through the possibility that the way that time is given to us (in terms of memory of the past, appreciation of the present to the extent that this is possible, and anticipation of the future) might be a clue regarding how time is given to God, with the provisos that God's memory is perfect, divine enjoyment of the present is preeminently enhanced through omnipresence, and God's awareness of future possibilities is vastly superior to our own. That is, on my view Augustine would have come closer to an understanding of the concept of divine omniscience if he had realized that this attribute consists in knowing possibilities or probabilities *as* possibilities or probabilities. To claim to know future possibilities as already actualized (on the classical theistic version of omniscience) is to misunderstand the future, which is not here yet to be known in minute detail and with absolute assurance (Hartshorne 2000, 91–92).

On the neoclassical or process theistic view, time is asymmetrical. The past refers to what did exist, but the future refers to the not yet existent. The future exists now primarily in anticipation or hope or dread, as Augustine almost noticed. We forget as much or more as we remember about the past, but the greatest knower would not forget what has actually happened. There is no compelling reason, however, to think that the greatest knower is aware in any detail of what will happen in the future if it is not here yet to be known. In different terms, our sense that the future is at least partially open does not refer merely to our ignorance of what is already in the cards or preset in stone. Reality is in process, both for us and for any other, including the greatest conceivable. What this means is that we have no defensible alternative to generalizing our ideas of memory and anticipation when we try to understand the relationship between God (as temporal) and the (temporal) world (Hartshorne 2000, 92–93).

To say that reality is in process, contra the classical theistic view of Augustine, is to say that at each moment future determinables are becoming determinate in the clutch of vivid immediacy in the present. Anticipation of the future necessarily involves indeterminacy of some sort, only an outline of what will probably (at best) happen. Strictly speaking, there just are no future events, only the possibility or probability of such. As Hartshorne puts the point: "When the future is present, it will be definite" (Hartshorne 2000, 94). We have clear experience of memory and anticipation, but we do not have any experience whatsoever of a grasp of what was, is, and will be "all at once." Or again, of necessity literal decisions are made in the present, where some possibilities are cut off so that others remain. If God's memory is perfect, then in a way nothing is lost, but because of the asymmetrical nature of time something is created at each moment. As William Wordsworth famously put the point in his immortality ode, what having been must ever be. Of course death involves the discontinuation of a certain series of events, but it is not a destruction of the events themselves, at least if God has ideal retention of what has happened (Hartshorne 2000, 95–96). But this is quite different from "retaining" that which has not yet come into actuality.

Just as Philo set the classical theistic tone for Judaism that later reverberates in Maimonides and other Jewish thinkers, Augustine sets the tone for both Catholic and Protestant thinkers, the latter through Martin Luther, who was an Augustinian monk and a theoretical follower of Augustine. The pervasive influence of classical theism in the Abrahamic religions cannot be overemphasized (see Armstrong 1993, 118–124; Bowker 2002, 258–261; Capetz 2003, 62–69). This influence is unfortunate, as I see things, in that classical theists such as Augustine did not combine the best in Greek philosophy with the wisdom of ancient Palestine. For example, by assuming that divine omniscience refers to God knowing with absolute assurance and in minute detail everything that will happen in the future, Augustine implies that everything we "choose" is part of a divine blueprint that is already settled. His view is in a troubling disequilibrium with much of our personal experience of volition. Or again, the Johannine view of God as sympathetic love is scarcely disclosed in Augustine's concept of God, although it understandably creeps in when this concept is relaxed for rhetorical or pastoral purposes. Therefore the philosophical problems Christianity raises are, despite the long history of this religion, fresh ones in need of attention: How can we develop a concept of God that can deal well with the claim that God is love? Such a revised, neoclassical concept of God would enable us to avoid being impaled on the horns of various classical theistic dilemmas: How is creaturely freedom compatible with classical theistic omniscience? How can there be evil in a world ruled by a classical theistic omnipotent God? And the questions go on. As before, however, neo*classical* theism is compatible with the claim that we do get very important half-truths in Augustine (Hartshorne 1953, 24; 1962, 19; 1983, 70, 149; 1984a, 11; 1991, 597).

3

St. Anselm

(1033–1109)

Consider the conjunction in Anselm in the eleventh and twelfth centuries in Canterbury between the classical theistic concept of God and his famous ontological argument for the existence of God. Elsewhere I have defended the latter if not the former (see Dombrowski 2006). Anselm was led by the force of modal logic to conclude in chapter 3 of his *Proslogion*, on my interpretation, that of the three apparent options regarding the modes of existence (the existence of X is impossible, the existence of X is contingent, or the existence of X is necessary), one of them drops out in the divine case. If "God" is defined as the greatest conceivable (a definition that is perhaps agreeable even to atheists and agnostics), then the second of these three options makes no sense in the divine case. This is because if there were a being whose existence is merely contingent, such that there might be some factors in play that could prevent its existence, it would not be the greatest conceivable. Or again, if "God's" existence were merely contingent, then the being in question would not really be God.

The idea that contingent existence is incompatible with deity is Anselm's great discovery on Hartshorne's account. But this great discovery still leaves us with intellectual work to do in that we are still left with the question whether God's existence is either impossible or necessary. Although this book is not centered on the existence of God, but rather on the concept of God, the neoclassical or process use of the ontological argument for God's existence uncovers some important features of the concept of God. Hartshorne's greatest contribution to philosophical theism may very well be his distinction between divine existence and divine actuality, between the claim that God is necessarily

25

and how God is from moment to moment, respectively. To be clear, Anselm himself was a monopolar, classical theist who thought that the ontological argument showed not only that God exists necessarily, but also that every aspect of God was necessary. That is, Anselm would only acknowledge the terms on the left side of the diagram in chapter 1 as divine attributes.

By contrast, the neoclassical or process view is that although the existence of God is necessary, the actuality or concrete reality of God from moment to moment as God re-sponds to creaturely experiences is contingent. As before, a living God cannot be strictly necessary or changeless in every aspect. Furthermore, one of the familiar criticisms of the ontological argument is avoided in its neoclassical use. One often hears it said that a problem with the ontological argument is that it moves (illegitimately) from a mere concept of God to the actuality of God. But once existence and actuality are distinguished, then the most that can be said is that, as a result of a modified (neoclassical) version of the Anselmian argument, one moves from the concept of God to the conclusion that God exists necessarily. The argument does not, however, move from concept to actuality in that no abstract argument can tell us in detail about concrete actuality or how God exists from moment to moment or how God experiences creaturely suffering. Although we can know abstractly something about God as a result of a modified version of Anselm's argument (*that* God exists necessarily), we cannot as a result of this argument learn about the concrete actuality of God (*how* God feels or the tenor of divine omnibenevolence as it occurs concretely in the divine life).

Of course my goal in these brief remarks about the ontological argument is not to convince those who are skeptical regarding this argument, but rather to suggest that the argument does not make the giant leap from the abstract to the concrete that many scholars assume that it makes. With the Hartshornian distinction between divine existence and divine actuality in mind, we can say that the modal version of the ontological argument moves from an abstract definition of God to the abstract conclusion that in some omnibenevolent fashion or other God exists necessarily. It does not take a further step to a conclusion regarding how God exists concretely at any particular time; such concreteness rests on various contingencies that cannot be predicted in any sort of detail in advance.

Anselm is typical of classical theists who paradoxically allege that God cannot experience compassion because, as a strictly permanent and active being, God cannot have sympathy or receive influence from others, on the one hand, and allege that God is eminently compassionate due to divine omnibenevolence, on the other. The latter claim is at odds with the monopolar and metaphysical character of the former. Or again, classical theists may at times say that God is compassionate, but they do an insufficient job of explaining how this claim is consistent with the opposite claim made more frequently that is dictated by their monopolar concept of God. By contrast, by ascending from lesser goods to greater ones we can trace a trajectory that points us toward God; as we move from compassionless beings to those with slight compassion, to those who are highly compassionate, we have an intimation regarding what divine Compassion might be like. Granted, in order to avoid hubris we need to apophatically temper our confidence here regarding our understanding of divine compassion, but this does not require or even allow us to say that God is compassionless, as Anselm himself almost saw. That is, although Anselm himself is clearly a monopolar classical theist, at times in *Proslogion* he gives evidence of a certain skittishness regarding his stance (see Hartshorne 2000, 98–103).

What is problematic in Anselm is not the idea that God is to be thought of as perfection, but rather with the assumption that perfection admits of an absolute maximum that is already accomplished; he seems not to have considered carefully the idea that there could be "perfect changes," as the title of a recent book in German on Hartshorne makes clear (see Enxing and Muller 2012). This failure to think in detail about divine dynamism leads to startling results, as in the idea that God helps those in misery without ever having suffered sympathetically with them. Although classical theists often say that they are thinking and speaking analogically about God, unsympathetic benevolence has no analogy in our experience. Hartshorne asks the following in this regard: "How can a being know what wretchedness is if no shadow of suffering, disappointment, unfulfilled desire or wish, has ever been experienced by that being?" (Hartshorne 2000, 104). An adequate, concrete grasp of particular suffering seems to require a sympathetic participation in that suffering.

We should note that process thinkers in the twentieth century were not the first to notice this problem. As early as the second and third centuries in Alexandria in Egypt, Origen made several astute dipolar observations: Love itself is, among other things, an affection such that the quintessential love as found in Jesus' suffering and death should provide for those who are theistically inclined (not only Christians) something of a model for divine passability (see Origen 1929, 15–16). Granted, God cannot suffer in the sense of passing out of existence, hence Origen and other dipolar theists can avoid the charge of "Patripassionism," wherein God ("the Father") suffers in an invidious sense. But Origen insightfully argues that God does suffer in what can be seen to be the divine actuality in terms of how God responds to human and other suffering. As Hartshorne sees things, Origen holds out hope that the undue influence of the despotism of the Roman emperors on the classical theistic concept of God could be mitigated: God need not be seen as a despot. The mutability of actual divine experiences of what happens in the world could, in principle, be made compatible with the everlasting character of the divine being who has such experiences (see Hartshorne 2000, 96–98, 103–104). In short, God is impassable in existence and passable in actuality.

Neither Augustine nor Anselm followed up on Origen's flirtation with dipolar theism. Despite Anselm's great discovery, mentioned above, his view did not involve a transition to a dipolar view of perfection. In ordinary cases both existence and actuality are contingent and this seems to have led contemporary Anselmians who are classical theists (see Rogers 2000) to think that in the divine case both existence and actuality are necessary (assuming for the moment that this distinction is even noticed). But there is another way to think through the logic of perfection wherein there are such things as perfect changes. The transition from a monopolar view of the ontological argument to a dipolar view is not as difficult as some imagine once the ambiguity in the phrase "none greater can be conceived" is noticed. The neoclassical or process theist interprets this phrase to mean that no other individual could conceivably be greater; this leaves open the possibility that this individual could be in a greater state than its present actual state (for example, by responding in the best way possible to new realities as they come into being). The classical theist, of course, interprets this phrase in static terms such that it means "unsurpassable by anything," in contrast to the neoclassical or process interpretation in terms of "unsurpassable save by itself." One wonders, however, if a being that is unsurpassable, even by itself, as an absolute maximum of value is even conceivable (Hartshorne 2000, 104–106).

Capetz does not help us much in the effort to figure out how the concept of God in Anselm could involve both compassion and lack of compassion. He seems to think that belief in divine compassion is a sign of our inadequate view of divine reality, which is compassionless. Likewise, Armstrong does not help much when she overemphasizes Anselm's rationalism to suggest that it encouraged Anselm to think that he could prove anything. On the neoclassical or process view, however, to argue abstractly in favor of God's necessary existence does not tell us much about God's concrete actuality, except to say that the divine actuality from moment to moment responds in the best way possible to creaturely affairs. Furthermore, in Armstrong's interpretation of Anselm's *nihil maius cogitari possit* (none greater can be conceived) she fails to note the modal character of the argument in chapter 3 of *Proslogion*, wherein it is not divine existence versus divine nonexistence that is contrasted (assuming for the moment that the latter can be conceived), but the different modes of existence that are contrasted when one thinks about necessary existence versus contingent existence. This is a crucial point to make if we are to appreciate Anselm's most significant contribution to the concept of God, acceptable to both classical and neoclassical or process theists: the claim that God does not exist merely contingently, but necessarily. The concept of having the possibility of not existing is quite different from the concept of not having the possibility of not existing (see Armstrong 1993, 201–203; Capetz 2003, 73–78).

To discuss God is, by almost universal usage, to talk about the best or supreme individual (or superindividual). But what does this mean? A seldom noticed implication of the classical theistic view is that if God is unmoved and compassionless then our love of God is ultimately for our own benefit in that it does not affect God. This seems to turn worship into a crass sort of egoism, despite religious believers' intent to the contrary. By contrast, on the neoclassical or process view, divine compassion is not something completely different from compassion as it is in Anselm. The key task involved in the ontological argument is to decide between the impossibility of the existence of God and the necessary existence of God. One notices this once the contingent existence of God is put aside as a result of Anselm's principle that perfection cannot exist contingently; this is because to exist contingently is to exist precariously, a precariousness or "iffyness" that is demeaning when attributed to the greatest conceivable or all-worshipful or perfect being. Contingency is a clearer example of a lack of perfection than mere nonexistence because of this demeaning precariousness, which is not exhibited by something that never existed; but contingency in an existing thing is a defect. Once again the purpose of this book is not to decide between divine impossibility or divine necessity. But it is crucial to notice that if God's existence is possible and hence, via the ontological argument, necessary, then this does not preclude contingency in divine actuality. In fact, no actuality can be necessary (Hartshorne 1941, 6; 1948, 54, 157; 1962, 51, 61; 1965, 102, 111, 166).

If the ontological argument goes through, or even if it does not, it is important to notice that it is essential to the concept of God to include the idea that to exist with nonexistence as a conceivable alternative is an inferior manner of existing compared to existing without such alternative; and only the latter is compatible with the Unsurpassable. That is, the ontological argument illuminates not only the issues regarding God's existence, but also some issues regarding the very concept of God. But not all of them. Both Anselm and Hartshorne defend a modal version of the argument, but the latter argues that a God unsurpassable even by self would indicate a purely absolute, nonrelative, and hence wholly unreceptive or insensitive, being. Although necessary existence inheres in the definition of Greatness, necessary actuality does not so inhere. We have seen that Anselm did not recognize that he needed the distinction between existence and actuality in order to consistently defend the claim that God is compassionate. There is quite a difference between "necessarily actualized somehow" and the "contingent how of actualization." As before, the necessary aspect of God refers to the abstract claim that some actual state or other will have to occur in the divine life, not to the precise character of each actual state. Divine necessity suggests that abstract traits such as omniscience or omnibenevolence must be realized in some concrete manifestation, but not in the manifestation that actually exists, given that the world is in process (Hartshorne 1965, 4, 10, 30, 32, 38–39, 48).

Anselm helps us to see clearly the debate between classical and neoclassical or process theists. Whereas the latter emphasize the claim that the classical theistic God is incapable of adapting or responding to new determinations as future determinables become determinate, classical theists emphasize the claim that there is no need for God to adapt or respond to these. And this debate is not resolved solely by appeal to negative theology in that partisans on both sides could claim that God is whatever it is better to be than not to be. By contrast, an overly aggressive version of apophaticism would lead to the cumbersome and indefensible claim that God is not what it is worse to be than not to be. The reason theists worship God is not primarily because of the defects God does not possess. But what I have said here does not imply an utter hostility toward negative theology, only an attempt to find its rightful place. Given the distinction between being actualized somehow (assuming the necessary existence of God via the ontological argument) and being actualized precisely as such and such, we can see that the latter requires a healthy dose of the apophatic. This requirement is due to the genuine contingency that characterizes reality with the process of actualization exhibiting brute facticity and a certain degree of capriciousness and undeducibility. One can defend the ontological argument without being a Leibnizian ultrarationalist. Claiming to know that God exists necessarily is much easier than claiming to know what and how God experiences concretely (Hartshorne 1965, 67, 69, 132, 185–186, 230).

Unfortunately, the incredible lucidity of Anselm's mind was not focused on the concept of God as much as it was on the necessary existence of God. On the one hand, more than anyone else, Anselm discerned the logical status of metaphysical ideas; on the other, he spoiled his best insights by assuming that divine necessity extended beyond necessary existence to include everything in the divine life. Think about how odd it would be to interpret the biblical command to "Be perfect" (Matthew 5:48) to be equivalent to the command "Be immutable." The contrasting notion of dynamic perfection leads to the modified Anselmian view that divine unsurpassability refers to unsurpassability by another, a view that has not been shown to produce antinomies. The task is to balance Anselm's genius and his lasting contributions to philosophical theism with his defects regarding the concept of God. He is certainly correct in implying that either God exists in all possible worlds or in none of them; contingent existence in some possible worlds but not others is contrary to the concept of God. In this regard Anselm prefigures Ludwig Wittgenstein in thinking that theology is, in a way, grammar. The word "God" refers to the being who is intended by those who adopt an attitude of worship; furthermore, the divine being who is the proper object of worship implies the crucial Anselmian concept of one who surpasses all others (Hartshorne 1965, 234; 1967, x, 18, 128–129, 136; 1970, 23, 55, 131–132, 261).

Modality of existence is always a predicate in that to say a being exists necessarily (or contingently) is surely to say something significant and informative about the being in question. For example, contingent things need a genesis, whereas necessary things do not. To exist necessarily is to be concretely actualized somehow, but this does not tell us how, in contrast to Anselm. God's very existence is noncompetitive with any actual state, but God's actuality at any particular moment is at odds with what could have been if previous decisions had been different. Only the necessary existence of God is settled by the meaning of terms, not divine actuality, which is settled by empirical facts. However, we have seen that the more cautious conclusion to the ontological argument states not so much that God exists, but rather that God's existence is either impossible or necessary. The neoclassical or process idea that the classical theistic concept of God involves logical contradictions is especially relevant in this regard in that if we had to rely solely on the classical theistic concept of God the impossibility of God's existence would be a live hypothesis (Hartshorne 1983, 94–100, 146). "The point is not that existing is better than not existing and therefore the unsurpassable being must exist; the point is rather that a being that cannot be conceived not to exist but can be conceived to exist is better than a being that can be conceived not to exist and also can be conceived to exist. In short, a necessarily existing being is better than one that, whether or not it exists, exists or fails to exist contingently" (Hartshorne 1984a, 215). The part of this quotation that asserts that we *can* conceive of a being who cannot be conceived not to exist presupposes, of course, that other aspects of this being are not contradictory, a condition that the classical theistic concept of God fails to fulfill. The static perfection of this concept is strongly analogous to the idea of a greatest possible number, which is surpassed simply by adding "1" to any supposed greatest number. Analogously, there is always one more moment with new experiences to be dealt with omnibenevolently by the one who is unsurpassable by any other. Because of the difficulties in the classical theistic concept of God, we should remain cautious and assert merely that on the basis of the ontological argument Anselm did not prove theism true, but he did in fact show that theism is either necessarily true or necessarily false (Hartshorne 1984c, 7; 1987, 15).

Whereas classical theists such as Anselm work on the dichotomy between essence (*what* a thing is) and existence (*that* a thing is), in neoclassical or process theism turning this dichotomy into a trichotomy of essence, existence, and actuality (*how* a thing is concretely from moment to moment) is important. Because of the enormous conceptual gap between contingent existence and necessary existence, one can say with confidence that there is an infinite gulf between "dogs exist" and "deity exists," thus preserving the best in the apophatic tradition. But we cannot say with confidence that "God exists necessarily" on a classical theistic version of the ontological argument because such confidence depends on a coherent concept of God that is not shipwrecked on the theodicy problem, the problem of divine omniscience and human freedom, and the problem of trying to make sense of omnibenevolence in an strictly permanent God who does not respond to creaturely suffering (Hartshorne 1990, 337; 2011, 104–105, 112).

Katherin Rogers is probably the most energetic contemporary defender of Anselm's philosophy in terms of his discovery of libertarian freedom in contrast to the compatibilism found in Augustine and Thomas Aquinas. But Anselm never really shakes off his classical theism in that the libertarian freedom found in his thought does not result in any contingency in the divine actuality. Rather, as in Augustine and Thomas, in Anselm there is the view of God as static perfection remaining unchanged by (yet supposedly not aloof to) creaturely changes, including the suffering ones (see Rogers 2000; 2013).

Distinguishing between two formulas in Anselm is important, as Donald Viney notes: God as that than which no greater can be conceived and God as greater than can be conceived. The second formula is a consequence of the first because a being who is greater than can be conceived is greater than a being whose greatness is completely conceivable. That aspect of God that is beyond our ken points to divine mystery, which is preserved in Hartshorne, Viney, and other neoclassical or process theists (contra Wildman). On the one hand, we do not want to overemphasize divine mystery in that such overemphasis in essence gives permission to those who would speak nonsense about God, but, on the other hand, we do not want to trivialize the degree to which there is genuine mystery in God. In Hartshorne's view, partially reliant on Anselm, the distinction between divine existence and divine actuality is one of logical type; hence the contingent states of divine actuality do not threaten the necessity of divine existence. Although we can know quite a bit abstractly about God, especially via the modal version of the ontological argument, we can know precious little about divine actuality (see Viney 2013a). For example, although we can know abstractly that the greatest conceivable would be omnibenevolent, imagining what engaging in love that is all-inclusive, unqualified, and noncompetitive would be like is quite difficult.

4

Al-Ghazzali

(1058–1111)

Despite the significant historical and cultural differences that surround Judaism, Christianity, and Islam, it is important to notice that the concept of God that has largely informed all three of these Abrahamic religions is classical theistic in character. Granted, there are some differences in what is said even about God in these religions, such as in the typical willingness in Christianity to see Jesus as divine or as in the muscular versions of apophaticism sometimes found in these religions (often punctuated with profuse kataphatic discourse). But the five characteristics of classical theism listed at the beginning of part I are noteworthy similarities regarding the concept of God that has dominated the intellectual histories of these religions.

Consider Anselm's Baghdad contemporary Al-Ghazzali. He, like Anselm, defends the categorical supremacy of God and assumes that this requires divine eternity in the atemporal sense. He also assumes that God's supremacy requires that God be an Aristotelian substance with no accidents, which, in turn, requires that there be no change whatsoever in God. Al-Ghazzali is quite willing to admit, as all classical theists should be willing to admit (but often do not), that God's knowledge (with absolute assurance and in minute detail) of what will happen in the future means that God determines all events. Even if one claims that God does not physically coerce human beings to behave as they do, the sort of omniscience found in classical theism implies that we are logically coerced to do what God knows (with absolute assurance and in minute detail) we will do. Al-Ghazzali's candor is refreshing in this regard. Whether he is equally willing to admit to the less than defensible implications of classical theistic omnipotence for the theodicy problem, however, is not clear (see Al-Ghazzali 1912, 8–13, 57; also see Hasan 2013).

In a sense, Al-Ghazzali's classical theism involves a more consistent sort of Aristotelianism than that found in Thomas Aquinas in that Al-Ghazzali, like Aristotle, inferred from the unmoved and changeless character of God (or the gods) the understandable conclusion that such a God (or gods) could not know concrete, changing particulars, in that any knowledge even remotely analogous to our own involves a sort of reaction to, or adaptability with respect to, the object known. For this and other reasons, Al-Ghazzali went through a famous religious crisis of doubt that concerned the relationship between philosophy and theology, a doubt that nonetheless did not prevent him from reaching classical theistic conclusions, including the idea that God is an immutable will who determines all events. This view, congenial to well-known Muslim fatalism, should in fact be the view of all classical theists who affirm the five characteristics listed at the beginning of part 1, especially monopolar permanence and divine omniscience with respect to the future, once again with absolute assurance and in minute detail (see Hartshorne 2000, 106–107).

Al-Ghazzali's intellectual honesty is also in evidence in his classical theistic identification of the worshipful with the powerful. This worship of naked divine power is derived, of course, from admiration for naked power in politics, thereby making God something of an absolute despot who is pure cause, self-sufficient, unmodifiable. We will see that liberal theists in various religions, including Islam, legitimately find this sort of power worship problematic (see An-Na'im 1990). The liberal theists who are process thinkers understandably think that an omnibenevolent being would not intentionally cause or permit unnecessary suffering to occur in those sentient beings who are capable of receiving it. Al-Ghazzali does not take us very far in an attempt to understand the metaphysics of a God of love, but this is not so much due to the fact that he is Muslim as to the fact that he shares classical theistic assumptions regarding the concept of God. A God of love requires dipolarity in that any love that is even remotely analogous to human love means being an effect as well as a cause, being responsive as well as being dependable, and so forth. The divine aim, on a neoclassical or process account, is to foster intense and zestful living; the dynamic perfection of God would not be compatible with divine indifference regarding creatures who fell short of this aim (Hartshorne 2000, 107–110).

Readers might correctly suspect at this point that the divine trait that I find least objectionable among the list of five found at the beginning of part 1 is omnibenevolence. Indeed, Hartshorne makes clear that on the neoclassical or process view "love alone is the essential principle" (Hartshorne 2000, 110). However, although both classical and neoclassical or process theists agree that omnibenevolence is crucial, only the latter develop a concept of God that makes this positive valuation of omnibenevolence intelligible. In fact, classical theists have done a good job of convincing neoclassical or process theists that they (the classical theists) value omnipotence more than they value omnibenevolence. Conversely, neoclassical theists value omnibenevolence above all and find the very concept of omnipotence problematic for several reasons discussed later. On the neoclassical or process view, God does not deliver rewards and punishments to tragic humanity as much as God shares the tragedy with us (although obviously not in the sense that God could cease to exist as a result). Love, like virtue, is its own reward, just as lack of love is, in a way, its own punishment. Importantly this dipolar concept of God, wherein divine omnibenevolence is made intelligible, is not Al-Ghazzali's, who, along with classical theists, in general, implies that divine power (and causation, justice, and so forth) is prior to and more important than love (Hartshorne 2000, 111).

The aforementioned spiritual crisis in Al-Ghazzali's life that led him to skepticism seems to have been due to many factors, but one of these surely was the difficulty involved in reconciling his concept of God with either religious or personal experience. Whether this crisis was due to certain epistemological inadequacies that confront human beings, in general, or to the assumption that we have to rest content with the classical theistic concept of God, in particular, is an interesting question. For example, Al-Ghazzali worried about why God (Allah) would, as a strictly immutable and self-sufficient being, want to create anything in that in principle nothing in addition to God could add to the already complete, static divine perfection that had existed "from" eternity. Although Bowker is insightful regarding Al-Ghazzali's worry, he does not trace Al-Ghazzali's predicament here to certain classical theistic assumptions regarding the concept of God (Bowker 2002, 356–359).

Likewise, Armstrong's careful treatment of the numerous differences between Al-Ghazzali, on the one hand, and other Muslim thinkers who preceded him, such as Al-Farabi (870–950) and Avicenna or Ibn Sina (980–1037), on the other, nonetheless might mislead us into thinking that these thinkers did not share the same concept of God. But all three of them shared a classical theistic concept. The internecine debates among these thinkers (for example, regarding whether we can know, as Al-Farabi and Avicenna thought we could, that God is a necessary existent who brings others into being in neoplatonic fashion as many emanations from The One) are like those between Thomists and Calvinists in that, from a neoclassical or process perspective, we find more similarities than differences. The similarities are those that classical theists, in general, share. Al-Ghazzali is like many classical theists in thinking that, because rationality cannot extricate itself from the conundrums that face it when dealing with God, the only escape can come from an arational mystical experience. My point here is not to trash mysticism or religious experience, as we will see, but rather to question whether the problem lies with rationality itself or with a bad theory regarding the concept of God. Unfortunately, despite her brilliant depiction of the debates among famous Muslim thinkers, Armstrong tends to think that the problems (including Al-Ghazzali's) primarily lie with rationality itself and not with its application in the classical theistic case. In this regard, Armstrong insightfully argues that Al-Ghazzali's rejection of rational religion prefigures Immanuel Kant's and Søren Kierkegaard's views, in addition to Armstrong's own (Armstrong 1993, 174–176, 181–192, 201, 229, 314–315; Bowker 2002, 352–359).

5

Maimonides
(1135–1204)

Like Philo, Maimonides tried to reconcile Judaism with Greek philosophical views. Furthermore, like Philo, Maimonides alternated between the apophatic indescribability of God and classical theistic assertions. Not surprisingly, Maimonides runs into standard classical theistic problems. For example, on the neoclassical or process view, no knower, not even the best one, could know with infallible accuracy an object that could have been otherwise. If the object of knowledge could have been otherwise, the knowledge of it could have been otherwise. This contradicts the pure necessity of divine knowledge in classical theism. Mutability or nonnecessity of the object known means mutability or nonnecessity in the knower. Maimonides's way of dealing with this critical problem is to say that in the divine case there is no positive content to knowledge of the world. That is, God's knowledge is *completely* different from our knowledge, in which case one wonders why we should call it "knowledge" (Hartshorne 2000, 111–112; also see Seeskin 2013).

In his classic *The Guide of the Perplexed*, Maimonides from Cordova both prohibits description of deity and offers a monopolar, classical theistic description: God is unmoved, substantial and devoid of accidents, completely unified without parts, unrelated to creatures (although they may be related to deity), incorporeal, active and not passive, actual and not potential, ruler but not subject, eternal in the sense of existing outside of time altogether, and so forth (see Maimonides 1885, I, 174–222).

Maimonides's fear, in part, is that if we ascribed a plurality of attributes to deity, we would run the risk of polytheism. But this seems to confuse levels of discourse in that a plurality of properties does not imply a plurality of individuals who exhibit these properties. A property is not a deity. What Maimonides has unwittingly discovered is that a strictly abstract "perfect" being without accidents cannot really have any positive attributes, not even essential ones, hence his exaggerated apophaticism. But a living God, a personal God who is dynamically perfect, would have an infinite number of successive experiences of concrete events, which of necessity would involve accidental features. God's very existence may be nonaccidental even if the experiences of this everlastingly evolving God would be accidental (Hartshorne 2000, 116).

One should not conclude, however, that God's essential goodness is accidental. Omnibenevolence is everlastingly inherent in the divine nature as perfect, whereas the particular ways in which this supreme goodness is exhibited are accidental in the sense that they are responses to particular creatures, here and now, in some idiosyncratic event or even crisis in their lives. God cares even for the fall of a sparrow, as one biblical claim from the Christian scriptures has it (Matthew 10:28; Hartshorne 2000, 116).

Maimonides is a bit clearer than Philo in thinking that if God really is immutable, then one cannot have it both ways regarding real divine relations with the world: God cannot have these even if creatures do have real relations with God. The creatures are really related to God, even in negative theology, by way of divine otherness. But the absoluteness of the classical theistic God precludes real relations on God's part with transient, changing, accidental creatures. The problems here could have been solved if Maimonides had seen essence and accident, say, as correlative notions that needed each other in order to be intelligible. Monopolar theists such as Maimonides either ignore or reject this dipolar insight, however (Hartshorne 2000, 117).

I would like to reiterate that there are good reasons to take negative theology seriously, especially when discussing the details of divine actuality. But serious problems arise when an aggressive apophaticism is used to hide the defects involved in the classical theistic concept of God. By analogy, saying that a rectangle consists of several sides is not too precise, but it does tell us something accurate about rectangles. Likewise, saying that God has knowledge (indeed supreme knowledge) is more accurate than saying that God is nescient. That is, efforts to convince us that we ought not have any confidence in what we say about God are very often not borne out of a humility regarding human cognition as much as they arise out of desperation regarding a concept of God riddled with contradictions (Hartshorne 2000, 118).

Several Jewish thinkers have struggled with the problems involved in the classical theistic view of divine knowledge. For example, in Gersonides's thought (1288-1344), as in the later works of Augustine, can be found a tendency toward determinism. This is a result of Gersonides's thinking through the implications of the classical theistic versions of eternity and divine omniscience regarding the future. However, determinism obviously puts into disequilibrium many of our strongest intuitions regarding the need to make choices, the need to hold people responsible for their choices, and so forth. In effect, although determinism makes sense once we start with the classical theistic concept of God, we pay too great a price for a defense of this position (Hartshorne 2000, 118; 1976, 7; also see Dorff 2013).

Two types of knowledge of the future can be distinguished on the supposition that there are particular free acts. The first is knowledge of what may or may not take place in the future, and the second is knowledge of what will, in fact, take place in the future with the same degree of assurance that one can have regarding what has, in fact, taken place in the past. Whereas classical theists always have to be tempted by the second sort of knowledge (and most classical theists have explicitly claimed that God has such knowledge), neoclassical or process theists deny that any being, even the most perfect being, could have such knowledge (Hartshorne 2000, 118).

I am not claiming that classical theists have only one response to the problem of trying to reconcile classical theistic divine immutability with God's knowledge of events in flux. Maimonides, if I understand him correctly, tries to resolve this problem by denying that God's embrace of contingent creatures really is a type of knowledge. Divine awareness of contingency is completely beyond our ken, on his view (see Bowker 2002, 218-221; Armstrong 1993, 194-196). Gersonides, however, concludes (in Aristotelian fashion) that God *does* have knowledge, but it does not embrace the contingent. The fact that Gersonides is somewhat skeptical of the classical theistic concept of God counts in his favor, on my view, in that he was on the cusp of the defensible view that the best way to "know the future" is to realize that it is always at least partially underdetermined and underdeterminable (see Eisen 1995). And Baruch Spinoza (1632-1677) from Holland—a Jewish pantheist who is clearly not a classical theist—denies any contingency. One pays a stiff price for each of these three resolutions to the problem (in Maimonides, Gersonides, and Spinoza) as it arises in the classical theistic concept of God. In Spinoza's case, his "solution" importantly does not work for the simple reason that contingency is obvious, ineradicable, and is presupposed by the very contrasting idea of necessity that is crucial to Spinoza's own philosophy (Hartshorne 2000, 118–119; also see 1941, 2, 5, 76, 98; 1948, 119; 1983, 75; 2001, 41–42, 160).

I argue that a more defensible way of looking at things is to hold the neoclassical or process view that God does have knowledge of the temporal and contingent; but, as a result, this knowledge itself is temporal and contingent, rather than eternal and necessary. Furthermore, this view is compatible with the abstract thesis that that God, as the dynamically perfect being, must necessarily know everything that is logically knowable, but the concrete acts of divine knowing are temporal and contingent as new events that are knowable come into being.

6

St. Thomas Aquinas

(1225–1274)

Thomas, the most influential Catholic philosopher, who came from Aquino in Italy and who taught for most of his career in Paris, is quite clear in part 1 of his magnum opus, *Summa Theologiae* (questions 1–26), that any relations between God and creatures are not a reality for God, even if they are real to creatures. The reason for this is that God, for Thomas, is entirely outside of the temporal realm. There is, of course, a nominal relation or a relation only in idea in God, but this is not a relation that is real. When explicitly considering an example similar to one that I have mentioned previously (that if an animal is beside a column, the column changes the animal but not vice versa), Thomas chooses to compare God to the column rather than to the animal, despite the animal's obvious superiority to the column in terms of levels of sentiency, nascent rationality, and so forth (Hartshorne 2000, 120–121; Thomas Aquinas 1972, 1.6.2; 1.13.7).

Rapprochement with Thomas can be reached when he claims that the most proper name for God is "The One Who Is." This loose rendering of Exodus 3:14 can be seen as a biblical way of talking about the necessary existence of God and of highlighting the neo*classical* dimension of the position I defend herein. In different terms, God's essence is to exist necessarily. This is not a hubristic claim because to say abstractly that God exists necessarily is not to say too much concretely about the actuality of God. But the necessary existence of God to which Thomas points is in partial contrast to the necessary existence of God that the neoclassical or process theist has in mind because the former, but not the latter, is an existence outside of time altogether. In this regard Thomas takes his cues from Augustine

(Hartshorne 2000, 121-122; Thomas Aquinas 1972, I.13.11; also see Kennedy 2013; Silverman 2013).

Thomas considers carefully Aristotle's view that an immutable God could not know anything outside of the divine nature itself in that doing so would be to sacrifice immutability. Thomas seems to reject this view in that, as omniscient, God has to know things other than the divine nature itself. However, a thing is known in two ways, he thinks: in itself and in another. Through this distinction Thomas tries to defend the view that although God may know the divine nature in itself, God knows others not so much in themselves but as they reflect the divine nature, on the analogy of objects in a mirror. The divine nature itself contains the similitude of things. Thus, Thomas ends up with a modified Aristotelian view in which the images of things are comprehended through divine nature. In this manner, Thomas thinks that God knows not only creatures, in general, but also creatures in their particularity, because to know things only in their generality is to know them imperfectly. So God knows things perfectly precisely because they are known not in themselves but as reflections of the divine nature itself. More technically, the created essence cannot sufficiently lead us to knowledge of the divine essence, but rather the reverse (Hartshorne 2000, 122-126; Thomas Aquinas 1972, I.14.4-6).

This is a clever response on Thomas's part to the problem of how to reconcile the strictly immutable God of classical theism with the knowledge of an obviously mutable world. Responses such as these lead Hartshorne to say that he learned almost as much from the Thomistic tradition as from Whitehead in that, even if Thomas is shipwrecked on certain rocks of contradiction, he has left us an incredible chart showing us the precise locations of the rocks (Hartshorne 1948, xi). In addition to what is mentioned in the previous paragraph, consider Thomas's response to the question whether God could know singular things. His response to this question involves another thought-provoking distinction, this time between human knowing as involving a crucial sort of passivity, on the one hand, and divine knowing, on the other. The latter sort of knowledge causes things to be what they are. That is, God's knowledge extends as far as divine causality. And divine causality involves the bringing into being of both formal reality and material reality; hence God does have knowledge of singular things on the assumption that singular things are individuated by matter (Hartshorne 2000, 126; Thomas Aquinas 1972, I.14.11).

Or again, Thomas is well aware of the criticisms that can be made against the claim that a strictly necessary God can know future contingents. For every conditional proposition, if the antecedent is necessary, the consequent seemingly would have to be necessary as well. For example, if God knows that X will be the case (not merely might be), then it will be. So whatever God knows is necessary in the sense that what is known could not be otherwise. In order to escape this objection, Thomas appeals to the idea that God is eternal in the sense of being outside of time altogether. Although contingent things become actual successively, God does not know them successively, but simultaneously, eternally. What we see in terms of past, present, and future from our temporal points of view, God comprehends in a single atemporal glance. In fact, the reality of future contingents is dependent on our limited (that is, temporal) standpoint (Hartshorne 2000, 126–127; Thomas Aquinas 1972, l.14.13).

Furthermore, Thomas distinguishes between God as supreme and necessary cause and more limited, proximate, and contingent causes. Here he analogizes between the sun as remote cause and the more proximate causality enacted in a plant by the germination of a seed. The things known by God are contingent by virtue of their proximate causes, while the divine knowledge of these contingent things is necessary. From Thomas's perspective, our temporality leads us to think that future contingents are not certain; for God they are already, from eternity, quite certain. God is like a being who sees a road from a height, such that what comes before and after a traveler moving at a slow pace can be seen at a glance (Hartshorne 2000, 126–128; Thomas Aquinas 1972, l.14.13–15).

Thomas holds that not all that God wills (causes, knows) is *absolutely* necessary, such as when a predicate forms part of the definition of a subject. There is also that which is necessary *by supposition*. An example of the latter would be when we suppose, say for the sake of argument, that God wills X. Here the predicate (wills X) is not part of the definition of the subject (God). Although God's goodness is absolutely necessary, things willed on account of God's goodness are not necessary; they are necessary merely by supposition. Thomas at this point is very close to Hartshorne's existence/actuality distinction, and he is in the neighborhood of dipolarity. But he stops short of these views because for him an effect is always deficient with respect to the cause and temporality is always a mark of imperfection. His hope is that he can maintain a concept of God wherein God does not will all things with absolute necessity (in part because God would then be responsible for all things, even the immoral and ugly ones). Nonetheless Thomas thinks that he preserves the perfection of God that would otherwise be lost if God were mutable in any way or if God were the effect of any other cause (Hartshorne 2000, 129–130; Thomas Aquinas 1972, I.19.3).

As I see things, Thomas confuses matters quite a bit when he says that it is not because proximate causes are contingent that things happen contingently. Rather, he thinks that God wills that some things be done necessarily and God wills that some things be done contingently, such that even the latter are a result of divine necessity rather than being due to the contingent character of proximate causes. From my perspective, only because of Thomas's genius does one hesitate to say that all of this is a hopeless muddle of oxymorons at best or contradictions at worst. As before, more than anyone else, Thomas shows us exactly what is problematic with the classical concept of God (Hartshorne 2000, 131; Thomas Aquinas 1972, I.19.8). Unfortunately, Armstrong, Bowker, and Capetz, although they commendably detail Thomas's great achievements, do not notice these problems. Instead, they attribute the conceptual difficulties in Thomas to rationality itself, rather than to its use in a classical theistic context (Armstrong 1993, 204–207; Bowker 2002, 266–269; Capetz 2003, 78–85).

How the Thomistic view can be consistent is unclear: God decides that a creature will perform act A; however, the divine decision is nonetheless that the act will be performed "freely" (Hartshorne 1984c, 11). One wonders what possible meaning could be given to "free acts" on the classical theistic view. By "free" Thomas seems to mean acts that an agent could have refrained from performing. But one cannot refrain from enacting the decisions of the divine will. Furthermore, Thomas seems to contradict himself as well when he claims both that God is pure actuality and that God is strictly infinite, on the assumption that infinity refers to possibility rather than actuality (Hartshorne 1987, 55, 92).

Thomas is like Philo in trying to fuse the prestige of Greek philosophy and the authoritativeness of the Bible, but such a fusion is reliant in both cases on an untenable view of God as wholly nonrelative. This is why Thomas develops the distinction between relations that are real (or internal) and merely logical (or external), because real relations, obviously enough, really relate one to something else. These real relations include the knowledge relation between knower and known.

Thomas's way of proposing a defense of both a completely nonrelative God and divine knowledge of others is to insist that divine knowledge is completely different from human knowledge because it involves creating from absolutely nothing the very object known. That is, as in Maimonides, and despite Thomas's defense of analogical language used when describing God, there is no common meaning between human and divine knowledge, and on this basis classical theists have dealt with divine knowledge in the 700 years since Thomas. The problem is not with Thomas's doctrine of analogy, which in fact is his greatest contribution to the concept of God, but rather with his failure to apply this doctrine in the divine case (Hartshorne 2000, 119–120).

Thomas, along with other classical theists, turns God into a super-object rather than into a supersubject. As before, the animal has a real relation to the column, not the other way around, hence something is amiss when God is seen as a nonrelative unmoved mover and is hence made to seem closer to a column than to an animal. The animal, rather than the column, takes account of its relations and is subjectively aware. Why make God into a super-stone rather than into a superorganic individual? Apophatic description is defensible, we should note, but only if it is harnessed to a dipolar logic of perfection rather than to its monopolar alternative (Hartshorne 2000, 131).

Hartshorne even claims that the key problem with the classical theistic concept of God is its inability to adequately explain how a completely necessary being could know the contingent. Thomas's attempt to deal with this problem, as we have seen, involves the questionable distinction between something being contingent in itself yet necessarily present in the divine mind. Here Hartshorne's criticism is quite sharp and on the mark: "But . . . either it is or is not a logical possibility that the thing might not have existed; if it is a possibility . . . [that] it had not existed, it would not have been present to God as existent" (Hartshorne 2000, 132).

The idea that all events, whether past or future, are determinate from the perspective of eternity involves what Henri Bergson famously calls the spatializing of time, in that all of time's parts would exist simultaneously and be seen together in a single glance, and hence would destroy the very notions of futurity and contingency. Furthermore complications set in when we realize that for Thomas and other classical theists, despite God's strict necessity, the divine creation of the world itself is entirely contingent! God could have avoided creating a world, we are told. Once again, Hartshorne is quite sharp and on the mark: "But then there are two kinds of volitions in God: those that are there necessarily and those that are there nonnecessarily. Yet all the being of God is held to be purely necessary" (Hartshorne 2000, 133). There can be no "ifs" regarding a being who is necessary in every respect, in contrast to the more defensible neoclassical or process theistic view that God, although necessarily existent, is contingent in actuality. As before, God *always changes* and both words are crucial.

Of course much is of value in thinkers who are classical theists, even when they are speaking of the concept of God. For example, in Christian thinkers such as Thomas much is admirable in what is said about Jesus or about the claim that God is love or about the necessary existence of God. The question is whether they can reconcile this discourse with their view of God as strictly supernatural and as pure actuality. The problem is not merely theoretical. If God's perfection means that God eternally realizes all possible values, the result is, in a sense, fatal to religion in that such a view makes human choice insignificant. In classical theism, infinite value will exist no matter what we do and "serving God" in this view ends up meaning serving ourselves. The Jesuit motto (which could serve as the motto for Abrahamic theists, in general) *ad majorum Dei gloriam*—all for the greater glory of God—makes no sense if we cannot really contribute anything to a God who exhibits eternal, static, fully actualized perfection. It is understandable, on this account, why many classical theists degenerate into various forms of idolatry, given the fact that one cannot really worship the God of classical theism. Especially problematic is that type of nationalist idolatry that Hartshorne calls "stateolatry." "Nor should we forget Hitler's Catholic [classical theistic] origin," on Hartshorne's troubling yet thought-provoking reasoning (Hartshorne 1937, 34, 42; also Dombrowski 2011, chap. 5).

We may acknowledge, nonetheless, that Thomas is the greatest classical theist because he did the most thorough job of thinking through the implications of classical theism and of trying to cut thin distinctions to save this view. As a result of such thoroughness, "the only way to beat Aquinas is to take as doubtful what he took as most certain": monopolarity, including the superiority of being to becoming (Hartshorne 1941, 71–72). What this means is that patchwork amendments to classical theism will not enable us to develop a concept of God that is in reflective equilibrium with everything else that has to be considered regarding the concept of God: religious experience, the theodicy problem, making sense of our freedom, and so forth. Only a systematic review of Thomism will do. But the "classical" part of neo*classical* theism is preserved when we realize that a systematic revision *of Thomism* is required. The sweeping negations in the concept of God in Thomas, as well as in other classical theists, are only part of the story. There are also positive claims regarding God's goodness and love and it is precisely these that Thomas does not account for well, if at all. In effect, Thomas has God say the following to human beings: I love you, but I am not really related to you and the loving relation I have to you does not affect Me in the least (Hartshorne 1941, 123, 235).

Thomas is not as consistent as classical theists think, nor is he as wrong as religious skeptics usually suppose. Regarding the former, consider the fact that the more advanced a being is, the more complex it becomes and the more passivity it is able to exhibit. In the divine case, passivity is the social relevance of God's sublime activity and to deny it altogether is to speak of some being other than the greatest conceivable. Or again, Thomas merely assumes that time has a settled character from the standpoint of eternity, when in point of fact that is the very issue in question. Thomas makes time itself superfluous or illusory or empty of meaning. His definite "will be's" from the perspective of eternity should be replaced with "may or may not be's." By contrast, the God of neoclassical or process theism genuinely lives in that on this view time is not so much created *ex nihilo* as it is the order of creativity itself, including but not limited to divine creativity (Hartshorne 1953, 24, 137, 201–202). If God is purely absolute and eternal and is in no way really related to creatures, then the being that God enjoys can be no other than the divine being itself (Hartshorne 1948, 15), as Aristotle realized. In this regard Thomas falls short of Aristotle's consistency.

The neoclassical challenge to classical theists who are also Thomists is to ask whether one can refer to God as an *actus purus* (pure actuality) and yet not view this God as an abstraction that is inferior in value to concrete manifestations of activity/passivity, permanence/change. Of course, some Thomists will respond by claiming that Thomas never alleges that we can have a perfectly clear and fully adequate concept of God, as is evidenced in Thomas's critique of Anselm's ontological argument. In response we should note that Thomas's concept of God is clear enough to enable him to defend a monopolar view, to speak in favor of divine omnipotence, and to indicate support for divine omniscience with respect to what are from a temporal point of view future contingencies, and so forth (Hartshorne 1965, 55, 230).

Although abstracting away from the concreteness of God's everlasting flux to talk about what is permanent in the divine life makes sense, this is quite different from the (idolatrous) identification of God with the abstract (Hartshorne 1967, 44). In the effort to differentiate between what is truly mysterious surrounding the concept of God and the "mysteries" that are due to inconsistent classical theistic reasoning or prematurely reached classical theistic conclusions, one needs to get clear regarding which of two options one is willing to adopt: Either one can believe that concrete events really happen or one can believe that they do not really happen, but always-already simply are in at least an abstract sense. Neoclassical process thinkers opt for the former, whereas classical theists opt for the latter. Or better, classical theists nominally opt for the former as well, except in the divine case, and herein lies the source of the disagreement because to opt for the latter in the divine case undermines any defense of the former. One of the implications of rejecting a ubiquitous event ontology is that as a result of such a rejection God as pure actuality cannot be seen as actualizing any antecedent potentialities and cannot be seen as going through any development, even if the creatures obviously develop. Thomas actually helps us to see the problems here because he, more than anyone else, makes us aware of the fact that the following contrasts all amount to basically the same thing: that God is strictly necessary whereas everything else is contingent, that God is infinite in every respect and creatures are strictly finite, that God is immutable in every respect and creatures are thoroughly mutable, that God is the sole creator and humans are merely creatures, and that God is in every respect self-sufficient whereas humans are utterly dependent (Hartshorne 1970, 10, 17, 70, 95; 1972, 18).

The neoclassical or process God is more of a Supreme Being than the classical theistic God found in Thomas because the latter is incapable of real relations with creatures. To make the same point in a different way, neoclassical or process theism embraces the best insights of classical theists such as Thomas (for example, regarding the necessary existence of God), but the reverse is not the case in that classical theists eschew divine mutability altogether, even with respect to the actuality of God (Hartshorne 1972, 69, 144, 168). Or again, the tragedy of classical theism is not that it got the concept of God entirely wrong, but rather that it mistook half-truths for the whole picture (Hartshorne 1991, 597).

It is fair to say that neoclassical or process theism involves a sort of "anti-Thomistic Thomism." The fact that Thomas thinks that the relations between God and the world are real relations for the world, but not for God, indicates why there is an anti-Thomistic side to neoclassical or process theism. Classical theism maintains that Aristotle was wrong to claim that God cannot know contingent or changeable things if God is a strictly necessary, unmoved, pure actuality. Neoclassical or process theism emphasizes the idea that knowledge involves a knower who conforms to, and depends on, the known, whereas classical theism reverses this order in the divine case, where the known depends on the creative power of the knower. Thomas thinks that because God is universal cause, by knowing the divine nature itself God would be knowing all of the other objects to be known. However, this begs the question as to how the contingent in nature can be known as contingent by consulting the eternal and necessary divine nature itself (Hartshorne 1976, 1–11; 1984a, 283).

I am arguing, against Thomas, that the following triad is inconsistent: (1) that the world is mutable and contingent; (2) that God is in all respects immutable and necessary; and (3) that God has ideal knowledge of the world. Aristotle removes the contradiction in this triad by denying (3), Spinoza removes it by denying (1), and neoclassical or process theists remove it by modifying, but not by completely rejecting, (2). The idea that God's existence is immutable and necessary is the "Thomistic" part of neoclassical or process theism's anti-Thomistic Thomism. Neoclassical or process theism also modifies classical theism's defense of (1) in that, although everything particular or specific about the world may have been different, it does not follow that there may have been no world at all, especially because the very concept of absolute nothingness makes no sense. To conceive of it, or to speak about it, is, in some fashion, to turn it into somethingness rather than absolute nothingness. To conceive of a different world is quite different from conceiving of (per impossibile) no world at all (Hartshorne 1976, 12–21).

The poverty of Thomas's view is evident when it is contrasted with the *dual transcendence* of neoclassical or process theism. Thomas's

God exhibits preeminence with respect to only one column of divine attributes found at the top of the present part of the book, whereas the neoclassical or process God is preeminent permanence as well as preeminent change, preeminent independence as well as preeminent dependence, and so forth. Importantly, the law of contradiction states that no subject can have the predicates "p" and "not-p" in the same respect. So there is no contradiction, as Thomists might allege, in saying that God is independent in existence and dependent in actuality. The two aspects are not on the same ontological level, hence the lack of competition between them. For example, at the level of concrete actuality in terms of how God relates to the multitudinous things that exist in the cosmos, God is supreme complexity, even if God's abstract essence as that than which no greater can be conceived is supremely simple. The complexity is largely due to the idea that God, as omniscient, is enriched by the knowledge of each new existent as it comes into being. However, this does not mean that God's knowledge at a previous moment was inadequate in that the future existents that eventually came into being were not there in the past to be known (Hartshorne 1976, 22–27).

To believe that we exist in order to contribute something to God, to the everlasting personal whole of things, is to presuppose that God can be enriched, that our contributions make a difference to God, contra Thomas's concept of God as an unmoved mover and strictly immutable. A wholly immutable deity can only be a means in relation to creaturely purposes. In the strongest terms: Whereas the logic of perfection should push us toward the idea that we should contribute to God, classical theists such as Thomas push us toward the idolatrous idea that God serves us. In different terms, Thomas made far too little use of the higher levels of experience found in love and sympathy and care when he analogized about God and concentrated exclusively on abstract properties like permanence and immutability (Hartshorne 1976, 43–48).

Like most medieval thinkers, Thomas overemphasizes both sacred writings and the finality of Greek philosophy. But the problem is worse. He does not even adequately preserve the best in either the scriptures (especially the claim that God *is* love) or in Greek philosophy, as we will see in part 2 herein. Thomas is at his best, in addition to his call for analogical discourse regarding God, in his moderate realism regarding the problem of universals. These are indications of the "Thomism" part of neoclassical theistic anti-Thomistic Thomism. Thomas unfortunately abandoned analogical reasoning regarding God when the topics in question were divine change, becoming, dependence, and so forth. And it must come as something of a surprise to learn that Thomas is an enlightened self-interest theorist in ethics with this judgment the result of an interpretation of his concept of God. Thomas encourages us to love God not because such love makes any difference to the divine life, but rather because, as classical theism maintains, we are enriched by our love of God (Hartshorne 1983, 74, 82, 87–88).

Thomas is nonetheless to be commended for lining up together the following terms: potentiality, contingency, change, temporality, and so forth. But because they are lined up, he can easily conclude that if a preliminary argument is produced against any one of them in the divine case, then they all come tumbling down together. Hartshorne had a fruitful debate on this topic with William Alston, one of his former students who is a major figure in contemporary analytic philosophy of religion. On Alston's account, Hartshorne gives us two complete packages: the classical concept of God and the neoclassical or process concept of God. Alston thinks that these packages are not as tightly bound as Hartshorne thinks in that one can pick and choose between monopolarity and dipolarity, depending on the contrasting attributes in question, such that his own view is a mixture of classical and neoclassical or process theism. He is thus a demi-Thomist, in contrast to Hartshorne's anti-Thomistic Thomism.

In this regard Alston contrasts two groups of contrasting attributes. In Group 1 we find:

a. absoluteness   relativity
b. pure actuality   potentiality
c. total necessity   necessity and contingency
d. absolute simplicity complexity

Whereas in Group 2 we find the following:

e. creation *ex nihilo*   both God and the world exist necessarily
f. omnipotence   ideal power
g. incorporeality   corporeality
h. nontemporality   temporality
i. immutability   mutability
j. absolute perfection relative perfection

On Alston's view, Hartshorne's criticisms of Thomistic monopolarity work, with qualification, regarding the contrasts in Group 1, but they do not work regarding the contrasts in Group 2, where the contemporary followers of Thomas can still defend classical theism. Thus, Thomas's neoclassical or process critique has much to commend it, especially regarding the idea that classical theism is not required by the practice of theism (Hartshorne 1984b, 67–81).

I am not going to say much about contrasts (a) through (d), which largely involve concessions to neoclassical or process theism regarding issues that have been treated in detail elsewhere in this part of the book. Like Hartshorne, Alston sees absoluteness in terms of nonrelativity, such that what it means to be strictly absolute is to be exclusive of all real relations with others (Hartshorne 2001, 68). One of the aforementioned concessions is found in the following argument Alston offers:

1. (A) "God knows that W exists" entails (B) "W exists."
2. If (A) were necessary, (B) would be necessary.
3. But (B) is contingent.
4. Hence (A) is contingent.

That is, Alston confirms Hartshorne's Aristotelian insight that we can totally exclude contingency in God only by denying that God has knowledge of anything contingent. This is too great a price to pay, as Alston and I see things, if the being in question is the greatest conceivable (Hartshorne 1984b, 81–84; also 2011, 95).

Regarding contrasts (e) and (f), Alston thinks that it is crucial that belief in creation *ex nihilo* has deep roots in religious experience and practice. The oddness of this claim is evident when one realizes that creation *ex nihilo* is not the sort of creation found in the creation stories in Genesis and enters into religious tradition only in the intertestamental literature. On a Whiteheadian view, it is perhaps due to the desire to model God on the imperial rule of Caesar (see Whitehead [1929] 1978, 342–343; Levenson 1988; May 1994), hence when Alston calls it the traditional view, we should be suspicious. If it is the case that belief in creation *ex nihilo* is integrally connected to belief in divine omnipotence, in that it seems that only an omnipotent being might be thought to be powerful enough to bring the cosmos into existence out of absolute nothingness, then the following five criticisms of omnipotence (and of creation *ex nihilo*) can be offered.

First and foremost, Alston hardly notices the metaphysical problems with omnipotence. Neoclassical or process theists in different ways have defended the definition of being in Plato's *Sophist* (247e) as the dynamic power to be affected by causal influences from the past and to creatively affect others in the future in however slight a way. That is, if being just *is* power, however slight, then no being, not even the greatest conceivable one, could have all power as long as other beings exist. To say (in neoclassical or process theistic fashion) that God has the power both to be persuasively influenced by all others and to persuasively influence all others is not to say (in classical theistic fashion) that God has all power (see Dombrowski 2005, chap. 2). The neoclassical or process stance is that God is perfect in all genuinely conceivable ways, but this does not mean that God is perfect in all mentionable ways, such as in classical theistic mention of divine omnipotence in terms of all the power that is (Hartshorne 2001, 32).

Second, and in a related way, we have seen that the concept of omnipotence seems to be integrally connected to the concept of creation out of absolute nothingness, in that it is one thing to create or persuade order out of the disorderly stuff that is already in existence, such as neoclassical or process theists believe, and quite another thing to create the disorderly stuff out of "absolute nothingness." The latter would seemingly require omnipotence. The problem is that creation *ex nihilo* is unintelligible, hence the above scare quotes. Even to talk about "it" (absolute nothingness) is to no longer speak about absolute nothingness, but about somethingness. This is why neoclassical or process theists hold that Plato was wise in the *Sophist* (256–257) to interpret nonbeing in relative terms or as a rough synonym for otherness (for example, this dog is nothing like that one), rather than in absolute terms in that the latter are unintelligible.

Third, the most familiar criticism that neoclassical or process theists receive from classical theists, including Thomists, is that the process God lacks power and hence is an unfitting candidate for the greatest conceivable being. However, many do not even notice that this criticism succeeds only if the previous two points are groundless. It assumes that the words "*omni*potence" and "all power" make sense in a world where there are other beings in existence with powers of their own. And because of the tight connection between omnipotence and creation *ex nihilo*, it assumes that we can make sense of the phrase "absolute nonbeing is" the substratum out of which God brought the world into being through His (the male pronoun is needed here) totalitarian coercive power. But there is no "lack" of power in the neoclassical or process God if these assumptions are defective.

Fourth, there is also a moral critique of omnipotence. Here the salient idea is that even if the concept of omnipotence made sense, whether it would be compatible with belief in divine omnibenevolence is not clear. Neoclassical or process theists have argued at length that it is by no means obvious that coercive power is more admirable than persuasive power, that to be a divine substance that needs nothing else in order to exist is superior to divine relational existence (how could God be benevolent if there were no one else to love?), or that we have greater ignorance of divine goodness than we do of divine coercive power. It is precisely because the neoclassical or process God does not possess all power that such a divinity can possess ideal power (see Loomer 1976; 2013).

The fifth reason to be opposed to omnipotence is related to the fourth. The theodicy objection to omnipotence is a powerful one that emerges directly out of David Hume's famous query regarding why an all-powerful God who is also all-good does not destroy evil, or at least destroy as much of it as possible and still preserve creaturely freedom. Of course, an all-powerful God could presumably destroy all evil and still preserve creaturely freedom. The debates regarding theodicy are well known and complicated. The point here is to emphasize the tendency on the part of neoclassical or process theists to return to the Platonic concept of God as all-good yet not all-powerful (although ideally powerful). The problem here with Thomism and other versions of classical theism is their a priorism: They start with the assumption that God has to be omnipotent and then try (unsuccessfully) to understand the existence of evil or tragedy on this basis. Neoclassical or process theists, by way of contrast, are more empirical by starting with the experiences of intense suffering, tragedy, and evil and then by allowing these experiences to help shape discourse about the concept of God. It is not viewed as a defect by neoclassical or process theists that their view is that even God, although necessarily existent, is in some sense a tragic being. Indeed in one sense God is the most tragic being in that there is no loss that is not felt by such a being in contrast to our feeble assimilation of loss (see Arnison 2012).

My purpose is to counteract Alston's claim that Hartshorne's criticisms of creation *ex nihilo* and of omnipotence are without substance

(Hartshorne 1984b, 85–86). Alston does little to bolster his Thomistic defense of the doctrine of creation *ex nihilo* by pointing out that this doctrine does not necessarily entail a temporal beginning of the world in that if creation *ex nihilo* refers to an eternal utter dependence of the world on God then we are still left with the issue as to how God could exhibit perfect love without creatures in the world to love and how such love does not include some sort of dependence on the creatures. Thomas and Alston ironically abandon analogical thinking and discourse when they talk about God, not the neoclassical or process theist.

Contrast (g) also involves the failure of classical theists to follow through consistently on the claim that God should be discussed analogically. A consistent application of analogy in the divine case would push us toward Hartshorne's view of God as related to the world on the analogy of mind related to body. The doctrines of divine omnipresence and omniscience are made more understandable as a result of such an analogy, whereas these doctrines are, as far as I can tell, completely unintelligible on a classical theistic basis. I defend this claim in detail later in terms of Plato's World Soul. Thomas, along with Alston, sees God as strictly incorporeal, rather than as animating the body of the world. Or again, and ironically, Hartshorne extends Aristotelian hylomorphism beyond the human case so as to speak of cosmic hylomorphism, with God as the soul for the body of the entire cosmos. On the hylomorphist view, we should speak of "mindbodies" or "soulbodies" because of the tight connection between the structure (*morphe*) given to the self by mind or soul, on the one hand, and body (*hyle*), on the other. In contrast, Alston continues Thomas's cosmic dualism, despite the latter's well-known debt to Aristotle in other areas. Unfortunately, Thomas's and Alston's cosmological dualism makes God into a supernatural fifth wheel, so to speak, which was easily discarded in the late modern period by many thinkers who saw strictly incorporeal supernatural intervention into the natural world as increasingly implausible. That is, the rise of modern atheism and agnosticism are not unrelated to the severe problems found in classical theism itself.

Contrasts (h) and (i) are closely related. The classical theistic view is that God exists eternally in an immutably nontemporal state, whereas the Hartshornian neoclassical alternative is that God constantly changes, but everlastingly throughout time. Alston agrees with Hartshorne that temporality and mutability stand or fall together in that God would have to undergo change if God were in time. What could remaining completely unchanged through a succession of temporal moments possibly mean? But Alston argues in a Thomistic manner that Hartshorne's view involves begging the question in that all that Alston is willing to concede is that if God is temporal, then God changes. But he is not willing to admit that God is temporal (Hartshorne 1984b, 87–89).

In defending the Thomistic case Alston also argues that the claim that God might have had a different relation to the world than the one that exists (assuming problematically for the sake of argument that God does have a real relation to the world in classical theism) is not to be conflated with the claim that God exists through a succession of temporal standpoints relative to each of which there is at least a partially open future. That is, Alston defends Thomas's view that God is not involved in process or becoming of any sort. Rather, God exists in a specious present, an "eternal now." However, Alston resists the neoclassical criticism that this means that God is static or frozen. God can be active and knowledgeable "in an instant," he holds (Hartshorne 1984b, 90).

Alston offers an illustration to help us understand his own and Thomas's view. Imagine the flight of a bee that is seen by us "all at once," rather than in segments, one after the other. All we have to do, he suggests, is analogize all of cosmic history with the flight of the bee in order to get some idea of the immutable divine eternal now. Needless to say, this is harder for me to imagine than it is for Alston, even in the case of a bee (in that I have a tendency to say that first the bee went left, then it went up, and so forth), and especially in the case of human, indeed cosmic, history. In any event, even Alston admits that this analogy has problems when we are trying to understand the *interaction* between a human being and God in that such give-and-take seems to be understood only in temporal terms. Many people have as data of their personal religious experience something like what happened to Job: First I received a test, then I responded to it, finally I grew spiritually as a result of the test. As Alston puts the point, "these back-and-forth transactions are not felicitously represented in the classical scheme" (Hartshorne 1984b, 91).

Later we will see that Alston's appealing to Whitehead rather than to Hartshorne makes sense at this point, given an internecine debate among process thinkers regarding the question as to whether the notion of a divine eternal now makes sense. Hartshorne famously opts for the view of God as an everlasting series of occasions of experience. Alston is instructive in the way that he pushes the Thomistic case as far as it can go: On the classical view one must be committed to something like the notion that there is a divine "process" (of knowing, willing, loving) that does not involve temporal succession. That is, Alston tries to weld Thomas and Whitehead together in terms of a single divine "concrescence" rather than in terms of a Hartshornian society of divine occasions of experience. On this view, although God concresces (to be discussed later), there is no transition from one divine experience to another.

In due course I examine the internecine debate within process theism that concerns those who want to defend the view that God is to be seen as a single concrescence, not as one who has a temporal transition from one concrescence to another. This single concrescence view is close to Boethius's (sixth century) famous formulation of divine eternity: the simultaneously whole and perfect possession of interminable life. This formulation has greatly influenced both Thomas and Alston. Although the key point here is that there can be process without temporality, one cannot help but wonder about the consistency in the above formulation of the use of "simultaneously" as well as "life" if the life in question is even remotely analogous to the organic, temporal lives with which we are familiar (Hartshorne 1984b, 94).

Contrast (j) is very much related to contrasts (h) and (i). Relative unsurpassability refers to the impossibility of being surpassed by anyone else, which leaves open the possibility that God might be surpassed by Godself at a later time as new events come into existence that elicit preeminent divine re-sponses. But a God who is not temporal could exhibit only absolute unsurpassability in that such a God would not exist successively through temporal moments. This classical God cannot surpass previous divine perfection because such a divine being does not move from one moment to another; for such a God there is no "previous." The classical God either simply is one eternal now, as in Thomas, or is one indivisible concrescing process of becoming, as in Whitehead, on Alston's interpretation of Whitehead (Hartshorne 1984b, 95).

The dipolar view of neoclassical theism can also be called a type of dual transcendence in that God is seen as preeminently permanent and preeminently changing, preeminently active and preeminently passive. By contrast, the classical view, as I have argued, is monopolar and monotranscendent. Alston is instructive precisely because he puts Thomas into meaningful dialogue with neoclassical or process theists. Alston's view is classical theistic and monopolar and monotranscendent with respect to contrasts (e) through (j). However, regarding contrasts (a) through (d) he is a neoclassical, process, dipolar, dual transcendence theorist. What is unclear in Alston, however, is how he justifies being a monopolar theist regarding some contrasts and a dipolar theist regarding others. Hartshorne is more consistent in that within all noninvidious contrasts there are parts of classical theism that make sense and parts that are problematic because the best insights of classical theism are not brought within a more reticulative neoclassical or process vision of divine perfection (Hartshorne 1984b, 98–99).

Another question for Alston (and Thomas) concerns exactly how one can finesse into the concept of God the dynamism that is required for divine-human *intera*ction if the monopolar God is strictly necessary. On this point Aristotle once again seems more consistent than Thomas or Alston in holding the view that accidents do not happen in eternity. As Hartshorne puts the point: "Aristotle's dictum . . . is about as intuitively convincing as anything so fundamental can be. I believe that our understanding of contingency is inseparable from our intuition that, whereas past events are settled and definite, future events are not settled or definite. Indeed . . . there are no such entities as future events. There are only the *more or less definite possibilities* or probabilities constituting the future so long as it is future" (Hartshorne 1984b, 99). The issue is crucial in the Abrahamic religions because divine love itself is crucial. Unfortunately, classical theism does not readily conceptualize the idea of divine love if what it means for God to love involves divine change, re-sponsiveness, and some version of passivity with respect to the beloved.

Love

7

Rene Descartes
(1596–1650)

We would be mistaken at this point to conclude that classical theism is primarily a medieval position in that its monopolarity, its emphasis on divine omnipotence as well as on divine omniscience with respect to the future, and so forth, continue to be influential doctrines throughout the modern and contemporary periods. To take one initial prominent example, French philosopher Descartes was a Catholic classical theist who, despite the enormity of his originality, contributes very little to the concept of God and retains a thoroughly classical theistic view of this concept.

For example, he assumes without argument in a monopolar way that God is strictly infinite and not finite, a one-sidedness I criticize momentarily. While Descartes contributes to an understanding of the ontological argument for the existence of God in that, although he has a flawed view of this argument in his *Meditations* that assumes that the major contrast in the argument is that between existence and nonexistence, in his *Second Replies to Objections* he makes clear that the relevant distinction in the argument is that between necessary existence and contingent existence and that the latter is at odds with the concept of that than which no greater can be conceived (Descartes 1988, 86-98, 154-155; Hartshorne 2000, 133-137; 1965, 165; 1962, 28, 48, 57).

But there seems to be no cognizance on Descartes's part that the necessity of God's existence does not extend into God's contingent actuality. This leads Hartshorne to speak of "the classical pseudo-idea of the divine nature" in that Descartes tells us nothing about how a strictly necessary divinity could also be a personal God who loves. That is, to the extent that Descartes and other classical theists view God as personal and loving they have implicitly affirmed dipolar theism, but this is a far cry from an explicit identification with neoclassical or process theistic principles (Hartshorne 2000, 136–137; also see Cunning 2013).

This negative judgment regarding Descartes's importance for the development of the concept of God is partially at odds with Armstrong's account. In one sense, she is correct that Descartes, as a scientific mechanist, had no time for mystery, but in another sense he unduly multiplies "mystery" in that every interaction between a strictly unified, infinite, eternal, supernatural God and the natural world is mysterious in the sense of being baffling or contradictory. Armstrong is also correct to notice that the omnibenevolence and omnipotence of God that Descartes affirms cannot be consistent with each other, given the theodicy problem and other difficulties. But she once again assumes that the problems here lie with the God of the philosophers rather than with a particular sort of concept of God defended by some philosophers, that is, the classical theistic concept (Armstrong 1993, 122, 301–302, 305, 312, 344).

In addition to the sheer necessity of God, Descartes's concept of God involves sheer unity, an apparently unexamined inheritance from medieval theology that is at odds with both God's real relations with diverse creatures (assuming that there are such relations) and with the complexity of the divine nature itself, say in terms of the difference between God's necessary existence and contingent actuality. This exhibition of the monopolar prejudice is not unrelated to the aforementioned idea that God is strictly infinite or unlimited and is in no way finite or limited. The problem here is that to reject all limit in God is to lose all concrete definiteness and to have God become indistinguishable from mere indeterminate or infinite potentiality. In the neoclassical or process concept of God, however, the greatest being is not only omnibenevolent, but loves this creature here and now. By uncritically accepting classical theism, and by identifying in classical theistic fashion God with the absolute (that is, with nonrelatedness), God's omnibenevolent concrete relations with creatures in some definite actual state or other are precluded (Hartshorne 1965, 168–170, 216, 227; 1941, 320).

Another problem with classical theism that is especially prominent in Descartes is that in his concept of God as strictly immaterial substance, finding any concepts or variables that are cosmic in scope is impossible, hence making dualism inevitable. On his view, nonhuman nature exhibits absolute order and is in no way free, whereas human beings exhibit partially free escape from order. God, however, is wholly free, on Descartes's view. In effect, Descartes's dualism of human nature is replicated at a higher level in terms of a cosmological dualism where there is no way internal to the Cartesian system to overcome the bifurcation of the world (Hartshorne 1972, 4, 10, 132).

This, in turn, made it famously (or infamously) easy in the late modern period to exorcize the ghost in the machine both at the level of the individual soul and at the level of the divine soul for the whole body of the world (Hartshorne 1937, 125). In addition, Descartes's view seems to be that God created not only all actualities, but also the potentialities out of which these actualities grew (Hartshorne 1941, 233), making his version of creation *ex nihilo* even more extreme than that in most previous versions of classical theism. Hartshorne was fond of pointing out that Descartes himself noticed that brilliant philosophers like to espouse absurd views because it provides an opportunity for them to display their brilliance in covering up the absurdities. One of the absurdities is that, although in the *Meditations* Descartes makes clear that God would not deceive us regarding the existence of the material world, his concept of divine omnipotence and creation out of absolute nothingness implies that God could have done so. Or again, Descartes's quite understandable defense of human freedom is hard to reconcile with his view of divine omniscience with respect to future contingencies. And Descartes's explaining sentience as a supernatural addition to a purely mechanical material world is almost comical (Hartshorne 1970, 45, 70, 96; 1983, 113, 335; 1984a, 129).

Even if Descartes is not the first modern philosopher, his name became identified with modernity such that a criticism of his concept of God can safely be seen as a critique of the God of modernity. (The point is ironic in that because he was a classical theist, Descartes's concept of God was much like that of most of the great medieval thinkers; he was not a great innovator regarding this concept.) Or again, Descartes was, in a sense, the Moses of modern philosophy, as Charles Sanders Peirce (1935) alleged, but not because of his concept of God or his desire to avoid heresy. Rather his innovation largely came from his Augustinian method of doubt, which had as its long-term implication the challenging of every tradition. Such a critique from a process point of view does not necessarily mean that there is nothing of worth in

Descartes; as before, neoclassical theism is, in fact, neo*classical* and deeply indebted to the great figures from the past. For example, Descartes may not have proved in the cogito argument that he existed as a substance or as a permanent ego, as he thought, but he did show quite convincingly in the cogito argument in the *Meditations* that there definitely are momentary experiences, which is a great boon from a process point of view (Hartshorne 1953, 11, 70; 1983, 68, 111, 368; 1984a, 6).

By claiming that Descartes follows a long line of classical theists I am not denying that he plays a very particular and historically significant role in the classical theistic tradition. In the late medieval and Renaissance periods, Christian thinkers with strong voluntarist views dominated the concept of God, a view that tended to accentuate God's omnipotent will. This sort of voluntarism did not fit well with a Thomistic hylomorphic stance wherein every natural entity had its own principle of motion within itself. But the voluntaristic version of classical theism fit well with Descartes's view of purely passive matter, wherein natural things moved only if they were moved from without. Herein lies Descartes's biggest difference in emphasis from previous classical theists such as Thomas Aquinas: In Descartes God functions as an external principle of motion, an omnipotent will that determines all motion. This view may very well be implicit in Thomas, but in Descartes this view has to be highlighted given his concept of supine matter (see Cobb 1991, 172).

8
Gottfried Leibniz
(1646–1716)

❖

Like Descartes, the German philosopher Leibniz is a philosophical theist who, in some senses, is thoroughly modern, while at the
same time a thorough classical theist. He is quite clear in his
Monadology and *Discourse on Metaphysics* that God's power, knowledge, and will are absolutely infinite. From a neoclassical or process
point of view, there is nothing objectionable in Leibniz speaking of
God as perfect. The problem lies in assuming that such perfection is
entirely absolute (that is, nonrelated to others) and infinite in every
respect. Furthermore, if Leibniz had thought that divine omnipotence
contradicted the presence of evil in the world, he probably would have
abandoned this divine attribute. But there really is no evil in the world,
on Leibniz's view; hence, there is no contradiction. There is sufficient
reason, he thinks, for everything that happens; hence, what is commonly called "evil" is ultimately either good or at least conducive to the
good in the long run. Precisely because God is omnipotent, omniscient,
and omnibenevolent, He created the most perfect world, on Leibniz's
view.

Leibniz is a classical theist also in his version of divine omniscience,
wherein God knows all things in a single, atemporal, immutable glance.
Likewise, what God has willed has been willed from eternity. So Leibniz's God sees all and wills all simultaneously from eternity. This view
understandably led Leibniz (as it led the later Augustine, Calvin, several
Muslim thinkers, and others) to defend determinism, contra Descartes.
All human action follows both from God's choice of the best possible
world and from God's knowledge, with absolute assurance and in
minute detail, of what will happen in the future.

Leibniz worked out for the first time in a consistent way two of the most important implications of classical theism: It leads to both an implausible determinism and an even more implausible, indeed unbelievable, claim that there is ultimately no evil in the world. However, this is obviously not the service he intended to perform (Hartshorne 2000, 137).

Leibniz missed at least three things. First, the claim that "God could not have done better" (in that God is perfect) is not synonymous, as Leibniz thought, with the claim that "God could not have done equally well, though differently." Some problems have more than one equally good solution. That is, Leibniz's principle of sufficient reason is itself without reason. Second, the claim that "God could not have done better" (although God could have done otherwise) does not imply that the world that results could not have been better. If one assumes that nothing is better than creating free beings, the world that results from a creator God who could not have done better nonetheless itself could have been better if creatures had made choices that were more responsible than the ones that were actually made. And third, Leibniz assumes that the divine creative act occurred all at once in a single act of creation. In this eternal act of creation, God in effect decides the details of the world for all time. However, if dipolar theism is more defensible than the monopolar theism Leibniz defends, then there are relative and temporal aspects of deity such that creation is not a single act, but an endless series of such (Hartshorne 2000, 140–141).

The following is a startling implication of Leibniz's view: Everything is as a perfect being would require it to be. By partial contrast, in neoclassical, process theism, the problem is not so much creating the best possible world (which assumes that God has to get it right the first time in that there is only one eternal creative act), but the task of trying to bring about the best possible successive state to a world already in being, with its own recalcitrant limits. Leibniz came close to this view when he urged that the value of the world consists in its integration of variety. The mutually contradictory possibilities insure that such integration will be difficult. God does all of the creating, on Leibniz's view, in that we are not, cannot be, cocreators with God. But this view runs afoul of our detailed experience of having made choices in life and of our desire to hold those responsible who have made bad choices (Hartshorne 2000, 141).

Leibniz admits in places that the perfection of the world is not static
and is in endless progress. The net value of the world increases over
time. But, once again, and incredibly from a neoclassical or process
point of view, he never shows cognizance of the idea that this admission
has implications for the logic of perfection and for the concept of God.
As Hartshorne insightfully argues: "The only way to relate this inex-
haustibility intelligibly to God's care for the world is to suppose that
[God's] perfection too is something not wholly and once for all actual,
but is rather, in one aspect, a law whereby [God's] actual achievement
is endlessly enriched by new achievement" (Hartshorne 2000, 142).

By contrast, Leibniz opts for the classical theistic view wherein a
strictly permanent God in a single act creates everything. This aspect
of Leibniz's thought influenced Martin Heidegger in his *Introduction
to Metaphysics*, which Armstrong notes. Whereas the ancient view that
informs neoclassical or process thinkers affirms that from nothing,
nothing comes, the Leibniz-Heidegger view is that *ex nihilo omne qua
ens fit*, from nothing, everything comes (see Armstrong 1993, 388). I
return to this implausible view in part 2.

Importantly, neoclassical or process theists have a certain fondness
for Leibniz's philosophy that they do not have for other versions of
classical theism. He offers the most lucid metaphysics of the early
modern period, his work in metaphysics is informed (as is Whitehead's)
by serious work in mathematics, and he refuses to have the prestige of
science abused by insisting that empirical methods are exhaustive of
what is important in the intellectual life. Furthermore, his panpsychism
is in many respects close to Whitehead's and Hartshorne's own views:
Mere matter, if such existed, would be a superfluous abstraction away
from concrete events in process. Leibniz is also helpful in his contribution to the panpsychist project of showing how active singulars can be
incorporated into either inactive composites or (in living macroscopic
organisms) active composites that are themselves concrete instances
of partially self-moving psyche (Hartshorne 1970, xii–xix, 48, 92, 112;
1962, 11).

However, the admiration that neoclassical, process theists have for
Leibniz can only go so far because he is adamant that a total reality is
already in existence, and it includes future events in full detail. This is
in sharp contrast with the neoclassical, process view that there are no
future events, strictly speaking, only the possibility or probability of

such. If future events existed now they would not be future. Leibniz's view of a total reality already in existence is especially hard to reconcile with his other view that this is the best possible world. The neoclassical, process objection here, in addition to the familiar worry that not all possibilities are compossible (that is, they are not all compatible with each other), is the concern of conceptual overreach on Leibniz's part when he moves from the idea that what is happening at present is the best possible way to reach the best possible world (say through the vagaries of human freedom, which in itself is a good thing) to the wildly implausible idea that it is already the best possible. A related difficulty is Leibniz's stance that there are always already self-identical individuals, rather than event sequences with a common line of inheritance running through them. Admittedly Leibniz follows through consistently in his defense of substantial selves by admitting that such could come into or pass out of existence only through a divine miracle. Once one admits contingency in an event sequence, however, one not only gives up on Leibnizian determinism, but also on the hope to find an a priori reason for the particularities of the world. There simply is no such sufficient reason for these. It is especially odd that Leibniz, as a panpsychist, reduces creaturely creativity to zero (Hartshorne 1970, 17, 30, 35, 70, 177, 180, 251).

The indistinctness of perception leads some people to automatically dismiss the panpsychism that process thinkers admire in Leibniz. For example, if we were able to identify the microindividual cells that experience light or sound, rather than clusters of such, then panpsychism might receive a more friendly reception. Leibniz's problem is not that he does not take panpsychism seriously, but rather that he joins it to an indefensible determinism. The latter is due to his adherence to the classical theistic version of omniscience. That is, individuals as such are sentient, but our inability to detect in sensory perceptions the minute perceptions of which they are subconsciously composed tends to prevent us from appreciating this microsentience. Although Leibniz did appreciate microsentience, he ruined his best insights in this regard by viewing all of reality as preset in the divine mind and hence as existing in an order of simultaneous coexistence. He would have been better served if he had emphasized more his nascent insight regarding the microsentient monads as interacting with each other through time. Some of them would have been sentient as wholes in addition to exhibiting sentience in the microscopic parts ("animate" beings) and some of them would have exhibited sentience only in the parts and would have been insentient as wholes (the supposedly "inanimate" beings). In this regard, even many contemporary thinkers are pre-Leibnizian (Hartshorne 1937, 180, 199; 1934, 66, 143, 269; 1953, 58, 133; 1962, 200, 213).

Importantly, Leibniz's determinism applies, or should apply if he is to be consistent, not only to human beings, but also to God. If there is no real alternative to what God "decides," then no decision has been made if this word literally refers to cutting off some possibilities so that others can go forward. If there is no range of possibility, then referring to what has to be "chosen" as a "possibility" is misleading (Hartshorne 1941, 43; 1948, 119, 137; also Leibniz 1931, 96, 114–115).

The ambivalence neoclassical or process theists exhibit toward Leibniz is especially evident regarding his defense of the ontological argument. He is like many thinkers in not noticing the modal version of the argument in Anselm's *Proslogion*, chapter 3, but instead relies (indirectly through other thinkers) on the nonmodal version in chapter 2. Unfortunately, this inadequacy exerts an influence even on Bertrand Russell (1945) in his famous (or infamous) *History of Western Philosophy*. Nonetheless Leibniz clarifies an important point regarding the ontological argument in holding that the "greatest" that is the subject matter of the argument refers to a qualitative, not a quantitative, maximum. All attributes that are capable of a qualitative maximum, and are compossible with other attributes that are capable of a qualitative maximum, are in God. Leibniz does not help much, however, regarding the crucial question regarding whether the existence of God is possible. On the neoclassical or process view, the God of classical theism is not logically possible for various reasons detailed in this part of the book. To cite just one example, Leibniz rejects all finitude in God; hence his God loses all concrete definiteness and is to be identified with sheer indeterminate (infinite) possibility. A strictly infinite God cannot also be a God who knows and loves particular creatures here and now (Hartshorne 1965, 13, 26–32, 52, 169, 178–180, 298).

Leibniz is astute enough to avoid defining God as the necessarily existent, which would beg the question with which the ontological argument deals, but rather he defines God in terms that are equivalent to Hartshorne's The Unsurpassable or The Worshipful. Once again, however, Leibniz engages in conceptual overreach when he uses the principle of sufficient reason to account for even the contingencies of life. There is no sufficient reason for these in that they are the result of capricious conjunctions of events or free choices or brute facts that are undeducible from previous reasons. They are not the conclusions to concealed syllogisms. The issue here is very much related to the cogency of the ontological argument in that the accusation is often made that this argument is the product of ultrarationalism. However, this argument cannot be defended until ultrarationalism is rejected. The a priori truth of theism that is involved in the ontological argument is not to be equated with the a priori truth of things in general, including the contingent aspects of the divine life. In other words, only the bare essence and hence necessary existence of God are treated in the ontological argument, not the contingent actuality of God (Hartshorne 1965, 185–186, 192).

The tendency in contemporary philosophy is to run to the opposite extreme from ultrarationalism, wherein, as Leibniz thought, there is sufficient reason for everything. In order to hold in check the excesses of ultrarationalism one needs to affirm the idea that reality, including divine reality, is one thing and the essential or the necessary is only one abstract aspect of it. Not everything about God is as necessary as the abstract existence of God. Identifying God's initial creative act with divine preservation of the world in a single atemporal act is a mistake on the part of classical theists. On the contrasting process view, reality, including divine reality, consists in definite steps one after another. This is another way of saying that God cannot simply choose a world in a flash, as Leibniz thought, in that a series of divine choices, as well as many series of creaturely choices, have to be taken into account (Hartshorne 1965, 188, 190, 192, 199–200, 243).

Leibniz, along with Whitehead, philosophizes about God with a scope of intellectual interest that is quite remarkable. For example, both were world-class mathematicians as well as philosophers. And both tried to bring the whole of nature into their systems, which in Whitehead's case, at least, is a fallibilist system that experience can modify as time goes on. But Whitehead, along with other process thinkers, is skeptical of Leibniz's claim that God is statically actual, even if God is admittedly supremely actual. Although he is often classified as a rationalist, Leibniz has vestiges of materialism that surface in his denial of creativity in any being other than God. His monads (distantly analogous to Whitehead's actual occasions) are simple individuals without creative relations with others in that they have "windows" only to God. Admittedly Leibniz explained endurance all too well, but he did this to such a degree that nothing new can enter an individual that is not already in its identity from eternity due to the classical theistic version of divine omniscience he defended (Hartshorne 1972, 2, 4, 10, 36, 49, 50).

The root of Leibniz's difficulties lies in his neglect of temporal asymmetry such that when confronted with the choice between claiming that happenings are in beings (Aristotle's approach) or claiming that enduring being is abstracted from an ordered string of happenings (the process approach), Leibniz chooses the former. The old self always possesses (at least implicitly, once again due to classical theistic divine omniscience) everything that will occur later. That is, only by neglecting temporal asymmetry could Leibniz suggest that an individual substance has at all times the same totality of qualities (Hartshorne 1972, 51, 120–121, 182).

Because Leibniz almost saw that true singulars have internal power, which calls into question classical theistic omnipotence, he is the quintessential intermediary between classical theism and neoclassical or process theism. The fact that he identifies individuals with their careers, however, pulls him back toward classical theism, specifically toward classical theistic omniscience; whereas his realization that the powerful basic units of nature are analogous to our own self-awareness pulls him toward neoclassical or process theism and its critique of classical theistic omnipotence. Another feature of his thought that pulls him back toward classical theism is his belief that this is the best of all possible worlds, a belief that Hartshorne thinks is a caricature of theism that plays into the hands of unbelievers such as Friedrich Nietzsche. But these pulls toward classical theism are balanced at the other end by pulls toward process panpsychism or panexperientialism. Once again, the confused character of perception leads to the conclusion that nature must be explained in terms of substances in that matter is assumed to be made of bits of insentient stuff. Leibniz's analysis of the grossness that characterizes sense perception is remarkable given the fact that cell theory had not yet been discovered. The lack of specificity in the given hides, he realizes, pervasive subhuman experience. Once the powers that characterize this pervasive activity are acknowledged,

becoming a process, neoclassical theist for a Leibnizian is easy (Hartshorne 1983, 28, 91, 105, 181, 243, 274, 312, 369, 375).

Because of Leibniz's determinism, this is not only the best of all
possible worlds, but it is also, in a way, the only possible world. But
this renders his philosophy pragmatically meaningless in that nothing
we can do will alter what will inevitably occur as God knows it will
occur with absolute assurance and in minute detail. The very distinction between better and worse is undermined as a result of Leibniz's
view in that if nothing could be better or worse about the world as
it is, judgments of value start to look pointless. As before, we are in
Leibniz's debt regarding his idea that our awareness of ourselves as
experiencing animals is our only definite model for individuality in
general. This view enables him to avoid the theological implication of
dualism: Reality is composed of insentient matter, at one end, and God
as pure spirit, on the other. On this Cartesian view, the alleged mixture
of the two found in human beings is utterly unintelligible. Despite
Leibniz's genuine advance over Descartes's dualism, his classical theism
and the practical implications of this view severely limited his genius
(Hartshorne 1984a, 17, 50, 67, 152, 213, 274).

In different terms, Leibniz saw that we are the most instructive
samples of reality, which pushes him toward the process panexperientialist (or panpsychist) view, as does his realization that apart from all
experience there would be "absolutely nothing," so to speak. Because
he viewed truth as timeless (as a result of the classical theistic version of omniscience), he misunderstood each one of us as a changeless
substance who was to be identified with its career (Hartshorne 1984b,
67, 123–125). Hartshorne is so impressed with Leibniz's anticipation of
process panpsychism or panexperientialism he claims there are two
classes of philosophers after Leibniz: those who do and those who
do not realize that we should ask not only about whether a whole is
sentient, but also about whether the parts of the whole are sentient
at a microscopic level. In this regard Leibniz also anticipates William
Wordsworth and the romantic reaction to dualism and mechanism, a
reaction that is at the heart of the process, neoclassical view (Hartshorne 1990, 229, 372; 1991, 590).

Once Leibniz's principle of sufficient reason is trimmed, one can
nonetheless admit a certain predictability regarding what happens in
the world as long as the statistical nature of this predictability is not
inflated into deterministic hyperbole (Hartshorne 1991, 580–581).

The aforementioned anticipation in Leibniz of the romantic reaction found in both Wordsworth and process thinkers is also evidenced in Leibniz's view that science ironically both enriches and impoverishes experience. The latter is due to the indistinctness of perception modern, mechanistic science encouraged. But a purely mechanical account of either experience or nature is an illusion on the Leibnizian, romantic, and process views because of the common belief that reality is essentially activity and appearances to the contrary are due precisely to the indistinctness of perception (Hartshorne 2011, 16, 34, 60, 62).

Leibniz is certainly instructive in viewing necessity in terms of what all possibilities have in common. On this basis cosmological dualism is incompatible with the necessary existence of God. At times Leibniz seems to agree with this view, especially when he sides with some of the later scholastics (for example, Tommaso Campanella) in trying to relate analogically categories that apply to both the divine and the nondivine. For example, talk about divine power does not preclude power in the creatures, as sometimes occurs in dualism; indeed, if the creatures exist in any fashion whatsoever they have a certain degree of power on their own. Yet Leibniz unfortunately negates some of his most insightful moments when he identifies an individual with its career, thus ignoring the dynamic, temporal pulse of the universe wherein monads should not be viewed as substantial, unchanging entities but rather as momentary, powerful expenditures of energy. To make these monads windowless, as Leibniz does, is unfortunately to render classical theism incompatible with personalism (Hartshorne 2011, 45, 49, 61, 116, 124; 2001, 14; also see M. Griffin 1994).

9
Immanuel Kant
(1724–1804)

Kant is the most famous critic of philosophical theology. One not so famous feature of his thought is an implicit argument for the existence of God, which he nonetheless forbids us to follow. In this implicit argument for the existence of God, however, the German philosopher Kant can be seen as assuming a concept of God that is classical theistic in character.

The implicit argument for God is found in Kant's first critique, the *Critique of Pure Reason*, where he assumes that sensory intuition is passive in character, while intellectual intuition is active and creates its objects. In familiar Kantian terms, appearances are called "phenomena," whereas things-in-themselves are called "noumena." But we cannot distinguish between things as they appear and things as they are unless we assume that there really is a form of knowledge not reliant on sensation but that has as its concern strictly objective reality. That is, appearance is nothing in itself and indicates a relation to something that is. The sort of intuition that is assumed here is divine in nature (Kant 1930, 298–304).

Given the aims of this book, my point here is not to assess Kant's implicit argument for the existence of God, but to determine what this argument says about Kant's concept of God. We see immediately that he assumes that God is a strictly nonmaterial being. Indeed, he elsewhere says that "the transcendental nonempirical concept of God as the most real being is unavoidable in philosophy, abstract as the idea is, since it is essential to the understanding" (Kant 1921, 16–18). Words such as "nonempirical" (more on the divine body later) and "abstract" (to the exclusion of concrete divine actuality) are indications of a commitment on Kant's part to monopolarity as described previously. God for Kant is the *ens realissimum*, the most real being (not the most real becoming) who is the ground of all reality. Although the nature of God is ultimately beyond our ken in Kant, he nonetheless, like apophaticists in general, indicates quite specifically a concept of God that is in conformity to the classical theistic tradition.

Although Kant is skeptical of any theoretical analogy between God and creatures, he seems to think that if there were a God, such a supreme being would exhibit supreme nonempirical understanding. If the doctrine of analogy is used in philosophical theology, it would have to involve not an imperfect similarity of two things, but a perfect similarity of relation between two quite different things, one that relied on the empirical and one that did not (Kant 1933, 129).

Kant also has a famous explicit argument for the existence of God by way of postulation. The *summum bonum* or greatest good discussed in Kant's second critique, the *Critique of Practical Reason*, involves both virtue (worthiness of being happy) and actual happiness. The supreme cause of nature, God, is presupposed as a condition of the Kantian *summum bonum* in that the virtuous are often not the recipients of happiness, at least not in this earthly life. God is here characterized as a supreme paymaster who has supreme intelligence and will, and one who will eventually reward the virtuous with happiness. To be clear, assuming the existence of God is morally necessary in Kant, in that without such a view we would be left with the unsatisfactory result that virtue might not be rewarded with happiness (Kant 1996, 135, 150–152).

Kant's treatment of philosophical theology presupposes a classical theistic concept of God that goes back to Philo in that God is assumed to be absolute, eternal, and independent. That is, Kant seems to identify any conception of a temporal God as anthropomorphic. In different terms, he subscribes to the half-truths of monopolarity. The problem here can be noticed when we consider the dipolar alternative regarding the contrast between independence and dependence. There is a significant difference between claiming that God is independent as to existence and essential individuality, on the one hand, and independence as to concrete content of the divine life, on the other. One can preserve the former in neoclassical, process theism, but there is no compelling reason to think that the latter needs to be preserved, as in classical theism, including Kant's version of it (Hartshorne 2000, 146).

One of the prime reasons that Kant, along with other classical theists, is skittish about whether God can be positively conceived is that on classical theistic assumptions one ends up in various conceptual problems, antinomies, even contradictions. To be explicit, Kant's famous and hugely influential skepticism regarding any theoretical knowledge that is possible regarding God is not unrelated to the untenable concept of God that he has in mind. This point is not noticed by those (both theists and nontheists) who themselves assume that the concept of God is definitively settled in terms of classical theism. However, Kant is to be thanked for pointing out that all of our positive conceptions involve the temporal. Difficulties arise when he assumes without argument that God must be wholly nontemporal. But if one supposes that God is the categorically supreme example of temporal reality, such as in neoclassical or process theism, the terrain of philosophical theology looks much more promising (Hartshorne 2000, 146–147).

Just as Kant is correct to think that our positive conceptions involve the temporal, but incorrect to identify God with the nontemporal, so also he may be incorrect in thinking that God must transcend any sort of embodiment, as we will see regarding the neoclassical or process idea that God's body is the universe itself. At every turn Kant ends up with classical theistic problems. For example, his assumption that God would have to be omnipotent drives him toward a sort of utopianism wherein life does not really make sense unless virtue is rewarded with happiness. Somewhere, somehow, it is assumed, there has to be an escape from evil and from the tragedy of life. Neoclassical, process theists do not make this assumption. If we are free, we are bound to make decisions that get in each other's way such that clashes of freedom lead to tragedy. "One must find joy in tragedy, or one will not find it, and this is true of God" as well (Hartshorne 2000, 149). A Platonic theodicy influences this Hartshornian view, which is treated in part 2.

Hartshorne sums up well the neoclassical or process assessment of Kant's view:

All in all, Kant is a classical or monopolar theist who emphasizes the theoretical difficulties in this position more than his predecessors but hopes to save it by appeal[ing] to a construction of the moral law. . . . His God becomes a cosmic magistrate and policeman who sees to it that the good are given their deserts—an anthropomorphic conception, indeed, of the ultimate end of existence! What remains valid is Kant's insistence that we cannot rightly renounce the notion that there must be some supreme end to which in ethics we may adjust our purposes. (Hartshorne 2000, 150)

Unfortunately, Armstrong, Bowker, and Capetz do not fully appreciate the fact that Kant is a classical theist and that his skepticism regarding philosophical theology is largely due to his classical theistic assumptions. For example, Capetz provides a standard view of Kant as rejecting rational religion to make room for faith, but he does not show any familiarity with the idea that Kant's rejection of rational religion is really a rejection of such on a classical theistic basis (Capetz 2003, 112–113). Bowker seems to have a similar view (Bowker 2002, 357). And Armstrong follows her usual inclination to think that the problems in philosophical theology are caused by the inadequacy of reason in general to deal with the concept of God. In this regard she is herself ironically quite Kantian in that she has a tendency to confuse problems with reason, in general, with problems associated with its particular exemplification in the classical theistic case. She is astute, however, to emphasize that the moral argument for God in Kant is something of an afterthought and that Kantian autonomy could easily be extended just a step further than Kant was willing to extend it to dispense with God altogether. By destroying rational religion, Kant made room for faith *or* the lack thereof. Since Kant some thinkers have been willing to take a leap of faith, but many are obviously not leapers (Armstrong 1993, 314–318).

In contrast to Armstrong, Bowker, and Capetz, neoclassical or process theists are likely to identify God with nature as infinitely loveable as well as with nature as infinitely intelligible. To say that nature is godless (the atheistic or agnostic view) or to say (as in Kant) that we cannot have any theoretical, in contrast to practical, knowledge of God is to say that nature is basically unintelligible or that it might be so. In this regard Armstrong, Bowker, and Capetz are, in spite of themselves, very Kantian. But if scientific knowledge itself assumes and points us toward a unified set of principles that governs nature, then it is implied that nature can be seen by a single, integrated experience:

> To say nature is godless is to say that it is not basically intelligible. . . . Now the more unified the world is conceived to be, the more it is conceived

to approach the maximum case in which all diversity is embraced in a single experience integrated by a single purpose or value. No other form of unity approaches this in degree. All other conceivable forms are, as Kant pointed out, loose or chaotic by comparison. To say God is not, is to say that the intelligible unity of the world is slight, not simply for our understanding but in itself. This attitude discourages the attempt to enlarge our comprehension of nature, for it makes it always possible that our failures to do so are results of defects in nature as a whole, and not merely in ourselves as parts of nature. (Hartshorne 1937, 23)

Just as Kant's philosophizing in light of Newtonian physics needs to be reconsidered in light of developments in twentieth-century science, so also Kant's philosophizing in light of eighteenth-century assumptions in religion needs to be reconsidered in light of contemporary alternatives to classical theism. In this regard Derek Malone-France is correct to alert us to the fact that Whitehead's *Process and Reality* is in many ways a magnum opus that does for relativity physics what Kant's first critique did for Newton's *Principia* (see Malone-France 2007; also see Hartshorne 1967, xi). For example, it is noteworthy that the determinism of Kant's first critique is in some sense qualified by the indeterminism of the second critique, but the freedom discussed in the latter book is strictly nontemporal. That is, Kant is quintessentially a nonprocess philosopher. As Hartshorne puts the point, "Kant . . . did not so much as dream of neoclassical theism" (Hartshorne 1967, 27).

As before, Kant assumes that if the traditional arguments for the existence of God were to work they must point to the existence of a most real being who is wholly infinite, timeless, and absolute. Believing in such a divinity, importantly, is not only not supported by rational argumentation, but it also cannot even be consistently affirmed on the basis of faith, contra Kant. If the classical theistic God is utterly changeless, then such a God would be completely unmoved by our faith and our worship, such that the point to these would seem to be for our benefit, thus turning theistic belief into a sort of egocentrism (Hartshorne 1967, 32–33). However, I am not necessarily criticizing the primacy of the practical in Kant. Rather, what is problematic is the primacy of the practical based on classical theistic assumptions about the concept of God as well as the assumption that the primacy of the practical excludes any theoretical argument regarding either the concept of or the existence of God. But why should we assume that God must eschew receptivity or change (Hartshorne 1967, 48–49, 54)?

Kant's view that concepts without percepts are empty is very instructive. But he does not apply this insight to the divine case. It is one thing to have a concept about God's (necessary) existence, but it is another thing to have the concrete feelings that God has from moment to moment. In effect, Kant, like classical theists in general, has a concept of God that is too abstract because of its monopolarity and because of its failure to distinguish between the permanence of divine existence and the fluency of divine actuality (Hartshorne 1967, 76).

The neoclassical or process view is that there cannot be a strictly immutable being who is also living; hence we should not be surprised that Kant, whose concept of God was that of a strictly immutable being who lived, thought that the concept of God necessarily led to paradoxes and hence had no real rational content. One can legitimately infer from this that Kant had a failed concept of God. Or again, one can agree with Kant that time is a positive idea and that all of our ideas involve temporal succession, especially modal concepts like "may or may not have been," "must have been," or "could not have been." But by assuming that God is completely outside of time one necessarily ends up with paradox at every turn. However, he correctly notes that we cannot conceive of the very first stage of process in that such a supposed first stage would be an exception to the metaphysical principle that each event arises out of its predecessors; claiming that the first event arose out of "absolute nothingness" reduces metaphysics to something like magic (Hartshorne 1970, 38–39, 62, 65; 1972, 87; 1991, 578, 681). In response to Kant's first antinomy in the first critique, one must admit that we must either suppose a first moment of all becoming or an infinite or indefinite number of past events. The neoclassical or process theistic idea is that, contra Kant and in conformity with the ancient Greek notion, an actual infinity of already elapsed events is a tenable concept (Hartshorne 2011, 77).

Unfortunately, Kant thought of time as strictly phenomenal or linguistic, rather than as ontological. This view was facilitated by his viewing God as altogether timeless. Why view time as ontologically real when God could escape it? His classical theistic view of God as timeless also facilitated the concept of God as an absolute maximum of value in contrast to the more defensible view of God as asymmetrically superior: With each new moment God incorporates more of the world into the richness of the divine life. On the neoclassical or process view, God is modally coextensive in the sense that God knows all that is actual as actual and all that is potential or probable *as potential or probable*. In this regard we can more easily understand the rise of agnosticism or atheism after Kant in that the most universally experienced reality (God) is not the most obviously experienced. We take God for granted in the way we take air for granted in that it is always there; in contrast, note how readily apparent some things are because they are rare, as in intense pain or as in a bright red object (Hartshorne 1970, 137, 225, 247; 1991, 41).

Kant does not seem to have thought about the idea that God's existence is quintessentially noncompetitive in that no fact could cause God not to exist, yet God's concrete actuality from moment to moment is competitive in that one actual state (say an awareness of a creature in pain) can be at odds with some other actual state (say the same creature avoiding the accident that caused the pain). Divine actuality, however, presupposes the sort of ideal passivity that Kant, along with other classical theists, denies. To put the point in the sharpest Hartshornian terms: What Kant thought of as theism is actually nontheistic and idolatrous if God is seen as the supreme, nonmoving, impassive abstraction. In a peculiar way, Kant realizes this when he indicates that theism has no rational content, which is another way of saying (unwittingly) that classical theism is a failure. Not to be influenced by sentient creatures is to be ignorant, at best, or morally perverse, at worst (Hartshorne 1970, 253, 277, 279; 1972, 63, 87; 1984a, 212).

The difficulties with classical theism are not "merely" theoretical, but existential as well. Theists hope that by living well they can give something to God (and they fear that by living poorly they disappoint God); by optimizing their gifts they hope to enrich an everlasting life that is not timeless, even if it is unborn and undying. If the theist is correct, we serve a primordial, deathless, and all-cherishing God. This is what Kant should have meant by the *summum bonum*, but he was unable to do this because of his classical theism, where God has no need of enrichment because the divine being is already and eternally superenriched. Nor can we get Kant off the hook by suggesting that it would have been too much to expect him to question classical theism in that Spinoza, the Socinians, and others had questioned it before Kant, as we will see (Hartshorne 1991, 573, 705).

Regarding the concept of God, Kant is very much a traditionalist. His chief criticism of classical theism is not that the concept of God that was passed down from the Middle Ages is defective, but that belief in such a God could be justified only as a postulate of philosophical ethics. Additionally, the determinism of Kant's *Critique of Pure Reason* is compatible with the classical theistic claim that God's initiative settles everything. In fact, Kant admitted freedom only as noumenal and hence as beyond our ken, even if there is a practical necessity to believe in it. "How our noumenal freedom was to be understood or related to phenomenological determinism or to the creative action of God was, he thought, entirely beyond our possible comprehension" (Hartshorne 1983, 170). As is well known, trying to reconcile the realms of the phenomenal (how things appear to us) and noumenal (how things are in themselves) in Kant has tremendous difficulties. Hartshorne's snappy way to put the point is to say that "Kant's view is that, while it is absurd to suppose that what appears is merely the appearance itself, nevertheless, we cannot even reasonably guess in what properties, if any, the reality is like the appearances" (Hartshorne 1983, 171).

Thinking that Kant's enormously influential theory of knowledge was divorced from his concept of God would be a mistake. Hartshorne reconstructs his argument as follows:

1. The only kind of knowledge of the way the world really is in itself (quite apart from how it appears to us) would be divine in character.
2. Divine knowledge is, by definition, independent of what is known. In fact, divine knowledge is (as it was for Thomas Aquinas) what really creates the world. However, the world does not create or even influence God; herein lies the origin of the (in)famous classical theistic doctrine of divine impassibility.
3. Thus, our knowledge is almost the opposite of God's knowledge in that our knowledge is, in a way, produced in us by the things that we are trying to know.
4. It is precisely the passivity of our knowledge that explains why we can know only appearances rather than the noumenal world in itself. Reality is what God alone could know, since only divine knowledge creates its own objects (Hartshorne 1983, 172).

From the perspective of neoclassical or process theism, the first claim is unproblematic. But neoclassical theists reject the second and fourth claims due to the confusion that results from a simultaneous adherence to the dicta that we know reality because it exists, whereas the world exists because God knows it (Hartshorne 1983, 173). The third claim is especially problematic in suggesting that our knowledge is almost the exact opposite of divine knowledge. The neoclassical or process alternative claims that divine knowledge is analogous to our knowledge. In different terms, the weakness of our knowledge is not due to the fact that it is passive, but rather to the fact that it is not passive enough, not receptive enough to all that exists.

If knowledge (understandably) consists, at least in part, in being determined by the object known, then God creates us not by knowing us, as classical theists think, but by persuading us into existence, in Platonic fashion, out of primordial chaos. That is, contra Kant, the model of creation is dialogue wherein God is not conceived, as in classical theism, on the analogy of someone who wishes to be heard but who does not hear. "This is the benevolent despot ideal that Kant avoided in his political theory but not in his theology" (Hartshorne 1983, 173-174). Kant is ironically in the line of medieval theologians.

The irony is that one suspects that Kant could have been turned into a process thinker because he took time very seriously. The only proper use we can make of concepts is to apply them to spatio-temporal things. This is another way of saying that we should be concerned with becoming and not with mere being, even when thinking of God. Or again, the ultimate principle is genuine coming-to-be rather than mere accidental changes in relatively static substances (Hartshorne 1983, 176-178). This irony is intensified when it is considered that one can imagine a case for panentheism on a Kantian basis, especially when the third critique (*Critique of Judgment*) is considered (even if such a position was not Kant's own): Kant's God is moral and the phenomenal world is *in* the noumenal world of God as moral (see Palmquist 2013).

Just as assuming that Kant's concept of God is unrelated to his epistemology would be a mistake, so also it would be a mistake to assume that it is unrelated to existential concerns as they surface in his philosophy. We have seen that the real *summum bonum* to which rational beings should contribute is God, specifically God's ideal union of goodness and happiness. All human beings, and not merely the malicious ones, fall short of this ideal. The degree of goodness in the world is largely dependent on the decisions of innumerable creatures on many levels "and these no law of nature, no advance planning by deity or creature, can settle beforehand," despite Kant's defense of determinism in his *Critique of Pure Reason* (Hartshorne 1983, 185, 187).

Kant was a bit glib in his assumption that faith was not in need of theoretical support, which is odd considering that classical theism is a ripe target for theoretical disproof. That is, the rise of contemporary agnosticism and atheism is not unconnected to the pervasive influence of Kant's fideism (that is, to his faith in God without rational support), which in turn is due to the contradictions that necessarily surface in the classical concept of God (Hartshorne 1983, 234).

Part 2

Ancient Greek Theism

Contrasting Hume and Kant on the concept of God will help segue into part 2. The latter, I claim, has a classical theistic concept of God. But Hume, although a religious skeptic, has a more catholic view of the concept of God wherein alternatives to the classical theistic concept are taken seriously. For example, Hume's *Dialogues Concerning Natural Religion* (1980) criticizes the cosmological dualism typical of classical theists, wherein the cosmos is seen in a two-tiered manner with an eternal, immaterial God hovering above a temporal, material world. An alternative to this view considered in Hume's dialogues is the ancient Greek view of God as the soul not for this or that body, but for the body of the world as a whole (see Hartshorne 2000, 422–424). In fact, Plutarch tells us that belief in God as the World Soul was the dominant one in antiquity, held by *all* of the great ancient philosophers except for Aristotle and the atomists (see Plutarch 1870, 3. 133). This is a remarkable claim. Plutarch refers to a type of cosmological hylomorphism wherein, contra the classical theistic view, God is not seen as entirely separate from the material world but as animating it in its entirety by providing structure (*morphe*) to the material stuff of the world (*hyle*).

Part 2 helps us to: (1) understand the ancient Greek roots of both classical theism and neoclassical or process theism; (2) grasp how certain intellectual moves (I would say mistakes) made among ancient Greek philosophers themselves made it more likely that classical theism would become the dominant philosophical and theological view in the Abrahamic religions; and (3) comprehend better the sedimented process whereby certain Greek concepts were accepted and transmitted to later ages whereas others largely fell by the wayside, as in serious consideration of God as the the World Soul. I will be concentrating on the thought of Plato especially, but also that of Aristotle and Plotinus.

10

Plato

(427–347 BCE)

Omnipresence

Whitehead is famous for his aforementioned observation that "the safest general characterization of the European philosophical tradition is that it consists of a series of footnotes to Plato" (Whitehead [1929] 1978, 39). This observation is especially applicable regarding the concept of God. Unfortunately, the process perspective on Plato's view of God has largely been neglected and this neglect impoverishes both our view of Plato and our view of what could or should be said regarding the history of the concept of God and what could or should be said in contemporary philosophy of religion and theology regarding the Platonic concept of God.

As the quotation from Royce in the introduction indicates, we contemporary thinkers are not as original as we often think. That is, thought about God is historical thinking in the sense that we never start thinking of God de novo, but are always reacting to or modifying the concepts of God that have been passed down from generation to generation. No thinker has been more influential in the development of the Western concepts of God than Plato, and hence there is something bold in the process claim that most, but not all, interpreters of Plato's theism over the centuries have either not noticed, or have underemphasized, the dynamism of his theism (Dombrowski 2005, 3).

Plato's thoughts on the concept of God have two facets, one static and the other dynamic, with the latter largely forgotten. The first facet has a distinction between the immutable and the mutable or between the formal and the material. Both soul and God are put into the former elements in each of these pairs, in monopolar fashion, for reasons to be discussed momentarily. However, in the second facet of Plato's thought on God, motion is granted to soul, including to God as the World Soul. The opposition here in the second facet is between independent and dependent mobility. Granted, within the World Soul there is a principle of immutability in that God everlastingly remains the soul for the body of the cosmos. By contrast, this principle of immutability characterizes divine soul per se in the first facet. Dipolar contrast between categories in tension with each other must be seen as inherent in the Platonic framework. Reality, including divine reality, is one, but this unity can only be discursively or metaphysically understood as two.

In the first, and more famous, facet of Plato's concept of God he flirts with ontolatry, the worship of being. Several Platonic texts come to mind in this regard (for example, *Phaedo* 80a-b; *Republic* 380e, 381b-c, 381e, 382e; *Laws* 797d; *Epinomis* 982d-e, 985a; and so forth). This facet sees something inherently perilous about change from the perspective of divine fixity. Furthermore, in this facet of Plato's thought about God there is no need for God to change in that if such a change were to occur, it would indicate something imperfect about God in that a perfect being would have no need to change. The second facet of Plato's concept of God flirts with gignolatry, the worship of becoming. Here soul, including God as the World Soul, is defined as self-motion and vitality. That is, soul, including God as the World Soul, is anything but reified substance, but rather has the power or *dynamis* of self-motion (see the *Phaedrus* 245–246; also Book Ten of *Laws*; and so forth). But not even in this second facet does Plato succumb to gignolatry in that even in this facet God *always* exhibits self-motion, indicating a consistency to divine *dynamis*.

Even before I examine Aristotle's concept of God I would like to highlight the following quite ironic shift that occurs in the transition from Plato to Aristotle: Plato is famous for a dipolar categorical scheme, wherein form is contrasted to matter and being is contrasted to becoming, but he ends up with a cosmological monism wherein the divine animal (the World Soul) includes all; Aristotle, conversely, is famous for a monopolar categorical scheme of embodied form, yet he ends up with a cosmological dualism more severe than anything found in Plato's dialogues (Dombrowski 2005, 65). That is, the identification of Plato's view with the first facet in his thought on God is misleading in that, like a child begging for both, Plato declares through the Eleatic Stranger in the *Sophist* (249d) that reality (as dynamic power) is both at once: the unchangeable and that which changes. This view has significant consequences for theism (Dombrowski 2005, 71).

Plato's theology turns on two principles: the "pure being" of the forms and the "supreme mobility" of soul. The unchanging deity (including such deity's knowledge of the forms) of the *Phaedo*, *Republic*, and parts of the *Parmenides* is the supreme instance of fixity; the self-moving deity of the *Phaedrus* and *Laws* is the supreme instance of mobility. Alluding to the aforementioned passage in the *Sophist* (to the effect that Plato, like an entreating child, says "Give us both"), Hartshorne claims that the two poles of Plato's theism are brought together with almost equal weight in the *Timaeus*. But the word "together" is problematic in that Plato mythically fixes the correlative categories in different beings, the Demiurge and the World Soul, to be discussed again momentarily (Dombrowski 2005, 73).

There is nothing objectionable about the view of divine perfection found in the *Republic*, wherein a perfect being is assumed not to change, as long as such a view is placed within a more inclusive, dipolar view of God. As before, God *always changes* and both words are needed. If God were an *ens realissimum*, a most real being that could not at all change, either by improvement or by influence from others, as Kant thought, God would come dangerously close to violating the definition of real being as dynamic power in the *Sophist* at 247e (Dombrowski 2005, 74). The problem does not lie in the assumption found in the *Republic* (381b) that God is in every way the best possible (*ta tou theou pantei arista echei*), but rather with the assumption that the best possible would be changeless in every respect. Although Plato himself is partly to blame for travelling as far as he did down the road to ontolatry, he took other journeys in his dialogues that are worth revisiting.

The whole point to neoclassical, process, dipolar theism is that there is a way to reconcile the exaltation of both being and becoming in terms of Hartshorne's distinction between divine existence and divine actuality: the former concerns the mere fact of God's permanent existence, whereas the latter concerns how God exists dynamically from moment to moment. Given this distinction, one is tempted to say that when the topic of conversation is God's bare existence, one can legitimately claim that God is unchanged, self-sufficient, invariable, indissoluble, and abides forever. We cannot change the fact that God always exists. However, when we consider divine actuality, the texture of God's existence or how God exists, describing God in terms of becoming and change makes sense. Just as I constantly change, yet retain a relatively stable identity as "Dan" throughout these changes (see *Symposium* 207d-e), analogously God everlastingly (or sempiternally) changes from moment to moment as a result of God's omnibenevolent and omniscient relationships with creatures, yet retains a stable identity or permanent being as "God" throughout these preeminent changes (Dombrowski 2005, 77–78). God's being refers to an abstract feature that applies to all of the concrete moments of becoming in the divine life.

God's bare existence is quite abstract because it has infinite variations and flexibility. In different terms that are compatible with Plato's dipolar theism, God is coextensive with modality as such: God is related actually to all actual things and potentially to all potential things. God is, because of the definition of being as dynamic power in the *Sophist*, influenced by and influences everything. Thus, modal coextensiveness is equivalent to the notion of the unsurpassable (Dombrowski 2005, 93).

Before moving to a fuller discussion of divine omnipresence in this chapter, and discussions of divine omniscience and a Platonic argument against divine omnipotence in the following chapter, we should note two provisos. First, I will not be treating in any detail my assumption that there is a chronology to Plato's dialogues such that his most insightful comments regarding the compatibility between being and becoming are found in later dialogues such as the *Sophist* and *Timaeus*. Likewise, I also assume without argument here, although I have argued the case elsewhere (Dombrowski 2005, 5–11), that Plato's view is not entirely absent in his writings, despite the fact that he primarily wrote dialogues where he does not appear as a character. And second, I also assume here that, despite the fact that Plato's dialogues waver between the singular and the plural when talking about the divine (*theos* and *theoi*, respectively), monotheism is close to the surface in his thought, especially when the World Soul is considered. That is, when Plato refers to gods he seems to have popular piety in mind rather than the conceptual problem of how to account for a unified cosmos (see Dombrowski 2005, 11–12, 84–89).

Let us now consider divine omnipresence. Does God have a body? To deny that God has a body, as classical theists insist, intimates that one would lean in the direction of cosmological dualism, even if one were not a dualist with respect to human nature. In cosmological dualism God's awareness of the world (through knowledge or love or both) is radically different from, not even remotely analogous to, our awareness of it. By contrast, the Platonic World Soul points us toward a cosmological monism wherein God is the mind or soul who animates the entire embodied cosmos. On this view the ubiquity of deity is not the problem it is in classical theistic cosmological dualism. This belief in God as the World Soul appears in at least five of Plato's later dialogues (*Statesman, Philebus, Timaeus, Laws,* and *Epinomis*), despite the fact that contemporary philosophical theists largely ignore this belief.

By the World Soul Plato seems to mean the idea that God is a living being endowed with preeminent reason (*phronesin*). His mythopoetic way to put the point regarding his dipolar theism is to locate the facets of deity in two different beings with two different names. Applying the principle of charity to these two, we can say that God is the besouled character of the cosmos in general (the World Soul) that has the capacity for reason (the Demiurge). The fact that God is seen as the besouled character of the cosmos leads one to think that the natural world itself in its entirety can be seen as the divine body or as the divine animal (*zoon*). The World Soul is diffused throughout the body of the world and hence does not have a merely parallel or epiphenomenal existence. Once again, soul is defined as self-motion; hence the divine World Soul is not only capable of self-motion, but the World Soul is also the supreme example of such in that divinity can make decisions regarding the whole of the natural world and not merely regarding some part(s) of it.

The following four-term analogy helps one to understand the organic and living character of divinity in Plato:

$$P1 : P2 :: P2 : P3$$

P1 is psyche at the microscopic level of cells, where a contemporary scientific view can vindicate Plato's flirtation with panpsychism. Although the ancient Greeks did not know about cells, they did speculate about nerves—*neura* (see Solmsen 1961). The nightmare of determinism has faded as organic reality in its fundamental constituents itself seems to have at least a partially indeterminate character of self-motion. That is, the sum total of efficient causes from the past does not explain the behavior of the smaller units of becoming in the world. Plato was wiser than he knew; little did he know that in contemporary science universal mechanism would give way to a cosmic dance.

P2 is psyche per se, psyche in the sense of feeling found in animals and human beings, whereby beings with central nervous systems feel as wholes just as their constituent cellular parts prefigure feeling at a local level. And feeling *is* localized. Think of a knife stuck in the gut of any vertebrate or of sexual pleasure. P2 consists in taking these local cellular feelings and collecting them so that an individual as a whole can feel what happens to its cellular parts, even if the individual partially transcends the parts. In the *Republic* (462c-d) Plato makes clear (through the character Socrates) that if one has pain in one's finger (note, not the whole hand) the entire community (*pasa he koinonia*) of bodily connections is hurt. The organized unity of the individual is such that when one part is hurt the human being who has the pain in her finger experiences pain as a whole (*hole*).

P3 is divine psyche. Plato shares with Hartshorne the belief that the universe is a society or an organism (a Platonic World Soul) of which one member (the Platonic Demiurge) is preeminent just as human beings or animals are societies of cells (or nerves) of which the mental part is preeminent. Because animal individuals must, to maintain their integrity, adapt to their environments, mortality is implied. But if we imagine the World Soul we must not consider an environment external to deity but an internal one: the world body of the World Mind (the Demiurge) or the World Soul. This cosmic, divine animal has such an intimate relation to its body that it must also have ideal ways of perceiving and remembering its body such that it can identify the microindividuals (P2) it includes. We can only tell when cells in our toe have been burned by the fire; we cannot identify the microindividuals (P1) as such.

In a way, all talk of God short of univocity contains some negativity in that God does not exist, know, love, and so on, exactly as we do. With regard to the divine body, however, classical theists have allowed this negativity to run wild. Hartshorne's use of Plato is an attempt to remedy this imbalance (Dombrowski 2005, 21). Admittedly, the tight connection between the World Soul and the Demiurge that I have articulated is much more explicit than anything found in Plato's *Timaeus*. However, applying the principle of charity to Plato's text makes articulating a coherent account of the World Soul possible in a way that might not otherwise be possible: the World Soul is the living, divine being who is also supreme intelligence (mythopoetically depicted in the *Timaeus* as the Demiurge).

God cannot suffer in the sense of ceasing to exist due to an alien force; hence the mind-body or soul-body analogies cannot be pushed to the point where a mortal divine brain is posited. The contrast between the brain and a less essential bodily part can be posited when an animal has an external environment in that the central nervous system is the organ that adapts internal activities to external stimuli, a function that is not needed in the all-inclusive divine organism. Every individual becomes, as it were, a brain cell directly communicating to the World Soul.

The scholar whose view of Plato's concept of God I find most instructive is Friedrich Solmsen, who makes clear that the background to Plato's theology is provided by a traditional view of civic religion whereby piety of a nonpolitical sort or a purely secular patriotism would have been contradictions in terms (see Solmsen 1942). The destruction of the old religion had both a positive and a negative effect: It not only made a more sophisticated, intellectual conception of God possible, but it also opened the door to atheism. Plato meant to close this door and to elevate religious discourse. This elevation would, given Plato's lifelong interest in politics, have to be able to establish some sort of rapprochement with civic religion even if the primitive identification of the interests of the polis with a particular deity would have to be dropped. Furthermore, this elevation would have to continue the pioneering work of the Presocratics in the two centuries before Plato, on whom Plato relied, and whose objective was to connect the deity (or deities) to cosmic processes in nature, a connection that very often led to belief in the World Soul.

Solmsen details how Xenophanes and Aeschylus partially prepared the way for Plato by indicating that God (Plato's Demiurge) was a mind who acted without physical effort. Euripides at times thought of God in cosmic terms. Anaxagoras and Diogenes of Apollonia dealt with an intelligent organizer of the world in that anything that serves its purpose well as a bodily organ cannot be the work of luck (*tyche*). This groping for a cosmic deity, as opposed to a political one, was characteristic of several Presocratic thinkers. A philosophical "science" was taking over the lead in the search for a new divine principle. This concept of God as cosmic was not threatened by political upheaval, and hence philosophy of nature was the chief potential source for new religious beliefs. Plato criticized the traditional gods in the construction of the Republic to make room for the World Soul/Demiurge in the *Timaeus*, as the beginning of this latter dialogue indicates.

Also important to notice is the way in Empedocles the cosmic sphere was given a divine status and how Thales, Anaximenes, and the Pythagoreans believed in a World Soul. Furthermore, there is a contrast between human learning of many things (*polymathia*), on the one hand, and the divine wisdom of the World Soul, on the other, a wisdom that is found in several forms in Heraclitus: *hen to sophon* (unified wisdom), universal logos, cosmic *gnome* (thought), and *kyberman panta* (world mind). The very idea of a cosmos leads to a belief in the cosmic God, the contemplation of which largely constitutes human wisdom; we are constituents of cosmic order. Heraclitus sometimes personified the cosmic principle as Zeus and at other times viewed it as a rarefied, all-pervading presence, like ether, a view the Stoics later made famous (see Dombrowski 2005, 24).

Indeed, we have seen that, according to Plutarch, *all* of the ancient philosophers, except for Aristotle and the atomists, believed that the world was informed with a divine animal soul! This is a claim that, even if an exaggeration, nonetheless shows how comfortable the ancients were with the World Soul, a comfort matched by classical theistic discomfort.

Plato's attempt to reform religion is initially seen in the effort to define piety (*eusebeia*) in the *Euthyphro*, a reform that was intensified in the *Republic*. At once, Plato's concept of soul preserves the best in the Orphic, Pythagorean, and mystery religion traditions regarding soul; it makes the soul the locus of political virtue; and it allows soul to be used to explain the cosmos in religious terms. The supreme soul, the World Soul, is Plato's attempt to connect the world of flux with that of sameness into an integrated theory of reality. Hence the function of God in the *Timaeus* is not so much to impart life to the universe as to make its life as excellent as possible. The philosophical contemplation of the beauty of the universe (through astronomy and music, where apparently discordant elements are brought into harmony) make the human soul at least akin to, if not homogeneous with, the Soul of the cosmos.

God (the supreme psyche with supreme *nous* or mind) confronts the elements of the world that remain discordant with persuasion (*peitho*), not force (*bia*). But God still has power (*kratos*), primarily the immense power to persuade the world by offering it a model of perfection. Although Solmsen is hesitant to identify the Demiurge with the World Soul on the evidence of the *Timaeus*, he is willing to see the two as aspects of one God that deal with separate functions: the World Soul with movement and life and the Demiurge with order, design, and rationality. In the *Laws*, however, such identification is legitimate in that in this dialogue mind presupposes a living soul, even if mind itself is everlasting (and even if the Demiurge is mythopoetically depicted as prior to the World Soul in the *Timaeus*).

Solmsen reinforces Hartshorne's notion of a personal deity: Once Plato's doctrine of a cosmic soul had taken shape, not only did it succeed in respiritualizing nature, but it also transformed the indirect relation between the individual and God into a direct and hence personal relationship. The ardor that this relationship fosters constitutes Platonic piety, which, as at the end of the *Euthyphro*, is a type of service (Hartshorne would say contribution) to God.

Paul Friedlander (1958) sees this respiritualization of law, art, and nature as the central task of Plato's life. Hence Plato can be said to metaphorically return to Thales's notion that all things are full of gods. Friedlander is also instructive regarding the similarity between the individual and God, for example in the *Gorgias* (505e). Plato indicates not only that there is a soul for the cosmos, but also that there is something like a cosmos or wholeness for the individual soul. That is, the best humans reflect the World Soul in that their common principle is the good (*agathon*). If the world is, as Friedlander notes many modern thinkers believe, a mere machine, then the appearance of a leaf or a caterpillar would be "miraculous" (Friedlander 1958, I. 31; III. 328, 348, , 363, 365, 436).

We should not be surprised that in *Laws*, Book X, the argument against atheism is described as a prelude for the whole body of laws. Religion is the basis of Plato's city here and plays a much more significant role than it did in the *Republic*. His goal was to refute three types of atheism: the denial of God altogether; the belief that divinity does not care for us; and the claim that God can be bought off with sacrifices. Plato's refutation is in terms of his own theological tenets, including belief in the divine animal. The World Soul in the *Laws* at times surfaces not as an individual entity (as in the *Timaeus*), but as a generic principle. Soul does not, however, manifest itself with equal distinctness in every phase of the cosmos; it is in some way intensified in animals, especially in human animals and in the divine animal. Hence the constancy of the world's organic functioning as due to the World Soul makes the cosmos different from a plant in that the cosmos can relay back to itself all the stimulations of sense experience. That is, the World Soul integrates the scattered multiplicity of the bodily, an integration that is similar to that found in Anaxagoras and Xenocrates among the Presocratics.

The Aristotelian conception of a self-sufficient God who contemplates only itself is entirely alien to Plato. God's *telos*, if there is such, is the best possible harmony for the sum of things: The parts are for the whole, but the whole only flourishes with healthy parts. God is like the good physician who does not give attention to a single, isolated organ, but rather to the body of the world as a whole. Although suggesting that Plato felt himself in his later years more at home in the cosmos than in the polis would be rash, admittedly he prepared the way for Hellenistic escape from politics into the life of the cosmos. Furthermore, the cosmic scope of the World Soul is, in many ways, a return to the Great Mother tradition in religion that existed before the bifurcation between Father Sky God and Mother Earth Goddess, a bifurcation that gradually tilted heavily toward Father Sky God, out of which Yahweh and God the Father grew (see Moltmann 1985).

Solmsen is quite explicit that the concept of a divine World Soul is the cornerstone of a whole new theological system based on physics. Before individual or political experience can be understood, the validity of religion itself has to be understood on cosmic grounds. This understanding makes considering oneself more of a citizen of the universe than a citizen of any mere political community possible. Law in a polis is indeed important, but only if it is seen against a larger background, specifically the theological background of the *Timaeus* and *Laws*, which were attempts to stem the process of disintegration in Greek culture that had been in existence for almost a century.

Here we should note that A. E. Taylor is instructive in his belief that the World Soul (God) is far more important in the *Timaeus* than in the *Republic* largely because the World Soul is a key part of a new cosmology without matter (an indirect way of saying that the later Plato was a panpsychist). Taylor also indicates that the language of God (here the Demiurge) putting soul into the body of the world is obviously not to be taken literally. God, the best soul (*ariste psyche*), is transcendent and immanent (that is, dipolar), with the former making it difficult to call Plato's God pantheistic and the latter making it difficult to limit God in a classical theistic way. Not surprisingly, however, Taylor uses Whitehead to criticize monopolarity, such as in his criticism of viewing soul at whatever level as "substance" (see Taylor 1928, 77–82, 103–105, 124, 255–256).

Sadly, Plato's thoughts on God have been obscured in the history of Platon*ism*. He was the last Greek to discuss God in the context of a political system, and after his death ancient theistic philosophers went in one of two directions: Aristotle moved toward a concept of divinity as strictly transcendent and the Stoics moved toward pantheism, leaving no one, as it were, to guard the Platonic fort. Solmsen agrees with Hartshorne that Christianity has largely followed the Aristotelian move, albeit designated at times as "Platonic," by relying almost exclusively on the first facet of Plato's thought on God.

The possibility of a genuinely Platonic type of Christianity, wherein the World Soul is taken seriously, is evidenced in Origen. He was a Christian theist in the third century, as we have seen, who avoided both impersonal pantheism and the view of God as supernatural (cosmological dualism). To briefly sample some of Origen's thoughts in this regard, consider his citation of a question from Jeremiah (23: 24), "Do not I fill heaven and earth?, says the Lord," and his use of a famous passage from 1 Corinthians (12: 12), "The body is one and has many members, and so it is with Christ." Christ is identified by Origen with an omnipresent *logos* (rationality), with the *agape* (spiritual love) that binds all things together, with the soul for the body of the world (Origen 1929).

Or again, Origen is clear that our one body (*corpus nostrum unum*) is composed of many members (*multis membris*) that are held together by one soul (*una anima*). Likewise, the universe is an immense animal of many members that are held together by God (*ita et universum mundum velut animal quoddam immensum atque immane opinandum puto, quod quasi ab una anima virtute Dei*). *Immensum* here entails something vast: the fact that God brings together the world within the boundaries of the divine body.

Perhaps Christians and other theists in the Abrahamic religions should be more sympathetic to the World Soul than they have been to date. If we start with the microcosm, we can then understand how cells are brought within the order of our "mesocosmic" bodies. But such an understanding was not always easy. Cell theory did not take coherent form in the work of biologists until the early nineteenth century and still has not been assimilated into philosophical theology. Moving to the other side of the mesocosm, where we can see ourselves as parts of a macrocosmic whole, is at least plausible.

Talk about the divine body is not only a consequence of the use of the soul-body analogy to understand the concept of God, but it is also logically entailed in Plato's metaphysics. Hartshorne has often claimed (contra Kant and others) that there are necessary truths concerning existence (for example, "Something exists"). The unintelligibility of claiming that "there might have been (absolutely) nothing" is derived from Plato himself, who, when he commits parricide on father Parmenides in the *Sophist* (241–242), only admits the existence of relative nonbeing or otherness, not the existence of absolutely nothing, which would be a logical contradiction in that *it* would then be something. Hartshorne agrees with Plato that all determination is negation (in that to say what something *is* is to also imply what it is not), but this inescapable element of negation is precisely Plato's form of otherness or relative nonbeing. The statement "Absolutely nothing exists" could not conceivably be verified. That is, a completely restrictive or wholly negative statement is not a conceivable yet unrealized fact, but an impossibility. Particular bodies can pass out of existence (or better, pass into another sort of existence), but the divine body of the universe has no alternative but to exist.

Furthermore, the concept of divine omnipresence is not unrelated to Platonic theodicy, as can be seen through a consideration of pain. The experience of pain in one's finger is both mine and something not mine in that it involves not only my life but also the lives of cells. Likewise, God can experience our pains without thereby becoming identical with us. This is why pantheism (literally all *is* God) should not be seen as exhausting all varieties of divine inclusiveness. Panentheism (once again, literally all is *in* God), such as when Plato suggests in the *Timaeus*, *Laws*, and *Epinomis* that body is in soul, rather than vice versa, is a type of divine inclusiveness that theists should no longer ignore. We are not in God as marbles are in a box or as an idea is in a mind. Rather, if we are to take seriously the Platonic idea of God as the World Soul who animates the body of the world—indeed he refers to it as the divine animal—then the sort of panentheistic inclusiveness to be considered is organic inclusiveness of bodily pain in a whole animal. It is not without reason that Whitehead traced the origin of his own philosophy of organism back to Plato's *Timaeus*, where it is not so much matter itself that is created, but rather a certain sort of order to the natural world that is congenial to the contemporary view wherein there has been a dissolution of material quanta into (partially self-moving) vibrations.

In any event, it is crucial to notice on the evidence of the *Timaeus* that there is only one cosmos (rather than one in an infinite series, as the ancient atomists believed) that is shaped in the image of the form of a living being, a form that is part of the content of the divine mind. Although scholars have been quick to notice the difference between the form of a living being and the perceptual world animal, they have generally not been as quick to notice that while the inclusion of ideas in the divine mind is somewhat like the inclusion of contents of thought within any mind, the inclusion of the world in God is actually organic inclusiveness, on the analogy of parts included in an animal body. This has significant implications for understanding the relationship between God (the World Soul) and the evils or pains that exist in the natural world.

11

Plato

(427–347 BCE)

Against Omnipotence

Whereas the previous chapter was intended to shed Platonic light on the divine attribute of omnipresence, this chapter sheds Platonic light on the unintelligibility of the divine attribute of omnipotence conceived as a monopoly of divine power. Consider the following crucial passage that I have mentioned previously from the Eleatic Stranger (presumably Plato) in the *Sophist* (247e): "I suggest that anything has real being that is so constituted as to possess any sort of power either to affect anything else or (*eite*) to be affected, in however small a degree, by the most insignificant agent, though it be only once. I am proposing as a mark to distinguish real things that they are nothing but power (*dynamis*)." For the most part process philosophers such as Whitehead and Hartshorne have done valuable work alerting philosophers to this passage in Plato hitherto undervalued.

Dynamis is the substantive answering to the verb "to be able" (*dynasthai*); hence it makes sense that it is the root of our word "dynamic," and it covers the power to be acted on as well as the power to act on something else. Thus, it would have been better if Plato had said "and" (*kai*) instead of "or" (*eite*) in the above quotation.

Whitehead thinks that in the above passage can be found "the height of his [Plato's] genius as a metaphysician" (Whitehead [1933] 1967, 5–6, 25, 83, 118–122, 129, 166–169). This is quite a claim. When Plato implies that it is the definition (*horon*) of being that it exert dynamic power and be subjected to the exertion of dynamic power, he indicates that the essence of being is to be implicated in causal action with other things, causal action that constitutes natural law as immanent rather than as externally imposed by a supernatural God. If Plato is defining being in terms of the agency in action and in terms of the recipient of action, then that which is not acted on (for example, an unmoved mover) is a mere external fixture rather than real immanent being. Action and reaction belong to the essence of being on this process interpretation.

Plato's genius here lies in his ability to provide a *tertium quid* between the external imposition of law on the world found in classical theism and the pantheistic immanence of the Stoics. That is, according to Whitehead, Plato's definition of being as power in the *Sophist* supplements his efforts in the *Timaeus* to find a moderate view between these (classical theistic and pantheistic) extremes wherein there is both: (1) an active and passive divine creator (who persuades the world and dialogues with it rather than delivers to it authoritarian dictation); and (2) the action and reaction of the other constituents of reality. Much can be said in favor of Whitehead's view of Plato in *Adventures of Ideas* (and in favor of Hartshorne's similar view) wherein the creation of the world (or better, the creation of civilized order) is the victory of persuasion over force. This victory, which Whitehead sees as one of the greatest intellectual discoveries, is made possible by the effort to incorporate both a doctrine of divine, persuasive lure toward order and a doctrine of divine immanence.

A second text where Whitehead treats the concept of "being as power" is in *Modes of Thought* (Whitehead [1938] 1968, 119). Here he emphasizes that power is the basis of our notion of substance (rather than the other way around) and that in Plato one finds a prominent place for power in metaphysics, even if Plato did not fully develop this concept of being as power and of power as the drive of the universe. Whitehead himself tries to develop these concepts fully, an effort that led him away from the view of the universe as static; or better, away from the view that all transition was ultimately due to "transition" among individually static realities. The concept of process itself involves the idea that the being of any actual entity is constituted by its becoming and its modifying agency/patiency. The stubborn facts of the world have power in Whitehead, as they do in Plato; specifically, the power to have the constitutions of other particulars conditioned and the power to be conditioned by other particulars. This power has profound implications for the concept of God.

If the term "metaphysics" refers, as Hartshorne thinks it does, to the noncontingent features of reality, such that any experience confirms these features, but none falsifies them, then "being is power" is a metaphysical claim. Its scope is as wide as reality itself, from the least significant existent to God. But if it is true that being is power, then it is not only the concept of being that is Platonic, but also the concept of God.

In their ultimate individuality, beings, if they are instances of dynamic power, can be influenced by God, but they cannot be utterly coerced. Power is influence, perfect power is perfect influence. Or again, to have perfect power over all individuals is not to have all power. The greatest possible power (that is, perfect power) over individuals cannot leave them powerless if being *is* power. Hence even perfect power must leave something for others to decide. We can understand why Hartshorne claims that: "Power must be exercised upon something, at least if by power we mean influence, control; but the something controlled cannot be absolutely inert, since the merely passive, that which has no active tendency of its own, is nothing; yet if the something acted upon is itself partly active, then there must be some resistance, however slight, to the 'absolute' power, and how can power which is resisted be absolute" (Hartshorne 1941, 89, also xvi, 14)? If being is power, then any relation in which one of the related things was wholly powerless would be a relation in which "the thing" was absolutely nothing: an impossibility. No matter how lowly a thing may be if it is a real individual it reacts upon things; cells, molecules, and electrons do not provide exceptions to the view of being as power.

Hartshorne agrees that God has universal relevance, and this is largely due to divine omnibenevolence. Hence there is nothing completely uninfluenced or completely outside of divine influence or love. But this Platonic view of a God who benevolently creates *ex hyle* (from beings already in existence) is a far cry from the view of God who omnipotently creates things *ex nihilo*. We can utter the words "God is omnipotent" or "God has all power," but we cannot really conceive what these words mean if there are other beings in existence, as Hartshorne eloquently argues: "That God cannot 'make us do' certain things does not 'limit' [divine] power, for there is no such thing as power to make nonsense true, and 'power over us' would not be power over *us* if our natures and actions counted for nothing. No conceivable being could do more with us than God can . . . and so by definition [divine] power is perfect, unsurpassable. But it is a power unique in its ability to adjust to others" (Hartshorne 1941, 294, also 205, 232, 244).

Jon Levenson (1988) shows that the doctrine of creation out of chaos (that is, creation *ex hyle*) is reflected not only in the first chapter of Genesis, but also throughout the Hebrew Bible in that this doctrine was central to the cultic life of the Hebrew people. Christian scholars, too, have long accepted the fact that creation *ex nihilo* is not to be found in Genesis. This view does not emerge until the intertestamental literature, particularly 2 Maccabees. Gerhard May (1994), for example, shows that Christian thinkers did not defended the doctrine of creation *ex nihilo* until the end of the second century as a response to Marcion's Gnosticism. Until that time Christian thinkers considered the biblical view of creation to be quite compatible with the creation out of chaos found in Plato's *Timaeus*. In effect, just as Plato's apparent belief in God as the World Soul is similar to the view found in some biblical passages and finds echoes in St. Paul and Origen and in the traditional divine attribute of omnipresence, so also Plato's apparent belief that being is dynamic power (a belief that is at odds with the claim that God is omnipotent in the sense of having a monopoly of power over the powerless and who creates the world *ex nihilo*) is compatible with the biblical view of creation *ex hyle*. For all we can tell, creativity or Platonic self-motion (whether divine or nondivine) is itself uncreated.

On Hartshorne's view, this critique of divine omnipotence (which amplifies what was said earlier in the chapter on Thomas Aquinas) does not demean God. The key is to hold that God's power is not separate from divine beauty and goodness; indeed, divine beauty and goodness *are* the divine power to inspire worship. Moreover, divine agency in the world is persuasive, rather than coercive, as evidenced in the *Timaeus*. The supposed recalcitrance of the material, on this view, is actually the problem of harmonizing the self-motions of an infinite number of partially free centers of dynamic power. God's actuality (that is, how God exists concretely), if not God's bare existence, is conditioned by states of affairs of which God is not the sole cause. Whitehead sees Platonic divine persuasion especially revealed in Jesus.

Some classical theists will no doubt object to the effort here to Judaize or Christianize Plato's view of God. Divine supremacy, they will allege, requires that God be sovereign over everything in the world, including evil. Of course this logically leads to the perennial question concerning why an omnipotent God does not eliminate the evil.

The lack of complete order in the world is at least partially explained by there being many self-movers. These many self-active agents imply indefinitely great, if not complete, disorder unless a supreme soul persuades the many lesser souls to conform to a cosmic plan. They cannot completely fit such a plan if they are at least in part self-determined. Process theodicy is essentially Platonic because the divine plan cannot be completely definite and detailed. The meaning of "God has power over us" only makes sense in a Platonic view if God is a self-moved mover of others who is partially moved by these other self-movers. God can "rule the world" by setting optimal limits for free action. The divine can control the changes in us by inspiring us with novel ideas; by molding the divine life God presents at each moment a partly new ideal. *Omni*potent power would therefore be a monopoly of power over the powerless; but Hartshorne agrees with the Platonic claim that being *is* power, and hence to be an individual is, in a way, to decide. Decision, once again, means the cutting off of some possibilities rather than others (a literal de-cision), a cutting off that is not necessarily done self-consciously.

The divine reality is distinctive not in terms of creativity as such, but rather in terms of the extent and quality of its creativity, of the ability to act in a qualitatively superior way on or with a greater number of beings than the rest of us. God's creative effort to bring order out of what would otherwise be disorderly chaos is fair (*kalon*; *Timaeus* 27c-29d, 68e). Indeed, the cosmos is as perfect as possible (*Timaeus* 39d-41d), given multiple self-movers and given the recalcitrance of the material dealt with by divine persuasion. Our ability to think makes us especially like the divine among created things in that we can be reflective cocreators of an orderly life (*Timaeus* 44d). Without rational planning, whatever harmony that exists, either in our own lives or in the cosmos in general, would be purely accidental (*Timaeus* 44d, 69b-c, 74d, 75d, 76c, 91a). Although our ability to create an orderly pattern only results in a semblance (*phantasma*) of the ideal, whereas God can create a true likeness (*eikon*) of the ideal, human beings nonetheless are clearly like God in having at least some creative power allied to reason (*Sophist* 265b-268d).

Ancient chaos reasserts itself whenever the divine principle of limit is abandoned or forgotten or rejected; at these times our lives hover on the brink of destruction. In any event, the cosmos at any particular time is a mixture of limit and unlimit, a besouled world that orders in as good a way as possible its diverse self-movers (see *Statesman* 273b–c; *Philebus* 27b–c, 28d–30d). At no point do we see evidence that God controls everything that happens, a view that would be at odds with the definition of being as dynamic power.

Of course Plato does not go out of his way to have one of the characters in his dialogues state explicitly an opposition to divine omnipotence, conceived as a monopoly of power, as does Hartshorne in his book *Omnipotence and Other Theological Mistakes* (1984c). The reason is simple: No one before Plato had asserted such a doctrine, and hence there was no need to refute it. However, such an opposition is often implied in Plato's dialogues, an opposition that surfaces in the oddest places, such as when Agathon in the *Symposium* argues that even love (Aphrodite), the mightiest of all, must contend with necessity (196d-197b). In the *Republic* any rational agent is clearly confronted eventually with the spindle of necessity and the fates, which are mythically depicted as the daughters of necessity (616c, 617c, et al.). And in the creation myth of the *Timaeus* can be found the most extensive Platonic treatment of the necessity that resists any besouled agency, whether divine, human, or subhuman. The point is that God wants everything to be as good as possible insofar as this is attainable.

I assume that there is a family resemblance among several words for conditions that are beyond the ability of any good self-mover, even God, to control: necessity (*anangke*), fate (*moira*), chance (*tyche*), or destiny (*heimarmene*). The creation of an orderly, morally good, and aesthetically beautiful world is hindered by resistant chance and infinitely variable circumstances produced by multifarious beings with powers of their own. Self-mover A may be responsible for moving to spot X at time Y; and self-mover B may be responsible for moving to spot X at time Y; but no one is responsible for A and B accidentally crashing at spot X at time Y. The crash is "due to" chance or fate. Like a skilled navigator, one must negotiate one's way through the tempest. Or better, along with God we do not so much contend against necessity (which would apparently be futile) as work with it or cajole it to elicit as much order and limit and goodness as is needed to bring about a beautiful world: in ourselves, in our political institutions, and in the natural world.

There is always over and above law (whether divine law in the cosmos or human law in politics) a factor of the "simply given" or "brute fact." It is this surd or irrational element that Plato refers to as necessity in the *Timaeus*. When the evidence of this dialogue is considered in conjunction with that of the definition of being as dynamic power in the *Sophist*, one is tempted to think in a Hartshornian way that Plato was working his way toward, or at least he could have easily worked his way toward, the view that this surd is nothing other than the stubborn fact of a clash of a multitude of self-movers.

One feature of a Platonic case against divine omnipotence concerns the metaphysical status of Plato's forms or ideas, the most abstract objects of thought. According to the "extradeical" interpretation of Plato, the forms or ideas are outside of God and hence are at odds with the doctrine of divine omnipotence. Nonetheless my own view is "intradeical" in that if God is omniscient, then God would know everything that could be known, including the most abstract objects of thought. That is, forms or ideas are thoughts in the mind of the ideal knower. One of the reasons to be skeptical of the extradeical account, in which the forms or ideas are seen as "independent" of God, is that independence does not have any real meaning when comparing everlasting realities. If "X is independent of Y" is to have any sharp logical meaning, it must be that X could exist even if Y did not, which implies that Y is contingent. If X stands for the forms or ideas and Y stands for God, then the nonexistence of God is being taken as possible. But this possibility conflicts with Plato's treatments of God in the *Timaeus* and Book Ten of the *Laws*, along with Plato's flirtation with the ontological argument (Dombrowski 2005, chap. 5). If God's existence is not contingent, then not only are the forms or ideas envisaged by deity, but they also could not lack this status.

To say that forms or ideas (conceptual possibilities) are items in divine psychical process, indeed to say that they are known ideally by God, is to come close to the claim that God is omniscient in the sense of knowing everything that is knowable. (However, this does not necessarily commit one to the claim that the future is here now and hence knowable in advance.) Furthermore, divine omniscience is not unrelated to divine omnibenevolence if we take seriously Plato's famous intuition about the coextensiveness of knowledge and virtue. If one really knew how happy one would be if one lived a life of virtue, one would never choose vice; hence, on this view, omnibenevolence is analytic of the concept of omniscience (Dombrowski 2005, 59–60).

In two passages in the late dialogues (*Theaetetus* 176b–c and *Timaeus* 90a-d) we are encouraged to see the goal in human life as a becoming like (*homoiosis*) the divine as far as possible, both with respect to divine knowledge and goodness. In different terms, the World Soul and our own souls are remotely akin, thus the likeness in question is metaphysical as well as intellectual and moral. In this regard it makes sense to say that religious believers in the Abrahamic religions do not need to "dehellenize" their beliefs, as is sometimes suggested, but to "rehellenize" them along the lines of a more sophisticated Platonic philosophy of religion than the one that has been operative historically. In fact, Plato's World Soul can more easily be seen as a personal God than the strictly transcendent deity of classical theism. As before, the World Soul is not beyond the natural world of becoming, but *is* that world conceived and felt as an integral, besouled whole.

The key thing is to get beyond the simplistic alternative between either a classical theistic, omnipotent God who coercively moves the world, but is unaffected by it, on the one hand, and a world that is cosmologically directionless, on the other. Most human beings "prehend" (that is, they feel rather than intellectually "apprehend") God in the sense that they grasp implicitly meaning in the world; they feel that they are parts of a meaningful whole. On this Platonic basis prayer consists in an aspiration to adjust one's inner attitude to cosmic, divine harmony; it is an attempt to avoid being distracted away from what is really important in life.

12

Aristotle

(384–322 BCE)

Aristotle defends a single categorical scheme of embodied form, which at least initially seems to simplify the Platonic categorical scheme of form in a condition of separation (*chorismos*) from matter or of ideas in a condition of separation from things. But this simplification is apparent rather than real when it is realized that Aristotle defends a cosmological dualism that is unnecessarily complicated. Indeed it is indefensible. Nonetheless, features of Aristotle's concept of God are instructive for any defensible version of philosophical theism, such as in his treatment of God as a final cause who induces change in the creatures due to divine attractiveness; or better, due to divine perfection. This final causality, however, should not be understood as a necessary end stage such that natural beings inexorably grow from seed to maturity in mechanical fashion (Hartshorne 2000, 58).

The substitution of a single conception of substance for Plato's apparent dualism nonetheless leaves us with an opposition that is unbridgeable: that between temporal substances and God (or gods) as the atemporal Unmoved Mover (or unmoved movers). That is, there is a shift in the locus for duality in the transition from Plato to Aristotle. Importantly, however, the problem here is not with the very distinction in Aristotle between form (actuality, immutability, activity, and eternity) and matter (potentiality, mutability, passivity, and temporality, respectively), but rather with the Aristotelian claim that form has its supreme instance in a deity who is in no way mutable or passive. Aristotle's mistake was not in contrasting form and matter, but in identifying pure form with the most exalted being and with contrasting this being with ordinary beings who are sullied by matter (Hartshorne 2000, 58–59; also see Olson 2013).

God for Aristotle is wholly actual, immutable, and eternal and hence stands in sharp opposition to the world of substances, which is qualified by potentiality, mutability, and temporality. In fact, ordinary living things are characterized by genesis and death, in contrast to God, who is eternal and necessary in every aspect. Furthermore, God for Aristotle is a completely self-sufficient actuality. As before, Aristotle's cosmological dualism is more severe than any duality in Plato, yet Aristotle's view, which preserves the worst aspects of Plato's view of God, endures through the Neoplatonists in the work of the great classical theists. In Plato's World Soul, by contrast, both being and becoming find a place in the divine life. Indeed, by defining soul as self-motion, Plato ensures that his World Soul will be a dynamic God. Aristotle seems to work with a concept of soul that has a family resemblance to Plato's concept, but Aristotle feels the need to deny besouled becoming to God. Whereas ordinary substances are dipolar in Aristotle (being composed of both actuality and potentiality, activity and passivity), his God is monopolar (Hartshorne 2000, 59–60).

Aristotle agrees with Plato that time is the measure of motion such that if there is always time, motion must always exist. Thus, when Aristotle speaks of God as the first cause or as the first mover, he does not mean that God is prior to the series of past causal phenomena, but that God is behind the scenes in any present series of causal phenomena. God imparts motion now, but nonetheless remains unmoved by that which is moved. Aristotle is quite explicit in the *Physics* that whatever is in the process of becoming is imperfect; likewise, linear motion is inferior to the perfection of a circle, whose center can remain still as all of the points on the circumference move around it (see *Physics* 251b–267b).

Although God is the ultimate object of human desire in Aristotle's *Metaphysics*, God moves others without being moved. Thinking is the touchstone here, but because God cannot change in Aristotle, the only thing that God could think about is the changeless divine nature itself. Although we do actions for the sake of God, this does not mean that any of our actions affect God in any way. In this regard Aristotle followed through on the implications of monopolarity in a way that is far more consistent than is found in those classical theists whom Aristotle influenced, whether explicitly or implicitly (through the Neoplatonists). The world of nature clearly depends on God, as Aristotle sees things, but

God could never know natural beings because to know them would entail that God would be changed by them; and all change in a perfect being would be for the worse. In an allusion to Oedipus, Aristotle declares that some things are better not seen; likewise, it is better for Aristotle's God not to think anything other than the divine nature itself. Aristotle is equally as inconsistent as the classical theists he influenced, however, in thinking that God as unchanged could be a living being. Imagining what it would mean to be a living being who is outside of time and who does not in any way grow and who is utterly impassive is difficult. Aristotle's God does not alter; such a being is unalterable. God's well-being is exhausted by the divine nature itself (see *Metaphysics* 1072a-1075a, 1244b-1245b).

Aristotle even goes so far as to say that viciousness is due to changeability; even the perceived need for change is vicious. Divinity is blessed and happy because such an exalted being is above alteration. Nonetheless, God is active, but this activity is not a dynamic one, whatever this might mean. Rather, divine activity involves contemplation of that which is beyond alteration (*Nicomachean Ethics* 1154b, 1178b).

We will see in the following part of the book that in neoclassical or process theism, contra Aristotle, becoming is much richer than being if the latter merely marks the line of continuity found in the former. It is in the very fabric of things that every entity has a past and be oriented toward some future or other. Even Aristotle realized that a first moment in time would contradict the nature of things in that it would signal a reality that arose out of "absolutely nothing," whatever that might mean. Rationality requires the impossibility of time's having a beginning or end and thus requires the necessity of processual contingency itself (Hartshorne 2000, 68–69).

The very reality of Aristotle's God is not problematic, but rather the nature of his Unmoved Mover. From the defensible claim that something exists necessarily, it does not follow either that this something is complete actuality or that it is an actual thinking that has only itself as an object of thought. A defensible concept of God involves a genuine divine life, rather than an abstract divine ideal. Unfortunately, Aristotle identifies the divine ideal with the divine life. This is an odd life, however, in that it constantly returns upon itself, as in a circle, the most perfect geometrical figure, according to Aristotle. This view contradicts experience, however, which indicates that life and intelligence involve sensitive responsiveness. Hartshorne helps us to realize the less than desirable tendentiousness of this Aristotelian concept of God: "To exalt the mathematician over the statesman or psychologist or priest who understands individuals not only generically or collectively but individually or distributively is mere expression of the typical philosopher's bias for his own type of mental activity, which indeed tends toward the abstract and universal" (Hartshorne 2000, 71).

The enduring being of things or persons exists abstractly, but only momentary events or experiences occur concretely or are strictly speaking actual. This is the familiar neoclassical or process distinction between existence and actuality. The existence of an individual is thus not identical with the actuality of the momentary experiences of the relatively permanent individual. In different terms, to speak of a necessary existent is to speak of something quite different from a necessary actuality; hence Aristotle led classical theists astray when he spoke of God as pure, necessary actuality. If Aristotle and classical theists are correct, then by imitating God we would be trying to care less and less about other individuals and to care more and more for ourselves to the extent that we approximate perfection. By contrast to the Aristotelian view that has exerted such a strong influence on classical theism, a concrete actuality must always be a novel becoming. The common aspects of a process that exhibits a line of inheritance among these novel becomings constitute the being or identity of this line of inheritance. In the divine case, God is more than the merely immutable in that this divine attribute is derivative from the evolving series of changes in the divine life (Hartshorne 2000, 72–74).

Aristotle himself was not a classical theist, despite the fact that his theism exerted, and still exerts, a profound effect on classical theism. He is not himself a classical theist because of his belief that God is not omnibenevolent and does not know nondivine things and is not omnipotent. His view was replaced in the Middle Ages by a classical theism that nonetheless continued his monopolarity and his preference for being as opposed to becoming.

Capetz not only barely notices the complexities involved in the concepts of God found in Plato and Aristotle, but he also tends to deemphasize the influence of these thinkers on the development of classical theism. When Capetz does notice the ancient Greek influences on what I have called classical theism, he does so by concentrating on the short distance between the Platonic concept of God and dualistic Gnosticism. This seems to assume the facet of Plato's concept of God that identifies divine perfection and immutability. The practical difficulty with this facet, as Capetz himself notices, is that on its basis reconciling monotheism with the existence of evil in the world is difficult in that the static world of divine perfection cannot be reconciled with this world of woe (Capetz 2003, 34).

Likewise, Bowker underemphasizes the crucial roles Plato and Aristotle play in the classical theistic concept of God because he thinks that what Plato and Aristotle really thought about God is not really all that clear. This part of the book addresses this concern. When Bowker opines about the Platonic concept of God it is, once again, the facet of Plato's concept that identifies perfection with static immutability that gets privileged. That is, Bowker interprets both Plato (problematically) and Aristotle (understandably) as monopolar theists. Furthermore, Bowker even wonders whether the Platonic Demiurge is divine; even worse, he ignores altogether the Platonic World Soul. This misunderstanding of the Platonic concept of God, including the dynamic perfection that characterizes one facet of this concept, affects Bowker's view of Aristotle. Bowker does not blink an eye when he asserts that whereas Plato puts ultimate reality "outside of the world" (despite the Platonic World Soul), Aristotle has a concept of God that is more easily reconciled with natural processes. I argue for the reverse. However, Bowker is to be commended for calling attention to the Aristotelian view that by intellectually seeking for the truth (via mind or *nous*) we are, in a way, participating in the divine life (Bowker 2002, 154, 230–232).

Although Armstrong deals in much more detail than Bowker and Capetz with the pervasive influence of Plato and Aristotle on the development of classical theism, she, too, says some questionable things. Whereas the great philosophers and theologians in the history of Abrahamic theism almost all rely heavily on Plato and Aristotle, Armstrong identifies such influence solely with the thesis that a perfect being would not, could not, change. Here she quite intelligibly thinks that this unchanging deity would be at odds with the God of biblical revelation. She notes that Aristotle was temperamentally quite different from Plato, such that the former took a more "earthbound" approach than the latter. But she does not notice that Aristotle ended up with a cosmological dualism much more severe than anything found in

Plato. This is due to her failure to deal straightforwardly with the Platonic World Soul or with the facet of Plato's concept of God that relies on an intuition regarding dynamic, rather than static, perfection. She correctly notes, however, that the contemplative life (*theoria*) of a human being leads us to become more like the divine. How exactly this could occur on the Aristotelian basis of a God who does not know particulars, only the divine nature itself, is nonetheless unclear. This points toward the familiar difficulty of determining the religious significance of a strictly immutable God, who could not, as in biblical theism, care even for the fall of a sparrow (see Matthew 10: 28). Armstrong at one point even intimates that the problem is not merely that the abstract, immutable deity of Aristotle and Plato (in one of the facets of his concept of God) is religiously remote, but rather that this God can be seen as despotic in light of divine indifference to creaturely suffering! Armstrong's strong language reminds one of Whitehead's and Hartshorne's equally strong language used when discussing the classical theistic concept of God (Armstrong 1993, 27, 35–39, 92, 174, 183, 230, 283, 330).

To be fair to Armstrong, in a work that appeared after her classic *A History of God* she notes the crucial roles Plato and Aristotle play in "the great transformation" or "the axial age" when mythopoetic religion was revolutionized by the birth of rationality and the magisterial efforts of the ancient Greek philosophers, among others, in the task of bringing intellectual skill and precision to an understanding of religion. Furthermore, she notes the cosmological unity Plato proposes in his *Timaeus*. These efforts on her part, as well as those of Capetz and Bowker, can be rendered consistent with the views of neoclassical or process theists. That is, all three authors of histories of the concept of God (Armstrong, Bowker, and Capetz) do excellent work, but it is work that needs the amplification and depth and "complexification" neoclassical or process theism provides (see especially Armstrong 2006; also 2009).

Aristotle's hylomorphism is instructive in claiming that if there is form, there must be that which is informed. If there is order, there must be that which is being subjected to this order. The problem is that in the divine case Aristotle defends the view that provides the core of classical theism: God is *pure* form and is strictly immaterial and immutable without qualification (Hartshorne 1937, 172). Aristotle rightly admits that pure matter all by itself explains nothing in that this concept only makes sense when integrally connected to form because formless matter is a mere idea that is abstracted away from some form-matter composite. The important thing to notice is that pure form is also an abstraction away from some form-matter composite. If we ask the question, what is it that everlastingly changes, the response should be: the divine World Soul/cosmic body composite (Hartshorne 1941, 258–259).

Plato was partially trapped in a verbal confusion in thinking that if God is perfect and free of any defect, then God would be immutable and incapable of wishing for any good not already possessed. Aristotle was wholly trapped in this confusion. The result of this confusion for classical theism was that divine love on this basis could only be an abstract "love" that had stilled all longing. How different intellectual history would have been if Aristotle's pseudo-Platonic simplification had not become normative for classical theists (Hartshorne 1967, 14–15, 28)! This speculation on my part is fueled by the thought that this counterfactual situation would have been possible, indeed likely, if Aristotle had followed through consistently on his own view, which is often referred to as the Aristotelian principle, that the abstract is real only in the concrete (Hartshorne 1970, 233).

Aristotle realized that the contingent aspects of something must be noneternal. Whereas past events are settled and definite, future events are not settled or definite. Contingent possibility and futurity are essentially one, on the Aristotelian view. We have seen, however, that Aristotle did not think that there was any contingency in God. This defect in his view should not prevent us from appreciating the fact that he nonetheless anticipated in an insightful way Anselm's discovery in the ontological argument: If there are no accidents in eternity, the everlastingly existing divine being could not exist contingently. This means that God's existence is either necessary or impossible. Although this conclusion is made explicit in a modal version of the ontological argument, it is at least implicit in Aristotle (Hartshorne 1984b, 99; 1984a, 224, 284; 1987, 15–16).

Although no universal can dictate all of the details regarding how it is to be particularized, for then it would be a particular and not a universal, Aristotle was nonetheless correct to hold that the universal can have being only if it is particularized somehow. And any particularization will have to arise out of its past conditions, which having been must ever be, in that causal influences from the past never altogether perish. Or again, facts about the past are immortal in the sense that what has been will always in the future have been. Anticipation differs from memory precisely because, whereas the latter concerns details, the former can only concern general tendencies or probabilities. By taking God out of time and out of the process of particularization, Aristotle insures that God as pure act will preclude any sort of social nature in God. However, being (including divine being) is ultimately in happenings (including divine happenings). The plurality of such happenings, which are organically connected to each other in a common line of inheritance, are the constituents of the internal social nature of divinity (Hartshorne 1972, 12, 51, 73, 120).

Both Plato and Aristotle were mistaken in thinking that there could be an actuality that was superior to any possible type of love. Aristotle's God is especially deficient in this regard in its thinking merely its own thinking, in contrast to the World Soul's sympathetic grasp of all that occurs in the cosmic body. Aristotle is at his strongest in holding (*On Interpretation*, chap. 12) both that contingency, necessity, and impossibility form a triad such that to affirm any one of these is to negate the other two and that this triad is not a mere fabrication on the part of human beings. In fact, five principles can be discerned in Aristotle's theory of time as objective modality, principles that, although quite defensible, Aristotle insufficiently integrates into his own concept of God: (1) There are no contingencies in the necessary aspect of a divine being. Or again, no everlasting being exists potentially. (2) Any event presupposes its causal antecedents, but not vice versa. (3) The future is a mixture of both necessity and contingency, such as in the claim that each mortal human being must die, but where and when and how is at least partially indeterminate while the human being is alive. (4) Point (3) can be put in modal terms: death is necessary for us, but the details are contingent. And (5) the concrete details of our lives or of any genuinely conceivable divine life, given temporal asymmetry, cannot be necessary (Hartshorne 1983, 29, 40–47).

Aristotle was not entirely clear on the points listed in the previous paragraph, even if it can be said that he implied them. For example, he is not as explicit as one would like regarding the idea that only the essential nature of God and the bare existence of God are necessary, along with the necessity of the world process itself. How God exists from moment to moment is not at all necessary. Unfortunately, Aristotle thought that the necessary as such is superior to the contingent, but this is a difficult notion to defend if necessity and contingency are correlative terms that do not make much sense without each other. Furthermore, the necessary is only one aspect of deity, not the whole of the divine life. Aristotle assumes that God is necessary in every aspect because of his questionable assumption that contingency as such is defective. As Hartshorne puts the point: "The contingent lacks duration and security; the necessary has these, but there are other things it may lack, for instance, concreteness, richness of definite content. . . . What indeed is the necessary but the common factor of all possible forms of concreteness?" (Hartshorne 1983, 50–51, also 49).

Classical theists distracted attention away from both Aristotle's theories regarding temporal asymmetry and the objective modality of time as encapsulated in the above five principles. This distraction was due to a mistaken idea concerning divine omniscience. The mere idea of omniscience does not entail the idea of the immutability of truth. But Aristotle made his own mistakes, too, such as when he assumed without argument that agency is necessarily superior to patiency (*On the Soul* 430a), which, once again, should be the motto of all those who like to talk, but not to listen. The idea that to be agent and patient is incomparably better than being either alone, when combined with Aristotle's theory of temporal asymmetry, leads to the conclusion that we are patients with respect to our ancestors, but agents with respect to our descendants. A God like Aristotle's which is purely active, could not really have memory of the past. Both Aristotle and classical theists erred in their monopolarity, even if the former escaped from the most egregious problems with the latter by omitting a concept of divine omniscience with respect to future contingents. For their part, classical theists continued the worst aspect of Aristotle's concept of God (monopolarity) without noting that this concept of God contradicts the view that God, as soul, would have to be analogous to human feeling and thinking. Aristotle's God is eminent, but it is the eminent abstraction (Hartshorne 1983, 52–54, 73–78, 176).

Aristotle is one of the chief causes of the classical theistic worship of immutable self-sufficiency, of agents over patients, of influencing over being influenced, and of controlling over loving. The antidote to these ills, quite ironically, lies in what is often called the Aristotelian

principle: Concrete reality includes the abstract just as the particular includes the universal. Although the neoclassical or process
concept of God involves an admiration for Aristotle's idea that God
moves and "orders" (or persuades) the world via divine beauty, the
emptiness of his God is evident when it is seen in monopolar fashion
as a universal that is adrift from any set of particulars (Hartshorne 1983,
234–235, 316, 378).

Aristotle's God is very thinly cerebral and aloof from worldly affairs.
This is far removed from the neoclassical or process God, but it is not
the polar opposite to Hartshorne's view. The polar opposite to Aristotle's God or the classical theistic view of God as eternal and outside
of time, on the one hand, is the strictly finite God of William James,
say, on the other. That is, Hartshorne's God is infinitely temporal and
omnipresent to the world. Aristotle and classical theists tend to notice
half-truths regarding God and finite theists such as James take notice
of the other half. The task is to put together the full series of dipolar
contrasts: being-becoming, infinite-finite, permanence-change, activity-passivity, and so forth. Aristotle's biggest mistake as a historian of
philosophy was to simplify the more complex Platonic dipolar theory.
The oversimplification still confuses the issue of philosophical theism.
Aristotle was correct in thinking that the greatest being thinks divine
thoughts, but such a being would also think about nondivine things
that are data or objective forms of feeling in the divine life (Hartshorne
1991, 315, 437, 597, 643, 645).

Divine changelessness is a half-truth because if divine stability is
taken as a value justifying worship, then the question understandably
arises whether the correlative concept of divine change also constitutes a value justifying veneration. One wonders what it is that divine
stability stabilizes if not the everlasting flux of moments of experience
that are in the line of inheritance of a supreme being-in-becoming.
Granted, some change is deplorable, but so is some stability, such as
in a rigid imperviousness to the feelings of others (Hartshorne 1990,
386–387).

We have seen that Aristotle ironically turns out to be much more
of an eternalist in his concept of God than Plato, despite the former's
reputation for lifelong concern for the natural world in flux. However,
Aristotle held back from determinism because his concept of God does
not include the classical theistic belief in divine omniscience, with

absolute assurance and in minute detail, with respect to the future careers of natural beings. And Aristotle is also to be commended for avoiding a defense of divine omnipotence and its attendant version of the theodicy problem at its nastiest. One cannot help but wonder how close Aristotle would have come to the neoclassical or process concept of God if he had followed through consistently with his own project of locating the abstract in the concrete and the universal in the particular. A consistent sort of hylomorphism, but at the cosmological level, would have brought Aristotle's concept of God into dipolar conformity with Plato's view when interpreted in the light of a principle of charity. Once again, Aristotle's God could not, in principle, be concerned with the fall of a sparrow (see Matthew 10: 28; Dombrowski 2000), whereas Plato's God could be interpreted as being capable of such concern. The strictly immaterial God Aristotle defends must remain uninfluenced by the details of the world. The only sort of relationship between Aristotle's God and other living beings is in terms of the former's admirable ability to act as a lure for creaturely striving, even if Aristotle's God remains unchanged by such striving (Hartshorne 1984c, 8, 15, 43, 46, 78, 81). Aristotle does not, like classical theists, deny that matter is a given in the constitution of the cosmos. Nor does Aristotle, like classical theists, deny that to know something is to be influenced by it (Hartshorne 2001, 34, 87).

Aristotle implies a view of personal identity between Hume's view that there is merely a succession of perceptions, but no stable self that endures, on the one hand, and Leibniz's view of a substantial self and a rigid identity wherein implicit in one's past experiences is all that will happen to one in the future, on the other. The latter view, as we have seen, depends on the classical theistic version of divine omniscience. The Aristotelian view is that we are in part constituted by what happens to us in the past (contra Hume and supported by Leibniz) and that we are not constituted by what might happen to us in the future (supported by Hume and contra Leibniz). Or at least this view can be reasonably abstracted from Aristotle's texts without much of a stretch. One way to appreciate Aristotle's genius here is to say that we should reject both the excessive necessitarianism implied in classical theism and the excessive contingency implied in Hume and many of his twentieth-century followers in analytic philosophy. Unfortunately, Aristotle's genius did not follow him when he described God is strictly necessitarian terms. Indeed, Hartshorne thinks that Aristotle was the very first thinker to define God in strictly necessitarian terms, devoid of any of the contingent features of the world. He did legitimately see that knowledge of something depends on that something, and hence he denied that God knows the contingencies of the world, including knowledge of Aristotle himself as a mere chance existent (Hartshorne 2011, 5, 22, 45, 53, 94–95, 120, 123).

13

Plotinus

(205–270 CE)

Thus far, this part of the book details how the thought of Plato and Aristotle has both prepared the way for classical theism and nonetheless provided the intellectual basis for an alternative view of God that improves on the concept of God found in classical theism. Plato especially facilitates this improved view, but Aristotle's views of temporal asymmetry and hylomorphism are also major breakthroughs in the history of philosophy that can be enormously helpful in developing a defensible concept of God.

This chapter adds a third ancient Greek thinker into this mix. Plotinus was perhaps the greatest thinker after Aristotle and before Spinoza in the seventeenth century who was free from ecclesiastical and creedal commitments. In one sense he reaffirms Plato's view of three aspects of ultimate reality as found in the *Timaeus*: the form of the good (and other forms), the Demiurge (the divine mind who contemplates the forms), and the World Soul. These correspond to three aspects of ultimate reality in Plotinus: The One, Intelligence or *Nous*, and the Plotinian World Soul, respectively (Hartshorne 2000, 211; also see Kenney 2013b).

The One is what is left when we transcend all duality or distinction. Intelligence or *Nous* contains at least a minimal degree of duality in that in any act of knowledge that is even remotely analogous to human knowledge, there is some distinction between the knower and the object known. And besouled agency involves distinctions between things at every turn. In Plotinus's view there is descent, although not necessarily degeneration, from The One to Intelligence to the World Soul. To what extent Plotinus's view is similar to Plato's is subject to debate. Although Plato's *Timaeus* has passages where the Demiurge is depicted as superior to the World Soul, we remember from Plato's *Laws* that the argument for the existence of God depends on the nature of soul. Perhaps the biggest problem with Plotinian theism is that it can mean all things to all theists. If one wishes an apophatic deity beyond all change, one can worship the Plotinian One. However, if one wishes a divine intelligence, one can worship Plotinian *Nous*. And if one wishes a living deity who experiences all of the details of besouled agents in the world, one can worship the Plotinian World Soul. One can also develop a process version of Plotinus's philosophy, as we will see momentarily (Hartshorne 2000, 212).

We can then understand why Plotinus values unity so highly in that to refer to any individual as such presupposes the concept of unity. This is why he thinks that The One is anterior to everything else and that above everything else there is something utterly simple. We often consider what is unitary in an animal, a human being, or even the cosmos. What is problematic is when Plotinus sees The One as an abstraction that is beyond essence and is ineffable because The One is beyond all multiplicity, including the multiplicity necessarily involved in words. The One or The Good is at times identified with God in Plotinus and is seen as in no way in need of anything else. That is, God is *causa sui* or cause of itself. Despite the fact that Plotinus is often referred to as a Neoplatonist, at times he is seen more accurately as a Neoaristotelian, especially when he says that The One can think only of itself. This is because if The One thought of anything other than itself it would be involved in multiplicity, as in the distinction between knower and known when the known is different from the knower (*Enneads* III. 7–8; IV. 9).

In addition to the monopolarity embedded in Plotinus's concept of God, there is also his denial of temporal succession in God such that the future is always already present to God. Not only divine existence, but also divine knowledge is necessary in every respect. What is left unclear is how Plotinus's monopolarity and preference for necessity over contingency is compatible with his defense of the World Soul. Something can be said in favor of the interpretation that suggests that divine necessity is compatible with creation in that The One of necessity emanates out or diffuses itself throughout the cosmos, hence Hartshorne labels Plotinus's conception of God as a sort of emanationism.

The superabundance of unity in The One emanates or oozes out to Intelligence (or *Nous*), which in turn emanates out to soul, including the World Soul. Each descending level of unity has nonetheless a degree of oneness whose source is The One. Granted, soul in Plotinus is both unified and multiple, but because it can be spread out in several parts of the body simultaneously it is a fitting model for the World Soul or divine inclusiveness. Unfortunately, Plotinus confuses things quite a bit when he then alleges that the World Soul is outside of time altogether (*Enneads* V. 1–9; VI. 1–9; also see Gerson 1996).

Plotinus's view that *Nous* and the World Soul (once again, these are similar to, respectively, Plato's Demiurge and the World Soul in the *Timaeus*) are to be treated as lesser deities in comparison to The One (*To Hen*) has serious difficulties. As the spiritual aspirant advances, the goal is to become as changeless and immaterial as possible and to devalue the material world of multiplicity as much as possible. As Hartshorne notes in an effort to explicate the ashamedness Plotinus had regarding his body, which his student Porphyry mentioned in his biography of Plotinus, "this would mean [it seems] exalting mathematical truth over historical truth, science above friendship, intellect above emotion, celibacy above marriage, etc. Although Plotinus was a most wonderful character, still the narrowness of the ascetic and the hater of the flesh is not absent from him. 'He was ashamed that he had a body.' He preached philosophical salvation, not human salvation" (Hartshorne 2000, 219–220). Plotinus may legitimately ask, in effect, without unity what would things amount to? But just as legitimately, we may wonder, without multiplicity what would things amount to? In both cases the response should be: Nothing (see Hartshorne 1970, 43, 121)! Unity is always unity of something and even in those rare passages in his posthumously published classic *The Enneads*, where Plotinus speaks somewhat favorably of the divisible, material world in flux, he does so in a whisper, whereas he proclaims loudly The One.

Abstractions are certainly crucial, but are they more crucial than the concrete realities out of which they are abstracted? "Abstract" and "concrete" are concepts that complete each other, as do "intellect" and "emotion," as well as "contemplation" and "action." When Plotinus denied dreaded temporal change to his World Soul, he made this concept unintelligible to anyone whose concept of soul is analogous to the human soul. Furthermore, if *Nous* or divine intelligence is the only reality that can adequately grasp The One, then why is *Nous* an inferior deity in that any subject who adequately grasps an object of knowledge cannot be inferior to the object grasped (Hartshorne 2000, 220–221).

If the world (including *Nous*, the World Soul, and all of the material stuff) issues necessarily from The One, then Plotinus's emanationism is very close to the classical theistic doctrine, despite the voluntaristic character of the latter. Or better, classical theism's creation *ex nihilo* (creation out of absolute nothingness, whatever that might mean) and Plotinus's creation *ex deo* (creation out of the divine nature itself, as in the way that a lit candle emanates light to the furthest corner of a room) are barely distinguishable when both are contrasted to Platonic and Hartshornian creation *ex hyle* (where God persuades the world toward a better place by offering it a model of perfect goodness and beauty). This is because both creation *ex nihilo* and creation *ex deo* fail to account for the contingency in the actual world; nor do they acknowledge the resistance various centers of power can offer to any persuasive agency. Furthermore, the world inclusiveness implied in Plotinus's World Soul is at odds with the wholly independent reality of The One. His monopolarity prevented him from appreciating the idea of both a supreme independence (of God's existence) and a supreme dependence (of God on creatures for God's actual enjoyment of the world). Plotinus himself seems to be caught between two equally unpalatable alternatives: Either God is world inclusive and, therefore, multiple and complex, or God is utterly transcendent and, hence, simple. Although Plotinus usually adopts the latter position, he also has a tendency to speak with a paradoxical ambiguity on the concept of God. This dilemma can be felicitously dissolved by claiming that deity has two complementary aspects (Hartshorne 2000, 222–223).

Ironically, Plotinus often uses metaphors and similes for The One that are drawn from the material reality that he appears to scorn. Hartshorne describes the irony in the following terms:

> One of the striking features about much Western theology is its combination of emphatic scorn for the physical, the "corporeal," which must, it holds, be absolutely and in every sense denied of God, who is pure spirit, together with a scarcely less decided preference for analogies drawn from our perception of physical things, inanimate objects, rather than from our observations of spiritual things (love, . . . memory, etc.) as

vehicles of theological meaning and reasoning. It could be shown that a rather crass materialism often, if not always, accompanies such extreme spiritualism. (Hartshorne 2000, 223)

One pays a significant price for this devaluation of love and memory, as I argue in part 3.

Capetz emphasizes Plotinus's strong influence on classical theism, in general, and his influence on Augustine, in particular. Augustine follows Plotinus in thinking that all things (the many) are emanations from a single ultimate principle (The One), from which they proceed (*exitus*) and to which they are destined to return (*reditus*). Everything has a common source, although some things are closer to the source than others. Strictly material beings are further from the source than living beings, which are further from the source than intelligent or spiritual beings. The lower ought to look upward to the higher, more unified reality (Capetz 2003, 60–61).

Bowker rightly sees Plotinus as a kind of fusion of Plato and Aristotle, although Bowker does not notice that Plotinus's concept of God may very well owe more to Aristotle than to Plato. The One in itself is absolutely transcendent and removed from the world. How the transcendence of The One is compatible with emanation and with the existence of a World Soul remains unclear in Bowker (as it remains unclear in Plotinus himself). In this regard Bowker sees a similarity between Plotinus's thought and dualistic Gnosticism (Bowker 2002, 233, 353).

As is often the case, Armstrong is more detailed than Bowker or Capetz in tracing the history of the concept of God. She notices that Plotinus and the great Christian thinker Origen had common teacher, Ammonius Saccas. Previously we had occasion to note that Origen defended a Christian version of the World Soul that relied heavily on St. Paul, indicated implicitly what some of the problems would be with classical theism, and pointed toward neoclassical or process theism. This leads us to wonder if similar tendencies are found in Plotinus, despite his distaste for Christianity. One feature of Plotinus's thought that is often noticed, but seldom emphasized, is that the return to The One could be seen not so much in hierarchical terms as an ascent up to a supersensible realm, but rather as an interior journey or as a "climb inward," to use Armstrong's useful language. On this line of interpretation, The One is not so much an alien object as our best self. This helpful suggestion enables us to avoid the view of The One as strictly transcendent, which leads to the strongest sort of apophaticism in that a one in complete isolation from others could not in any way even be said to exist because to do so would put The One in multiple relationships with other things that exist, hence destroying the absolute unity of The One. As Armstrong sees things, because nothing can really be said about The One, the reference to divine unity requires ecstatic (literally, to stand outside of oneself) mysticism. In any event, the timelessness and impassibility of Plotinus's deity is very much at odds with the best in biblical theism, once again as in the belief in God as love (Armstrong 1993, 101–104, 171).

As with Plato and to a lesser extent Aristotle, we find in Plotinus the makings of a defensible concept of God. To be specific, if he had both focused on the World Soul and made it explicit that the World Soul is God, he then could have been able to identify intelligence as one of the defining characteristics of the World Soul; and he could have seen the forms of unity and goodness as the most significant concepts entertained by divine intelligence (see Whittemore 1966). Instead of this living, dynamic deity that he could have defended, however, Plotinus's concept of God privileges The One (hardly a living being in itself) and then struggles to find a place for both intelligence and living, besouled agency in the world. Again, as with classical theistic appropriation of Aristotle and especially Plato, nothing was necessary in the way philosophical theists in the Abrahamic religions took Plotinus's thought in a classical theistic direction. In different terms, Plato, Aristotle, and Plotinus need to be rebaptized in a spirit of love that is more appropriate for that than which no greater can be conceived.

Plotinus's monopolarity, importantly, is both an intellectual and a religious mistake. God as actual is more than, not less than, the abstract, soulless, absolute unity Plotinus defends. An utterly relationless absolute unity, devoid of inner plurality, is hardly a being worthy of worship; indeed, it violates the logic of perfection, which starts with a careful consideration of what exactly it means to be that than which no greater can be conceived. Why the mere having of parts equals corruptibility, however, is not clear. Even on a strictly materialistic basis, the material world, with all of its parts, could be everlasting (Hartshorne 1967, 24, 106; 1965, 27).

Plotinus is to be thanked for reacting to the negative impact of ancient Greek skepticism, but he unfortunately continued the biases toward being over becoming and the abstract over the concrete. Indeed he carried these biases to their bitter ends. His supreme reality, The One, is not at all analogous to mind or even to life in that this completely unified reality is beyond awareness. This "beyond" quality makes his thought similar to that of some Hindu thinkers such as Sankara (788–820). It is one thing to analogize beyond human experience to talk about subhuman experience and, at the other end, divine experience. But it is another thing to try to get beyond experience altogether, an effort that is merely verbal and has no experience to back it up (obviously enough). This is not to deny that Plotinus's experiment has a sort of value in pointing out the blind alleys that a defensible concept of God should avoid. An improved concept of God would have to detail both the good and the bad ways in which something could be complex, in contrast to Plotinus's assumption that all complexity is evil. Furthermore, an improved concept of God would have to improve on Plotinus's pictures of (not exactly concepts of) The One's ability to emanate like the overflowing of a fountain or the radiation of light from the sun without the sun losing anything of itself (Hartshorne 1983, 59).

On Plotinus's view, pure being precedes, surpasses, and renders noncontributory and superfluous the variegated world that we know. By way of contrast in a process worldview, being is derived from, or abstracted away from, the actual world of becoming. In this regard Hartshorne thinks that Plotinus has a contemporary defender in the metaphysician Robert Neville who, along with Plotinus and others in contemporary philosophy and theology, emphasizes the eternalistic side to Plato (Hartshorne 1984a, 189, 267; 1984c, 8; also see Neville 1993). That is, Plotinus confuses the Platonic waters by precluding any sort of divine relativity (see Hartshorne 1991, 643, 721).

Part 3

Neoclassical
or Process Theism

The history of the concept of God presented thus far has concentrated on both the classical concept of God in the Abrahamic religions from the time of Philo in the first century CE until the present, as well as the ancient Greek roots of this position found in Plato, Aristotle, and Plotinus. But I have also argued that the monopolar direction Aristotle and Plotinus take was not the only way that Plato's rich thought on the concept of God could have progressed. That is, Aristotle and Plotinus largely ignored the dipolarity of Plato's concept of God; and what Aristotle did notice about Plato's World Soul was rejected. This started a pattern that continues in classical theistic circles until the present day.

There was nothing inevitable about classical theism as the traditional antipathy exhibited by biblical scholars, fideists, and mystics toward classical theism indicates. Things could have gone much better. We have seen that Origen, for example, defended a Christian version of the Platonic World Soul, and Gersonides exhibited skepticism regarding the classical theistic version of omniscience and so forth. Part 3 examines historical versions of dipolar monotheism that are nonetheless somewhat at odds with classical theism. In different terms, this part of the book contributes to the effort to insure that philosophical theism, which obviously has a rich past, will have a luxurious future as well. This effort requires that we understand that classical theism has not gone unchallenged by philosophical theists. We even find evidence from 3,400 years ago that Ikhnaton, the Egyptian pharaoh who is arguably the first monotheist, thought that God is most good and beautiful, but not omnipotent. Likewise, Nezahualcoyotl in Mexico before the Spanish conquest thought of God as a self-creating process (Hartshorne 2000, 29–30; 1981, 17).

We should not assume that the view of God found in the Hebrew and Christian scriptures is philosophically at odds with Ikhnaton's view. Granted, the Hebrew view did not select just one natural phenomenon (the sun) as peculiarly divine, as did Ikhnaton. And the scripture writers were clearly interested in an intense way, unlike Ikhnaton, with describing God in personal terms, such as love, knowledge, and will. Hartshorne urges the following regarding the Hebrew scriptures: "Those who insist upon simply combining utter nonrelativity of deity with the assertion that, metaphorically speaking, God knows and loves the world are speaking, in our judgment, not analogically but equivocally" (Hartshorne 2000, 34). In fact, the scriptural evidence in favor of neoclassical or process theism is just as impressive, or more so, as that in favor of classical theism. For example, the famous version of creation at the beginning of Genesis indicates not that an omnipotent God created the world *ex nihilo*, but rather that God persuaded as much order as possible out of the disorderly aqueous muck that was there "in the beginning" with God. This persuasive creation *ex hyle* brought about what was, for a while at least, a vegetarian paradise. Likewise, in the Psalms (for example, 103) God is depicted as eminently merciful and compassionate and one who does not (thankfully) treat us as we deserve to be treated. God is great in the kindness shown to those like ourselves who have great faults. And throughout the Christian scriptures these themes of personal love, knowledge, and will are repeated, expanded, and deepened, such as when 1 John (4: 7–9) claims that God *is* love and that God is revealed to us when love is present.

Some sort of gap will always exist between mythopoetic approaches to God, such as found in Ikhnaton and in the Judeo-Christian scriptures, and philosophical theism. But it is important that the best insights found in mythopoetic approaches to God at least be compatible with the concept of God philosophers and theologians defend. Indeed, part of the job of philosophers and theologians is to explicate and deepen understanding of the best insights in mythopoetic theism, such as in John's thesis that God *is* love. Or again, one would expect an explication of the biblical idea that divine creation does not start with sheer nonentity and that divine creative acts are successive rather than all at once. Among these successive acts are those related to "harvesting" as well as to "sowing" in dipolar fashion. An abstraction can be immutable, but it cannot love or be angry, such as in the biblical God. In sum, "in no simple objectively convincing way can Scriptures be shown to affirm monopolarity. And certainly they often seem to imply a dipolar conception" (Hartshorne 2000, 38; also see Timpe 2013).

Part 3 treats some of the major figures in dipolar theism in the modern period up until the mid-twentieth century from the Hartshornian perspective that dominates the entire book. Because the entire project relies on Hartshorne, no specific chapter is devoted to his thought. But I treat several major historical dipolar theists whose views are compatible with Hartshorne's. Again, because I treat dipolar theism in this part of the book, I generally do not include the monopolar theists, who are at the opposite end of the spectrum from classical theism; that is, monopolar theists who see God as strictly temporal or strictly finite with no eternal or everlasting aspect. These would include some famous examples, such as Samuel Alexander and others. I also largely ignore other sorts of theism that are outside of the debate between classical theism and neoclassical or process theism, such as in pantheists like Spinoza or Sankara, the latter a Hindu pantheist from the eighth and ninth centuries. Although I will not be able to address much of the history of the concept of God in this book, my belief (or at least my hope) is that the focused debate between classical and neoclassical or process theism is of wide significance for theists and nontheists alike. As before, I will not treat theists such as Hegel, whom I find impossible to classify in that they could easily fit the mold of classical theism, process theism, or perhaps even pantheism; nonetheless most experts acknowledge that Hegel exerted a great influence on thinkers such as Schelling and Pfleiderer, who clearly are neoclassical or process theists.

Part 4, the final part of the book, treats the thought of Bergson and Whitehead; these two thinkers are, along with Hartshorne, the greatest neoclassical or process theists.

14

Faustus Socinus

(1539–1604)

In addition to historical opposition to classical theism found in Origen, various biblical scholars, Gersonides, mystics, fideists, and so on, there is the critical perspective Faustus Socinus offered in the sixteenth century. His thought in many ways prepares the way for the thinkers in this part of the book by pushing the case for a temporal theism. Socinus realized that divine wisdom cannot consist in a survey of all time in a single glance in that on this basis there could not possibly be any new knowledge; but there *is* new knowledge that could not possibly be predicted beforehand, and hence the inadequacy of classical theistic omniscience. As in Gersonides, this position is not to be identified with the view that there is a defect in divine knowledge. Not surprisingly, Socinus and his followers were very unpopular due to their criticisms of classical theism, which had become the received view reified in several religious traditions. Indeed, the Socinians were widely seen as heretics (Hartshorne 2000, 225).

Socinus explicitly criticizes Boethius's view of divine eternity in the sense of being outside of, or above, time. That is, on Socinus's view divine omniscience itself is temporal in that knowledge consists in being aware of what is knowable and the knowable consists in what has reality in some manner or other. Hence the greatest knower would know the reality of the past as past, the reality of the present as present, and the reality of the future or the possible/probable as future or as possible/probable. Admittedly, God would know the necessary future as necessary, but this aspect of the future would only concern very abstract realities, such as in the realization that some world or other would have to exist in the future if absolute nothingness is unintelligible. But most of the future is the region of possibility or, at best, probability. In fact, God's knowledge is ideal precisely because God knows ideally the possible as possible or the probable as probable (Fock 1847, 427–439).

From a neoclassical or process theistic perspective, Socinus is on the mark when he claims that nothing in the world would be accidental or contingent if God already knew the future as determinate. Furthermore, he is understandably not convinced by St. Thomas's distinction between primary (divine) and secondary (human) causation, wherein all is necessary concerning primary causation and the contingent enters via secondary causation. The reason for this skepticism is that primary causation is decisive if God is omnipotent, as Thomas thinks. On classical theistic assumptions, everything should be seen as necessary and determined from all eternity. The later St. Augustine, Calvin, and various Muslim classical theists admit as much. But then on this basis there is no human freedom. And that is the difficulty of the situation. Rejecting belief in freedom puts into disequilibrium many other beliefs that we are not willing to (or perhaps are not even able to) relinquish, such as the belief that people should be held accountable for their free choices.

Socinus is well aware that the classical theist is likely to respond by saying future events will not occur because God knows them, but rather God knows them because they are to happen. The problem with this objection is that knowledge of the future can be determinate and necessary only if "the future" really is determinate and necessary. Another reply from the classical theist would be that there is no past, present, and future in the divine, only an eternal "now." But the Socinian perspective on this is once again telling: This means that events have permanent being and do not have the transitional sort of existence that is characteristic of becoming. If all that exists is just right now, then it is not only freedom, but also change, that is illusory. As I see things, one pays too great a price in terms of loss of reflective equilibrium for this ultrastatic Parmenidean view (Fock 1847, 439–442).

Although Socinus is a dipolar theist (see Hartshorne 1991, 701), his concept of God nonetheless has problems. The difficulties surround his defective sense of divine inclusiveness. He does not clearly affirm the idea that all changes and contingent things are included in (via divine omnibenevolence and divine omniscience properly conceived) the divine life. He clearly denies divine eternity in the Boethian sense of being outside of time altogether, but whether he affirms divine world inclusiveness is unclear. In different terms, if the world is conceived as existing outside of God, then mere "God" would be inferior to "God and world." The logic of perfection works against not only a strictly temporal theism, but also against a weak or nonexistent sense of divine world inclusiveness (Hartshorne 2000, 226–227).

Socinus is on stronger ground when he emphasizes that divine knowledge has to be changing knowledge, albeit preeminent changing knowledge. Scholars have largely ignored this great insight. Importantly, however, the real scandal in Socinus's own lifetime was not his critique of classical theistic omniscience, but rather his critique of trinitarian theology in Christianity. It was his criticism of the Trinity that led to his persecution and the need to flee from his native Italy to Poland. By being diverted by this "scandal," scholars have failed to appreciate his genuine contribution to the concept of God in terms of the idea that once real change is admitted in the divine case, there is a plurality of divine persons in the odd sense that God would be a slightly different person from moment to moment as all of the changes that occur in the world are assimilated into the divine life. However, in a peculiar way this leads not to a trinity, but to an infinite number of divine persons, albeit strung together with a strong line of causal inheritance (Hartshorne 2000, 227).

Although both Bowker and Capetz ignore Socinus, Armstrong cites his book *Christ the Savior*, where the doctrine of the Trinity is criticized. She does not cite Socinus's critique of classical theistic omniscience (Armstrong 1993, 280), despite the fact that this is what is most philosophically noteworthy about Socinus's thought. A great number of thinkers, including many theists, have not even thought about the possibility that a perfect knower would not have fully anticipated later states at an earlier time because until an event is actualized, it does not exist to be known. In fact, claiming to know as determinate that which is at present somewhat indeterminate is an error, not knowledge, as Socinus realized. Reality is essentially a creative process that contains futurity or partial indeterminacy (Hartshorne 1962, 42; 1965, 43).

Despite the fact that Socinus might not adequately defend divine world inclusiveness, Hartshorne lavishes praise on him by saying that to him: ". . . goes the rare honor of being the first thinker who explicitly, clearly, and with reasoned arguments accepted a contingent, changing aspect of God as a religious belief, justified by its being an implication of human freedom and responsibility. . . . [I]f we decide something of our lives, then, since God knows us, we decide something of what God is" (Hartshorne 1983, 91–92).

The apparent impasse between classical theists and neoclassical or process theists can be seen as being centered on the following question: Is knowledge of the past radically different from "knowledge" of the future? Neoclassical or process theists, along with Socinus, think that it is, whereas classical theists think of divine knowledge of the future in determinate terms that are not much different from the terms used to describe knowledge of the past. By contrast, God does not eternally know what we will decide tomorrow because until we decide there are simply no such things as tomorrow's decisions. Human words like "freedom" either have meaning or they do not; if not, we should (*per impossibile*) stop using them. God knows all things perfectly (the past and particular as past and particular, the future and potential as future and potential), but this claim differs significantly from the claim that God knows future contingencies as already actualized (Hartshorne 1984c, 26–27, 39, 73; 1984a, 18, 31, 155, 259; 1987, 28).

We can learn from the past and prepare for the future, but preparing for the past and learning from the future makes no sense. Socinus realized this. Quite ironically, mystics such as St. John of the Cross with their alleged otherworldliness realize it better than classical theists (see Dombrowski 1992). There is no contradiction in claiming that God is all-knowing and that God acquires new knowledge. In fact, the logic of perfection entails that God would have to acquire such knowledge if partially new realities come into being at each moment (Hartshorne 1990, 140, 386, 388).

There are qualities in God that might have been otherwise. If we have genuine freedom in the sense of self-determination, then when we decide something and if God knows our decisions once they occur, then we change God (not the very fact that God exists, but God's actual tenor of existence). On this Socinian view, God is creative-cumulative in actuality (Hartshorne 2011, 53, 77, 120–121; 1991, 705).

15
Friedrich von Schelling
(1775–1854)

The first modern dipolar theist who also defended divine world inclusiveness may well have been the German philosopher Friedrich von
Schelling. Although he is not always clear on the point, his best insight
is that the concept of God cannot be expressed in a single word, like
"first" or "necessary," but rather requires that we express this concept
in contrasting terms, such as "necessary and free" or "self-sufficiency
and relativity to others." This dipolar doctrine can also be called a type
of panentheism wherein all is in God, via divine knowledge and love,
yet God is not to be *identified* with the world. There is no contradiction in saying that there is something necessary in God (say, divine
existence) and something contingent. In fact, that there is something
nonnecessary in God is itself necessary. If our contingent suffering in
some sense is "in" God, as even St. Paul admits, then there is divine
contingency. Whereas suffering may be a universal category, wicked-
ness is not in that the latter requires the sort of rational responsibility
that is the hallmark of moral agency. The divine life involves a series of
transactions with free creatures. The best way to insure against a false
conception of omnipotence is not to suppress this freedom (Hartshorne
2000, 233–234).

The mix of divine necessity and freedom in Schelling is related to
the contrast between divine aseity (*seinheit*) or divine "ownness," on the
one hand, and divine love that reaches out to others as a partial negation of own-ness, on the other. Each term in the contrast is essential
and, according to Schelling, it is a sign of degeneration if one of these is
reduced to the other in classical theistic fashion. It makes sense to say
that God is unlimited (*ens illimitatissimum*), but it also makes sense to say

that God is limited both internally to the divine life itself and in relation to particular creatures. God responds in this way rather than that, here and now, to this or that sparrow or human being. Schelling explicitly defends his dipolar concept of God against the obvious objection that it is contradictory. It would be contradictory if he were claiming that God as such was permanent and changing, rather than uttering the more defensible claim that in one aspect God is permanent (or necessary) and in a different aspect is changing (or contingent). The contrasting predicates apply to different aspects of the divine life. Complete divine permanence would involve a deadly slumber of the divine nature itself (Hartshorne 2000, 234–236; Schelling 1942, 95–106; also see 2000).

Schelling is also insightful in *The Ages of the World* in his criticisms (albeit not free from obscurity) of divine "eternity," at least if this term refers to a complete absence of time in divinity. He notes that the ancient Hebrew word *naezach* conveys the successiveness involved in the divine life that is perhaps better represented in English as "everlastingness," rather than as an atemporal "eternity." There is movement, indeed progress, even in, especially in, the imperishable divine life. Furthermore, Schelling anticipates Whitehead's doctrine of prehension, wherein the past is never entirely lost, so the past is not so much annulled time as it is partially preserved time. If God is revealed spatially (as in the orderliness and beauty of the material world or as in the nuanced spiritual lives of certain human beings), then the spirit-matter contrast is yet another dipolar pair that must be included in any description of God that approaches adequacy to the subject matter in question (Hartshorne 2000, 237–241; Schelling 1942, 111–225; 2000; also see Wirth 2005).

The prime frustration involved in reading about Schelling's concept of God is that at times he does revel in contradiction and at times seems abstruse. A more cogent way to convey his legitimate insights is to say that sheer simplicity in a description of God would preclude any sort of intelligible relationships with the complex world in process that surrounds us. This frustration is outweighed by the astute way in which Schelling avoids the effort to ground becoming or process in something else, most notably being. Being is an abstraction away from becoming and consists in what is permanent in a strand of process or in what is permanent in process per se. If concrete reality is process or becoming, then being issues from it, rather than the other way around, as Schelling realized. In different terms, there is no such thing as absolute rest, only rest that is relative to motion; hence there is something wrongheaded in the classical theistic apotheosis of rest in a God who in no way changes (Hartshorne 2000, 242–243; 1991, 640; also see Ottmann 2013).

The need for the present book becomes apparent when we see both Armstrong and Capetz ignore altogether Schelling and several other dipolar theists in the nineteenth and twentieth centuries. However, Bowker at least mentions Schelling in an insightful way in terms of the resistance he offers to the Enlightenment thesis that science can explain everything. Even mythopoetic thought, as found, say, in Ikhnaton and the Bible, is valuable as something like a hieroglyphic expression of nature transfigured by imagination and love (Bowker 2002, 47).

Schelling is to be commended for realizing that, in addition to two widely noted possibilities (that there is no God and that there is a wholly immutable God), there is also a third, widely neglected, option (that God is not wholly immutable). A fourth option (that God is wholly mutable) is hardly tenable in that it could lead to the conclusion that God's very existence could change, in which case the being in question would not be that than which no greater can be conceived. The third option (that God's existence is immutable, but God's actuality is eminently mutable) is the one that is most compatible with temporal asymmetry: The past is the realm of accomplished fact, whereas the future is the realm of possibility as long as one does not assume that all possibilities can be realized. That is, possibilities compete with each other such that many of them are not compossible with others (Hartshorne 1983, 2, 203, 251).

Schelling's stumbling efforts toward a concept of God that finds a place for both divine necessity and divine freedom include the realization that God as abstract and God as concrete are not identical; rather the latter includes the former in the sense that God's abstract being refers to that which is constant in concrete divine becoming. This highlighting of divine becoming is, in part, meant to make sure that the concept of God refers to the God of religion. For example, the Christian ideal of suffering or sacrificial love does not make sense on the classical theistic view. To worship (classical theistic) absoluteness and independence is not exactly to worship God (see Hartshorne 1941, 141; 1948, 2; 1953, 20; 1962, 272; 1970, 294; 1972, 13, 187, 196).

Schelling realized that the merely infinite and eternal could not have knowledge of the finite and temporal without somehow being finitized and temporalized. In this regard his instructive dipolarity influenced other dipolarists in the tradition of neoclassical or process theism, as in Morris Cohen, who, in turn, greatly influenced Hartshorne. And although Schelling did not explicitly defend belief in God as the World Soul, he did support in his work *System of Transcendental Idealism* the related romantic idea that "force" rather than "matter" is the key idea in the understanding of Nature when conceived as a restless self-activity and a living, organic Whole (Hartshorne 1984a, 62, 183, 279; 1991, 512–513, 696; Schelling 1978; 2010).

In sum, Schelling is part of a vast international movement among scholars over the past two centuries to remove philosophy of religion and theology away from a still-influential classical theistic tradition that prevents a social interpretation of divine relations with the world (Hartshorne 2011, 141).

16

Gustav Fechner

(1801–1887)

At his best the German philosopher/psychologist Gustav Fechner defended a view of a world inclusive, everlastingly temporal deity, a view that indicates the complexity of the concept of God. God's environment is internal, rather than external, as Fechner sees things in agreement with Plato. The world inclusiveness that Fechner defends means that not only joys, but also tragedies, would be included in the divine life via God's omniscience and omnibenevolence. God must experience evil because of omnibenevolence even if God is incapable of doing it. Philosophers and theologians, including Armstrong, Bowker, and Capetz, unfortunately have largely neglected Fechner.

Because of divine dipolarity (or better, because of divine dual transcendence) one must be prepared to find more than one meaning for divine preeminence when various contrasting attributes are considered. As a unitary, inclusive spirit, God is superior to the individual spirits who are members of the divine life. Our individual bodies are but parts of nature, but we are also intimately connected to the divine life conceived as Nature as a whole. Fechner was well aware of the fact that many people experience the world in terms of material things scattered everywhere as a mere concatenation of disconnected stuff. Indeed, referring not to a cosmos or to a *universe*, but rather to a multiverse or a pluriverse, is currently popular. Where is the common center?, it will be asked. Fechner thinks it important to note, however, that natural laws do not tend to contradict each other from academic discipline to academic discipline, even if there is still the worry that there might not be any purpose to the various purposes in the natural world. This worry is often associated with a belief in divine omnipotence, in which case there should be a Purpose to everything that happens. In the neoclassical or process concept of God, however, which is devoid of the concept of divine omnipotence, there is only as much direction and purpose as is compatible with multiple freedoms in the world if the creatures are assistants in the precise character of the whole and who have powers of their own (Fechner 1922, I, 200–215).

The harmony of natural laws can plausibly be explained, Fechner thinks, in terms of a "highest law," quite apart from the issue of whether an omnipotent being delivers the highest law. Unfortunately, at times Fechner speaks as if this highest law *is* the result of an omnipotent being, a view at odds with his claim that creatures have legislative powers of their own, just as cells have powers of their own inside of our own bodies. Fechner himself acknowledges the tension between belief in divine omnipotence and belief in creaturely power and freedom. He is on somewhat safer ground when he uses the familiar figure of speech wherein God is seen as a shepherd, such that the "sheep" have their own volitions up to certain limits. But because God's environment is internal rather than external, a better metaphor than that of the shepherd is that of a divine, cosmic soul for the body of the whole world. And he partially escapes from the problems associated with belief in divine omnipotence by suggesting that the divine goal is not so much reaching a maximum as achieving a certain degree of progress. God heals and reforms a tragic world in flux (Fechner 1922, I, 217–249).

William James was a partial admirer of Fechner's work. What James liked about Fechner was his panpsychism, wherein lesser psyche are included in higher psyche. Because Fechner has at times been called the father of experimental psychology, his concept of God, not surprisingly, in effect involves a psychology of deity. Despite the fact that we are not really outside of God, our wills are different from the divine will. God does not so much will our volitions as God suffers them. This involves a sort of dynamic perfection, in contrast to the classical theistic static perfection. On Fechner's process view, although later phases of divine experience are richer than earlier phases, God is every bit as unrivaled as in classical theism in that God's experience is cosmic in character and preeminent in terms of knowledge and love (Hartshorne 2000, 254–256).

Fechner's argument for the existence of God is to be commended in terms of the degree to which it is stripped of divine eternalism and of the idea of a creation *ex nihilo* once and for all. That is, the argument from design can lose its bad reputation if it is seen in everlasting terms as the gradual result of the divine lure toward that sort of order that is beautiful. Unfortunately, at times Fechner leans back toward classical theistic determinism, so his view could have been improved if the following Hartshornian advice had been followed: "That every difference in conditions occasions a difference in outcome may be accepted by an indeterminist, but that every similarity in conditions means an equal similarity in outcome is scarcely acceptable as a basis of freedom" (Hartshorne 2000, 256).

The problematic influence of classical theistic tradition also surfaces in Fechner's thought when he flirts with the idea of a type of divine justice with rewards and punishments inherent for every action. This position seems to rely implicitly on a concept of divine omnipotence.

Fechner is remarkable precisely because he was able to move, in the great chapter on "God and the World" in his book *Zend Avesta*, beyond the Kantian view of God even if he did not, like other nineteenth-century German idealists, break with science. For example, Fechner did not think, like Kant, that the crux of religion was to be found in a paymaster God who ensured either immortality of the soul or resurrection of the body. These are secondary matters when contrasted with one's contributions to the divine life (Hartshorne 1953, 12, 123, 211).

There are a few differences between Schelling and Fechner, both because Fechner is clearer than Schelling and because he is more explicit in his defense of God as the World Soul. This defense illuminates the "feeling of feeling" that occurs at the animal level when a being with a central nervous system gathers at a higher level the microfeelings that occur at the cellular level and when God gathers at the highest level the feelings that occur in us. This feeling of feeling, which Fechner refers to as a "daylight view," is similar to Charles Sanders Peirce's sympathetic "agapism" (Hartshorne 1948, xi, 29).

Hartshorne goes so far as to say that the relations of God to the world are in many respects treated more ably by Fechner than by any other author. Fechner's success in this regard has to do with his combination of clear distinctions among the levels of feeling and careful attention paid to what we do in fact experience. For example, sometimes we experience very localized pains that indicate microfeelings *in* our body, sometimes we experience an overall bodily malaise, and sometimes we experience that we are parts of a cosmic whole that feels us. Although James noted Fechner's genius, and he even agreed with Fechner that limited minds were parts of some more inclusive Mind, James thought that Fechner slurred over the distinction between God and timeless absoluteness (that is, timeless absence of relations). But this distinction is quite alive in Fechner, who knew that the God of classical theism was an empty (that is, absolute) unity divorced from the otherwise chaotic plurality of the world. By contrast, in Fechner's theism every new child who comes into the world brings something new and fresh to God, hence God is both the oldest and youngest of beings (see Plato's *Symposium* 178a, 195a). God is also the richest being in the sense that God is "the most equipped with suitable background for diverse new [experiences], as the [human person] with a varied past is apt to have the most capacity [among creatures] to assimilate further variety" (Hartshorne 1941, 228). Or again, Fechner was perhaps "the first to see clearly that the choices of lesser minds, the voluntary acts, must appear in the highest or all-inclusive mind as involuntary 'impulses' upon which the choices of the highest mind, its volitions, will operate" (Hartshorne 1941, 291, also 209, 211; 1962, 203; 1987, 88; also see Fechner 1922, l, chap. 11).

Also insightful is that Fechner notices that the progress in divine actuality does not mean something was inferior about earlier stages of the divine life. At any moment God is the supremely excellent being-in-becoming who exhibits dual transcendence, but new moments bring with them new opportunities to exhibit preeminent divine knowledge and love. In Fechnerian terms, to view God's earlier existence as inferior would be to exhibit an inferior conception of inferiority. We are inferior to God because we do not, like God, assimilate all that is actual; but the future is not yet actual for any being, not even for a preeminent one. Events endure, as Fechner realized, but they endure in later events, not in any "future event" that is not here yet. Strictly speaking there really are no future events, only the possibility or probability of such (Hartshorne 1962, v-vi, 18).

Critics of the doctrine of the World Soul are likely to ask, where is the world brain? Fechner is helpful in responding to this question. Note how odd it is to assume that when we examine microscopic animals we must attribute to them all of the organs found in mesoscopic (midsized) animals such as ourselves. Might it be the case that there is something equally odd in assuming that when we are considering the cosmic, macroscopic, divine animal there has to be a super-brain? Microscopic animals have no internal organs largely because relations among their neighbors serve as something like organs for these individuals. Analogizing at the other end by claiming that everything contributes to the divine cosmic value in that there is no external environment in the divine case thus makes sense. That is, our central nervous system, including our brain, relate us to that which is external to us, but in the case of the World Soul there is no such external environment. "The world mind will have no special brain, but . . . rather every individual is to that mind as a sort of brain-cell. . . . The cosmic analogue of a brain will be simply the entire system of things as wholly internal and immediate to the cosmic mind" (Hartshorne 1962, 197–198). God's "power over us," on this view, at least in part consists in the power to be influenced by each of us when seen as analogues for brain cells, as it were (Hartshorne 1962, 275).

The perfection of God consists not in reaching some definite maximum, but in always seeking an unlimited progress. The logic of perfection in neoclassical or process terms points us not toward a strictly immutable being, but toward ideal perfectibility. In this concept of dynamic perfection it is important to notice that we are not only cocreators of the world, but cocreators of God's actuality if not of God's existence. This is the meaning of the transcendence of mechanical order that is freedom. It involves some slight injection of unforeseeable novelty into not only our lives, but also into the divine life itself. This is precisely why something is not only mistaken, but also something downright idolatrous in identifying God with an abstract aspect of God, such as absoluteness or aseity (Hartshorne 1970, xi, 277; 1967, 72, 113, 115, 127–128, 135).

If reality is essentially creative process, then necessity is merely what all possibilities have in common. Fechner more than hinted at the metaphysical ultimacy of creativity, and thus he is not only one of the greatest predecessors to Whitehead, but is also a major figure in his own right in the history of neoclassical or process theism. He does not shy away from the tragic element in God, as do classical theists. In fact, that God's perfection is dynamic, in addition to being tragic, is essential to religion itself, as I maintain throughout this book. The symbol of the cross in Christianity points toward this tragic element in divinity. One of the competing views is that nature is not so much tragically creative as it is machinelike, a view that Fechner calls the "night view" (Hartshorne 1965, 43; 1972, 13–14, 63, 72, 132, 154, 161, 167, 175, 187, 190, 192; 1984b, 186).

It is not merely the fact that we enrich the divine life that is noteworthy. In addition, for a theist such enrichment is the ultimate meaning of human existence. If this is correct (as in the motto of the Jesuits, which, once again, could or should be the motto for all theists: *ad majoram Dei gloriam*, all for the greater glory of God), then what one would want from a concept of God is some intelligible way to come to terms with our contributions to the divine life, which classical theism fails to do. No such contributions are to be found on a mechanistic materialist view, either. The parsimony of materialism is deceptive in that it achieves its simple end by restricting both our curiosity and the meaning of our lives, as Fechner realized. Neoclassical or process theism is admittedly complex in that it involves the analogy between the difficulty our cells have in understanding us and our own difficulty in understanding the concept of God. Fechner's favoring of dipolarity over monopolarity is an advance in this arduous task (Hartshorne 1984c, 27–28; 1987, 22, 24).

Fechner was perhaps the first scholar to think clearly about divine increase, an effort that pushed him toward both dipolar theism and a doctrine of dual transcendence. Once one gets over the mistaken idea that our minds are inextended (rather they are, in a way, spread over all of the cellular activity in our central nervous systems), we are in a better Fechnerian position to see that the divine mind is not entirely inextended, either (Hartshorne 1990, 388; 1991, 716; 2011, 68).

Fechner's insights in his 100-page chapter "Gott und Welt" in *Zend Avesta* can be seen as constituting a coherent worldview in the following terms: The only way to understand the world in its concreteness is to recognize something in it that is analogous to our own experience. This panpsychist or panexperientialist view is what we have seen him call the "day view," in contrast to the "night view" of mechanistic materialism, wherein reality is understood in the merely structural and nonqualitative terms of primary "qualities" like extension. The day view restores to us secondary qualities such as the joys of color sensations and painful experiences such as a burning feeling. Furthermore, Fechner acknowledged two types of panpsychism or panexperientialism: monadological and synechological. The former deals with the feelings of microscopic reality, whereas the latter deals with large entities like ourselves and nonhuman animals. Unfortunately, Fechner also attributes synechological psyche to trees, in contrast to Whitehead's more defensible view that trees as wholes are "democracies" devoid of (or almost entirely devoid of) sentiency, even if protosentiency or monadological sentiency can be found in cells in the tree. In any event, all of these centers of feeling are included in the divine consciousness. Hence, Fechner's view can be seen alternately as either a moderate pluralism or a moderate monism. He is not an extravagant monist in that cells and animals have their own feelings that are not swallowed up or obliterated in the divine whole. And Fechner in his defense of the World Soul, like German thinkers in general, was never tempted by extreme pluralism, which is more typical of British thinkers from William of Ockham to Hume to Russell (Hartshorne 1983, 248).

We have seen that Fechner's deity does not exhibit a timelessly complete perfection, but is the personal feature of a world inclusive, everlastingly progressive reality. God is constantly enriched by each new creature, yet is unsurpassable by others, even if God constantly surpasses each previous moment in the divine life itself. "Though beyond rivalry, the divine is not beyond growth" (Hartshorne 1983, 249). Becoming is real; indeed it is the most real. In Fechner's theodicy the divine does not omnipotently decide all that happens in that divine causality, although general, does not (indeed cannot) dictate the details. We have volitions that are taken up into the divine life as involuntary components that are ideally assimilated, albeit sometimes reluctantly so when these are ugly or cruel. In short, the evils of the world are due to us and to random clashes among the creatures, not to God. All of this is Fechner's effort to clarify the implicit Platonic scheme described in part 2 of this book.

17

Charles Sanders Peirce

(1839–1914)

Even more than in most thinkers, discovering a unified concept of God in the great American philosopher Charles Sanders Peirce's thought is difficult. His reflections on God are fragmentary, but the vigor and freshness of his thought is infectious, especially to those who are dipolar panentheists. Although Peirce distrusted theologians and the armchair character of philosophy of the seminary, seeing him not so much as a critic of theology, in general, as a critic of classical theism, is plausible although other interpretations of Peirce's theism are understandable (see Raposa 1989). Or, at the very least, Peirce is one of the chief exponents of the main theoretical supports for dipolar panentheism: He recognized potentiality as a real feature of the universe, he affirmed the primacy of becoming over being, he saw growth as the basic feature of the universe, and he defended a version of panpsychism or panexperientialism (Hartshorne 2000, 258; also see Kasser 2013).

Peirce has a fascinating line of reasoning for the existence of God called the "Neglected Argument" that starts in pure play or musement. Although the details of this argument for the existence of God are not my concern here, it is noteworthy that when the novelty of the argument is in full force, Peirce attributes growth to God as well as to everything else in the universe. It must be admitted, however, that at times Peirce reverts to classical theism. At his best Peirce is clear that if God is personal, and if personality involves being oriented toward a partially open future, then God must face a future that is at least partially open. By contrast, a machine exhibits the carrying out of predetermined purposes. Peirce's philosophy is genuinely evolutionary, from beginning to end and from bottom to top (God). A completely necessitarian concept of God is at odds with the assertions that God is personal and related to the primordial element in the universe: growth (Peirce 1935, vol. VI, para. 157, 457–459, 465–466).

Peirce points us toward the view that the concept of God should exemplify the categories of an evolutionary system. While he was convinced regarding God's existence in the neglected argument, his concept of God wavers between classical theistic omnipotence (problematically) and neoclassical or process theistic change in God. That is, he had a difficult time in recognizing in Whiteheadian or Hartshornian fashion that permanence and change could be reconciled if they referred to different aspects or levels of the divine nature. Or again, Peirce wavers between classical theistic and neoclassical or process theistic versions of omniscience. In his defense it should be emphasized that when he is original he leans in the neoclassical or process direction; he is quite wooden in his reiteration of classical theistic themes. To be clear, I realize that one can show originality in the defense of tradition, but Peirce does not do this. In different terms, he borrows from the very seminary philosophers that he despises when he speaks the language of classical theism; he saves his best prose for his neoclassical or process theistic insights, as in his stress on becoming rather than being and on the indeterministic and random feature ("tychism") of the universe. He realizes that the details of the divine purpose cannot, given the asymmetricality of time, be antecedently explicit; these details must develop over time (Hartshorne 2000, 268–269).

God, for Peirce, is *Ens necessarium*, a necessary being. But as a pragmatist Peirce must remain attentive to anything that might be said about God that would contradict what we must believe in practice, such as in the claim that there is real freedom in the world. This is one of the facts about the world of practice that always stares us in the face. Another one of these facts of practice is that at each moment the indeterminate future becomes the irrevocable past. Even Platonic forms or abstract concepts have a narrative and should not be seen as completely outside of evolutionary history (Peirce 1935, vol. VI, para. 162, 190–194, 484, 488–490, 492, 502–503, 508–509).

Although Armstrong and Capetz do not discuss Peirce, Bowker notes the important role Peirce plays in the analysis of religious signs, which are of three sorts. (1) An *icon* is a sign that contains some of the qualities associated with the thing signified, such as in maps or diagrams.

An example of a religious icon is a statue of a saint or a crucifix. (2) An *index* is a sign that is in a dynamic relationship with the thing signified, such as when a column of mercury indicates the temperature outside or when it indicates health or sickness in a human patient. An example of a religious index is a relic of a saint or a piece of wood from the "true cross." (3) And a *symbol* is a conventional sign with a commonly agreed meaning, such as when the color red symbolizes danger. An example of a religious symbol is a halo symbolizing holiness. These distinctions among signs are helpful not only in responding in a nuanced way to overly aggressive apophaticism, but also in overcoming the monopolarity of classical theism. We need symbols not only for divine permanence (a mighty fortress, an immovable rock, and so on), but also for divine responsive change (the flow of water, a mother's tender care, a living body, and so on). The dynamism characteristic of religious indices makes them especially helpful to neoclassical or process theists in the effort to understand the way in which current religious believers can prehend or grasp what has gone on before to keep alive what might otherwise be the antiquarian content of religious belief. Indices involve mutual dependency, and hence imagining how there could be religious indices on a classical theistic basis is difficult. And icons should be as much or more concerned with expressions of divine omnibenevolence as with divine power, especially if the latter is identified with coercive, perhaps even omnipotent, power. The important thing is to work against the assumption that religious signs are already established and reified, an assumption that may very well stack the deck in classical theism's favor. Realizing that knowledge of God has an indexical character on the neoclassical or process view that is reinforced by the history of mysticism or religious experience is also important (Bowker 2002, 39; also Hartshorne 1941, 296, 299; 1984a, 87).

The crucial thing from a Peircian point of view is not to block the path of inquiry and understanding in the hope that conceptual tensions and quandaries will eventually make sense. Granted, Peirce thought that in order to define our ideas we have to consider how they affect action, but this does not mean that the whole purpose of ideas is to affect action. There is still on Peirce's pragmatic account an important place for knowledge for its own sake; in fact, the love of nature is itself religious and an incitement to meditation and provides an occasion for an examination of religious feeling (Hartshorne 1934, 9; 1937, 79, 293).

The word Peirce uses to describe the inherently social character of the real is "agapism," such that each individual is not so much an absolute one as a Platonic one-in-relation with others. How odd on this basis to view God in classical theistic fashion as an absolute one who is immune to influence by others, which, in effect, turns God into the antiagapist. The sort of responsive love Peirce has in mind presupposes a partially open future characterized by objective indefiniteness and "real vagues." Of course the future will be detailed, but that does not mean that it is already full of detail in the divine mind. The contrast between past and future is that between actual and potential individualities; and being refers to the abstract, fixed aspect in becoming, to the identical element in all temporal diversity (Hartshorne 1948, 29, 107; 1941, 14; 1962, 248).

An important part of Peirce's philosophical project is the effort to avoid playing confidence games with ourselves whereby obvious flaws in widely held views are ignored. One such flaw is the view that there are such things as future individuals, rather than the more defensible view that there are future possibilities awaiting further individuation, as Peirce realized. Causality in general involves what he thought was a type of transcendence of mechanical order and predictability. That is, prediction of the future is limited not merely by our ignorance, but also by the meaning of the future as a region of yet-to-be-made decisions. Reality is predictable to the extent that it is not creative, rather mechanical, automatic, or habitual, but only to this extent. Determinism is precisely the view that abstracts away completely from the creative and partially free aspect of experience itself. The statistical nature of scientific laws, which Peirce defends, becomes problematic only when such laws are absolutized so as to haunt reality from all eternity, as encouraged by classical theistic omniscience. On the process view Peirce endorses, time, even everlasting time, is a positive idea that is negated by eternity and not the other way around (Hartshorne 1965, 18; 1967, 73, 115; 1970, 3–4, 29, 51, 59, 62).

The present, even the divine present, is nascent in the sense that it is a coming into being, rather than already in being. And the present, even the divine present, is intrinsically related to past experiences via memory. In fact, memory can be seen as the paradigm of experiencing in that even "present" perception involves a temporal lag, given the speed of light, that makes perception more like memory than memory is like perception. Only the most abstract features of the divine life can be seen to have a certain sort of independence of the concrete details of temporal existence, such as in the claim that God always exists. Life concretely lived, even a divine life, involves experience. Indeed, as Hartshorne puts the panpsychist or panexperientialist point that would have been acceptable to Peirce, "experience is not merely a bridge we may cross to reach reality; it is a paradigm case of reality" (Hartshorne 1972, 173; 1970, 109, 115, 120, 218).

Some thinkers are skittish about the possibility that philosophical theism would foster a closed totality, but on a Peircian basis there is no final sum of facts, things, or events, in that with each new moment a new "total" reality comes into existence that is constantly transcended. Peirce had a great deal of admiration for medieval thought in general (see Boler 1963) and for philosophical theism in particular, but he did not equate these with a finalized totality. Experience itself is in principle creative and partially transcendent of causal necessity in that out of a plurality of previous experiences a new unitary experience comes into existence at every moment. In different terms, the full description of any situation, including the divine situation, must be richer than a description of any of its predecessors (Hartshorne 1983, 46, 82, 90, 153).

God's persuasive power makes God into something like the poet of the world, on a Peircian basis (Hartshorne 1984c, 10). Peirce's theory of three categories is related to his concept of God as the poet of the world. Very briefly, "firstness" refers to the characteristic of independence, "secondness" refers to dependence, and "thirdness" (on Hartshorne's interpretation of Peirce's three categories) refers to futurity and to the temporal structure of all three categories in general. No reality, not even a divine one, depends on nothing else, hence classical theism is problematic because it denies altogether secondness to God. But this does not mean that neoclassical or process theism is deficient with respect to divine firstness in that God's abstract essence or necessary existence is independent of any particular creatures, although it is dependent on some creatures or other. Firstness refers to independence of future details: "Although there are no particular successors that an event must have, it does have to have successors, and some *general* features of these are settled in advance." God is like a poet in the ability to lure the world toward some sort of creative and harmonious configuration of such successors. Or better, given the autonomy and power of creatures, God is more like a playwright who brings about a performance where the various creatures can play their parts well or ill, on Hartshorne's interpretation of Peirce, much like a theater exercise where the actors do not merely mouth the lines they are given, but actually take responsibility for their own words and actions (Hartshorne 1984a, 81, also 78, 80, 89).

These considerations regarding the three categories led Peirce to see difficulties with the concept of God as completely immutable and immune to any sort of dependence, although his admiration for medieval philosophy is also a noticeable feature of his view. His status as a dipolar theist is made more secure when he speaks of secondness and thirdness in regard to God and when he cringes at the thought of a divine tyrant running the universe in a way that is impervious to evolutionary history. He is opposed to one-sided worship of independence, eternality, and causality without reference to divine dependence, temporality, and receptivity (Hartshorne 1984a, 89).

Futurity, including divine futurity, is the same mode of reality as generality; particularization occurs as determinables become determinate in each present. This is another way of saying that Peircian firstness, secondness, and thirdness are characteristics of any conceivable experience, including any divine experience. To prohibit secondness to God, as in classical theism, is to presuppose that there really are no determinables in that everything is already determined from all eternity. Or again, the creative dimension of psyche (including divine psyche, that is, the World Soul) is not so much an addition to mere matter as it is integrally connected to what matter is. As Peirce puts the point, there is something zoomorphic or animal-like throughout nature, including its religious aspect. The Peircian view "is that every singular active agent (there are no singular inactive ones, the seemingly inactive being composites whose constituents are active) resembles an animal in having some initiative or freedom in its activity" (Hartshorne 1987, 122, also 7, 16–17, 21, 120).

Divine contingency does not have to be a problem if it refers to something other than God's existence. Perhaps Peirce's biggest contribution to theism could be his emphasis on the facts of contingency and freedom, and hence risk, in the nature of things. A related contribution could be the realization that because freedom entails risk, any defensible theodicy must include some account of contingency, including divine contingency, along with pervasive human and subhuman contingency (Hartshorne 2001, 87; 1990, 140, 236, 329).

Peirce is wise to discuss order and chaos together, such as in the biblical account of creation in Genesis, wherein the earth was without form while divine agency hovered above the face of the deep. The togetherness of order and chaos in Peirce's thought is not unrelated to the fact that, as a dipolar theist, Peirce would have thought that God is both necessary and contingent in different aspects of the divine nature, as well as independent and dependent. On this view, actuality is not reducible to a set of repeatable predicates that are eternally envisaged by deity. This would make God into another being among beings, the worship of which would involve an idolatrous fetish for permanence. The Peircian view is not merely that the future is open for God because human beings are free. Rather, it is that all actors in reality, including the divine one, are dynamic centers of power in Platonic fashion, specifically the power to give as well as the power to receive. This dynamism involves the evolution of definite qualities out of a primordial continuum of possibilities, but at every stage of this evolutionary process there is both order and chaos. This evolutionary process is such that in our imperfect prehensions of the past there is inevitably loss, but not for God's uniquely adequate preservation of the past. The data of God's life are everlastingly preserved (Hartshorne 1991, 417, 593–594, 634, 662–666, 672, 681; 2011, 116).

18

Otto Pfleiderer

(1839–1908)

Although Pfleiderer's views are close to those of Schelling and Fechner, and although Hegel heavily influenced all three thinkers, there is something distinctive about this German thinker's criticisms of the classical theistic concept of God, criticisms that are as much religious as they are philosophical. If God genuinely cares for the world, he thinks, such care is real as the content of divine love and divine consciousness. That is, such care would be internal to divinity, not merely the raw material for relations external to the divine life. Christianity, in particular, he emphasizes, has no essential ties to classical theism in that the latter is an interpretation of the concept of God that is very much at odds with both the best in the biblical tradition and the testimony of the great mystics in Christianity and other religions. Furthermore, there is no necessary antagonism between Christianity (or other major religions) and dipolar panentheism. Pfleiderer uses this conceptual aperture to squeeze through his own version of neoclassical or process theism (Hartshorne 2000, 269–270).

We may legitimately claim that the most basic discovery of neoclassical or process theism is that the absolute (that is, nonrelative) aspect of God is a merely abstract component of the divine life and is not to be identified with God. Pfleiderer is one of the participants in this discovery. The abstract everlastingness of God is presented in scripture not as a Boethian eternity outside of time and history, but as freedom from the limitations of temporality (the beginning of time, the end of time), rather than as freedom from time itself. That is, Pfleiderer's insight here, despite some confusing terminology on his part, is that God is everlastingly temporal rather than eternal in the sense of

escaping time altogether. Furthermore, divine permanence is illuminated by biblical accounts of the dependability of God. To view God's
abstract aspect *as* God is to play into the hands of deism, a view that
separates God from the real world of time and history. Divine immutability of existence (everlastingness) and purpose (dependability) does
not mean that God does not change; indeed, God always changes, in
Pfleiderer's concept of God (Hartshorne 2000, 270).

Pfleiderer's dipolar theism is facilitated by his defense of something like God as the World Soul, a view wherein God's relationship
to the whole physical world is analogous to that of a human mind to
its physical organism. Such a being would have to be passive as well
as active, changing as well as dependable, and so forth. Likewise, the
(everlasting) temporality of Pfleiderer's God requires that the classical
theistic version of divine omniscience be criticized. If God's omniscience is articulated in terms of God eternally knowing everything
that will occur with absolute assurance and in minute detail, then any
analogy with human consciousness and knowing will be destroyed.
Knowledge of necessity involves succession of states of consciousness:
"If the temporal structure of successive development is essential to
the existence of the world, this structure must also be reflected in the
divine consciousness of the world" (Pfleiderer 1888, 71–72; also 69–70,
88).

Granted, knowledge of the past and present (the latter subject to the
realization that what is present epistemically may very well be something that is ontologically past, such as in the finite amount of time it
takes for something that really occurred to reach us, given the speed of
light, sound, and so forth) enables us to anticipate to some degree what
will happen in the future. This anticipation may even in a peculiar way
be termed a sort of foresight. But this is a far cry from classical theistic
omniscience, which, once again, involves absolutely certain knowledge
of what will happen in the future and in minute detail. Divine activity,
indeed any activity, occurs in time, and hence there is something deeply
problematic about the classical theistic version of creation *ex nihilo*.
Temporal activity, in general, is beginningless and endless (Hartshorne
2000, 270–271).

Given Pfleiderer's relative obscurity, Armstrong, Bowker, and Capetz
not surprisingly do not treat his concept of God. But there is a consequence to this neglect in that Armstrong, Bowker, and Capetz tend to

follow the familiar route of moving directly from the classical theistic view, in particular, to critics of theism, in general, such as Karl Marx and Sigmund Freud. But as I see things, this plays into Marx's and Freud's hands: By assuming an inadequate concept of God, showing that religious belief is an opiate of the people or an illusion is much easier.

Clearly, however, the "neo" part of neoclassical theism should not necessarily be interpreted as a rejection altogether of religious tradition. Within the traditions of Abrahamic theism a distinction can be made between religion and theology. The latter has been dominated by classical theism, but if "God" is both a religious term and a theological term, we should be on the alert to see if the theological use of the term is compatible with, or preserves the best in, the religious use of the term. "It is a belief of many today that the 'new' theology is more, not less, religious than the old" (Hartshorne 1941, 3, 52). In this claim Hartshorne has Pfleiderer especially in mind. Or again, Pfleiderer's neoclassical or process theism is quite different from both the old naturalism of the Thomistic natural law type and the old supernaturalism of classical theists and deists alike. The difference between Pfleiderer and classical theists largely concerns the effort to understand the relationship between the supreme religious value of love and the logic of perfection. The classical theistic preference for a motionless God who is purely self-sufficient, indeed who is utterly incapable of receiving influence from human beings, stretches to the breaking point any analogy with love as we know it (Hartshorne 1953, 22–23, 159).

Rapprochement between the supreme religious value of love and the logic of perfection is more closely approximated by thinkers such as Pfleiderer, who see God as both infinite and finite, immovable in existence and eminently changeable in actuality. To put the point more cautiously, if there are problems with neoclassical or process theism, they are quite different from the problems associated with classical theism, and hence religious skeptics do not necessarily discredit theism in general, even if they are successful in pointing out defects in classical theism in particular. In neoclassical or process theism there is no leap from the temporal to the eternal, from interacting individuals to a self-sufficient deity, and so on, and hence agnostics and atheists who have not read the great authors in neoclassical or process theism should not prematurely congratulate themselves on their accomplishments (Hartshorne 1967, 127–128, 135).

Pfleiderer's accomplishments, although not widely known in academic circles, and which rely on the even less-well-known Scottish thinker John Erskine, are nonetheless significant enough to lead Hartshorne to say that Pfleiderer makes it possible for us to see classical theism as a scandalous failure. For example, classical theistic immutable eternity (in contrast to neoclassical or process theistic dynamic everlastingness) is an empty abstraction that makes it impossible to say that God knows the creatures in that the latter are characterized by temporal alterability, as theists as far back as Aristotle realized. A God who exhibits dual transcendence is worthy of worship, not one who exhibits a monopolar transcendence that makes any relations between God and the world unintelligible. By seeing the relationship between God and the world as analogous to the relationship between a human mind and his or her body, Pfleiderer makes God's relationship to the world amenable to rational discourse and at least partial understanding. Likewise, in order to avoid utter unintelligibility, Pfleiderer sees ideal knowledge of the future as referring not to particulars, but rather to the essential features of the universal (Hartshorne 1972, 63; 1983, 251–252; 1984c, 39).

19
Nicholas Berdyaev
(1874–1948)

Eastern Orthodoxy, like Catholicism and Protestantism, has over the centuries been in the grip of classical theism even without a necessary connection between these religions and classical theism. This claim might sound counterintuitive to some scholars for two reasons. First, although the apophatic tradition of negative theology is found throughout the Abrahamic religions, it is especially noteworthy in Eastern Orthodox thought, and hence this reticence to talk about the concept of God might be assumed to inoculate Eastern Orthodox thinkers from being categorized as classical theists. And second, there is much talk about divine energies in Eastern Orthodox thinkers and this discourse regarding dynamism might seem to militate against the static character of God found in classical theism.

However, both of these concerns are misguided in that the major philosophical and theological concept of God that has been operative in Eastern Orthodoxy has been classical theistic in character. Consider several authors anthologized in *The Philokalia*, a highly influential collection of important texts in the Orthodox Christian tradition between the fourth and fifteenth centuries.

The fourteenth-century thinker St. Gregory Palamas is clear both that God's essence is incomprehensible to us and that we can nonetheless comprehend God through the divine energies. That is, through God's creative activity we can learn analogically about divinity through created things. That is, divine energy is revealed to us through that which God creates *ex nihilo* as a result of omnipotent coercive power. God's "energy," as Palamas uses this term, is "completely impassible": God alone acts without being acted upon. For this reason, there can be no accidents in God in that these involve either coming into existence or passing out of existence in a way that affects the subject of the accidents. God is "entirely changeless," such that any relations God has with others may be real to these others, but not to God. God is eternal (in the sense of being outside of time altogether in a "now" that is all at once) and immutable and simple. As is typical of classical theists, there is both a repeated proclamation of ignorance regarding God's nature and a repeated monopolar preference for being over becoming, immutability over mutability, simplicity over complexity, the infinite over the finite, the spiritual over the bodily, and so on, when the topic is the concept of God. Palamas assumes that all of these contrasts are contradictories (see Palmer et al. 1979–1995, IV, 343, 354, 359–360, 380, 384–385, 406–407, 414, 418, 427).

St. Maximos the Confessor in an earlier period (sixth and seventh centuries) likewise saw God as unchanging, infinite, and beyond all potentiality in that God is eminently active but not passive. As the author of time, God is not in the divine nature temporal. In this author it is clear that divine perfection clearly entails omnipotence. God is either being or (apophatically) beyond being, but not becoming. Like classical theists in all of the Abrahamic religions, Maximos thinks that God loves the creatures, but God is "absolutely independent" of them, otherwise dreaded accidents would enter into the divine life. God loves the creatures, but is "altogether . . . free from relationships," whatever this might mean. What is noteworthy is that Maximos, along with other classical theists, seems unaware of the tension between the claim that God is eminently loving and the claim that God is immutably self-sufficient and unrelated to creatures. Maximos defends divine impassibility even while admitting that the biblical God is passible; here the monopolar influence of Aristotle is most apparent. But Maximos is un-Greek in thinking that an omnipotent God creates the world (see Palmer et al. 1979–1995, II, 70, 87, 100–101, 114–115, 124, 132, 137–138, 165, 277, 280–281, 295–296).

The classical theism of Palamas and Maximos is found in several other major figures in the history of Eastern Orthodoxy, such as in St. Peter of Damaskos's twelfth-century observation that those who praise God gain more from the praise than God does in that God has nothing to gain; St. Thalassios the Libyan's affirmation that divine eternity means existing outside of time rather than through all of it (Thalassios was a contemporary of Maximos); and St. Antony the Great's alleged claim from the third and fourth centuries that God creates mutability and hence is not subject to it, which involves a sort of dispassionate nature that really is at odds with personal terms like "rejoicing" or "anger." The pattern is familiar: Claim ignorance regarding God and then claim that God simply does not, simply cannot, change, as in the eleventh-century thought of Nikitas Stithatos (see Palmer et al. 1979–1995, I, 243, 252; II, 332; III, 148,187; IV, 139–147).

The Russian Berdyaev both assimilated and criticized this Eastern Orthodox tradition. His theism is both "classical" and "neo." One difference between Berdyaev's relationship with the Eastern Orthodox tradition and the relationship between other neoclassical or process theists and their respective traditions is that the doctrine of world inclusiveness has often received a friendly hearing in Eastern Orthodoxy, even if this doctrine is frequently connected to the perhaps contradictory doctrines of divine omnipotence and creation *ex nihilo*. The tension between divine world inclusiveness and creation *ex nihilo* (the latter seems to presuppose omnipotence, the former seems to work against it) tends to be glossed over due to the fact that world inclusiveness is more of a component in mystical theology in Eastern Orthodoxy than in a philosophical discourse wherein logical precision is highly prized (Hartshorne 2000, 285).

That Berdyaev was heavily influenced by both the mystic Jacob Boehme and the dipolar theist Schelling is noteworthy. Berdyaev is quite frank about the fact that there is a divine history, a divine becoming, and most importantly a divine suffering. We obviously suffer and experience tragedy in our lives. This is a given. Do these sufferings and tragedies in some fashion accrue to God or not? Berdyaev's view is that only if they do accrue to God can we find some reticulative meaning in them. Only if God shares our pain can something other than suffering and tragedy have the last word, but not because God omnipotently, miraculously, and incredibly negates the fact that suffering and tragedy occur. Rather, although the suffering and tragedy are preserved in memory, the fact that they are taken up as parts of the divine life is what is noteworthy. Hartshorne puts the point regarding Berdyaev's view as follows: "This theodicy is scarcely like any that went before it. Here is something on a more sublime level than the usual cold-blooded justifications of evil. Evil springs from the indeterminacy which providence itself cannot banish. . . . This (our enthusiasm may perhaps be pardoned) is really a metaphysics of love" (Hartshorne 2000, 286)!

In Berdyaev's *The Meaning of History* he speaks histrionically about how each moment of time "murders" the previous one in the absence of divine memory. Although this seems to trivialize human powers of memory, such powers at times admittedly fail us. The key points here are that: (1) the perfection of divine memory means that our actions and tragedies take on an everlasting significance not found otherwise, no matter how successful or unsuccessful our human memories are; and (2) anticipation of the future is not an equal counterpart to memory of the past in that the open and indeterminate character of the future means that even an ideal knower would not be able to know it in advance in a closed and determinate fashion. The indeterminate is that which is yet to be determined. In fact, the idea that God knows everything in advance filled Berdyaev with nothing less than horror (Hartshorne 2000, 286).

Whereas the metaphysical ultimate for Whitehead is creativity, as we will see, for Berdyaev it is the related notion of freedom or spontaneous activity born out of the coming into being at each moment of a partially new reality. And like Whitehead, Berdyaev thinks that the origin of tragedy lies not in the conflict of good with evil, but rather with contested goods in the flux of events. Various things that are good are posed to us at each moment for our consideration and evaluation. Some must be accepted and some rejected; this need for selectivity applies to God as well, he thinks. When the conflicts within ourselves and with others result in suffering, some small solace is received in knowing that God shares our tragic joys. Indeed, Hartshorne thinks that Berdyaev offers an overall view of God similar to Whitehead's, but it is expressed with a more intense religious fervor (Hartshorne 2000, 286–287).

It is one thing to say that the meaning to human life is to contribute new realities to God's actuality that are virtuous and aesthetically valuable, but it is quite another to develop a concept of God wherein the divine life is amenable to such contributions. Berdyaev is instructive on both counts, whereas classical theists do not do much to help us understand the latter effort. The process of divine actualization is both beginningless and endless on Berdyaev's account (Hartshorne 2000, 287).

Although this book is not focused on the existence of God, it is appropriate at this point to note that for Berdyaev the rise of modern atheism and agnosticism is due to the faulty concept of God found in classical theism: "Atheism may spring from good motives and not solely from evil ones. The wicked hate God because [God] prevents them from doing evil, and the good are ready to hate [God] for not preventing the wicked from doing evil. . . . It is precisely the traditional theology that leads good [people] . . . to atheism (Berdyaev 1937, 31–32).

In a related vein, on the classical theistic view God foresaw from all eternity the fatal consequences of human actions, but did nothing to prevent these consequences: "This is the profound moral source of atheism" (Berdyaev 1937, 32). Furthermore, Berdyaev notes the intellectual dishonesty involved in responding to the disaster that is classical theistic theodicy by the sleights of hand involved in an overly aggressive apophaticism or in an appeal to mystery that is actually a ruse for unintelligibility.

As before, Berdyaev finds predeterminism terrifying because it makes a mockery of our sense that we are at least somewhat free and responsible for our actions and it fills life with an ominous sense that we are doomed, or at least that we are locked into a future that we cannot really alter, no matter how hard we try. He is instructive in the way he urges that it is classical theistic omniscience itself that leads one to this sense of doom. Furthermore, classical theistic omniscience leads philosophers and theologians to an exaggerated apophaticism. Once one realizes that, on a classical theistic basis, God already knows with absolute assurance and in minute detail everything that will happen to one in "the future," one has a very difficult, if not impossible, time reconciling this version of omniscience with human freedom. At this point negative theology comes on the scene to help the classical theist "to breathe more freely as though coming out of a prison house" (Berdyaev 1937, 33).

In a processual worldview one of the things that God does not create is freedom in that there has always been some sort of spontaneous activity in response to previous instances of spontaneous response. Although at times Berdyaev confuses things a bit when he falls back into classical theistic language regarding omnipotence and creation *ex nihilo*, a charitable interpretation of his thought would suggest that God's power consists in the ability to persuade the recalcitrant material that is always there and that has a limited degree of power of its own. That is, when Berdyaev sometimes speaks of creation *ex nihilo*, he does not have in mind creation out of absolutely nothing (*ouk on*), but creation out of relative nonbeing (*me on*) or the creation of something different from what was there before (see Berdyaev 1953). In different terms that take us to the heart of Berdyaev's greatest contribution to neoclassical or process theism, God is manifest not so much in terms of (coercive) power as in sacrifice, a sacrifice that itself has a certain degree of (persuasive) power. Berdyaev urges us to abandon the concept of God as monarchical or as a glorification of Caesar. Historically certain aspects of both Greek philosophy and the Bible have fueled this monarchical conception, but we have seen that both of these at their best can suggest something better than divine monarchy (Berdyaev 1937, 289).

Berdyaev notes that the concept of God as a static, pure actuality with no potentiality whatsoever is an Aristotelian view rather than a biblical one because the God of the Bible clearly has affective states as well as dramatic developments in the divine life. Berdyaev finds it odd that classical theists have been reticent to ascribe to God inner conflict and tragedy, but they have been willing to accept biblical accounts of God as angry, jealous, and vengeful. The overall task is to think through as carefully as possible the logic of perfection by trying to come to terms with the best in ancient Greek thought, biblical mythopoetic accounts of God, and philosophical and theological accounts of that than which no greater can be conceived. Or again, it is odd that some classical theists balk at dipolar theism while they accept as divine certain personality traits that are downright sinful when exhibited by human beings, such as in the aforementioned vengefulness. Of course some thinkers are reticent to ascribe movement to God because they think that movement implies a lack in something. It should now be clear, however, that this stance rests on a sort of monopolarity that can be called into question. Motion as well as rest admits of certain admirable traits (Berdyaev 1937, 37–40).

Tragic conflict in the life of God, far from being a sign of insufficiency, indicates perfection if it resides in divine actuality rather than in the very existence of God. Christians, in particular, should be especially amenable to persuasion on this point, given the prominence of the cross and of sacrificial love in that tradition. To deny tragedy in the divine life is to deny the importance of the crucifixion of Jesus.

Berdyaev, echoing Boehme, speaks of the theogonic process of living through tragedy, specifically through the conflicts among various creaturely freedoms. Deeper than the distinction between good and evil is the conflict between creaturely freedoms that pit some good versus some other good (Berdyaev 1937, 37–42).

If a commitment to human freedom is a nonnegotiable item in one's philosophy, as it is in Berdyaev, then both pantheism (as in the Stoics, Spinoza, and so on) and classical theism are problematic. The latter is especially problematic because of the contradiction between human freedom and the classical theistic version of omniscience. From Berdyaev's point of view, carving out a conceptual space for human creativity, which is a continuation of divine creativity and a vicarious participation in the life of God, is crucial. But we are not free to escape suffering, and hence religions that try to escape it (Buddhism and Stoicism on Berdyaev's account) are inferior to those that embrace it and try to find a place for it in the divine life (such as in Christianity at its best on his view). Although I have no desire to either refute or endorse Berdyaev's view regarding the superiority of one religion over another, the following quotation importantly helps clarify his concept of God: "Buddhism recognizes compassion but denies love, for compassion may be a way of escaping from the pain of existence while love affirms existence and, consequently, the pain of it. Love increases sorrow and suffering. . . . Buddhism renounces existence and seeks refuge in nonbeing. Buddhism does not know how life can be endurable if suffering is accepted; it does not know the mystery of the Cross" (Berdyaev 1937, 151). Once again, without entering into Berdyaev's preference for Christianity over Buddhism, the crucial point to acknowledge is his notable contribution to the logic of perfection: The greatest conceivable being would not only suffer, but such a being would also suffer preeminently and on a cosmic scale in contrast to our minimally decent suffering and on an attenuated scale.

The problem with classical theism, according to Berdyaev, is not that it views God in personal terms, but that it cannot consistently view God in personal terms, and hence it is not personal enough. And the highest quality of persons is love, that vital energy capable of converting evil passions into creative forces. Philosophy itself, as it was once conceived, is a love of wisdom that marks such a lover in the image and likeness of God (Berdyaev 1937, 178).

Although with less than optimal clarity, Berdyaev helps to make the case not only that monopolar terms such as "necessity" and "absolute" are not sufficient when explicating the concept of God, they are not even the most profitable starting points. For example, if we start by assuming possibility, then in a derivative way necessity can be understood as the abstract identity common to all possibilities. Once again, the two poles in dipolar theism are correlative and mutually reinforcing. Ultimately neither pole can be understood without the other (Hartshorne 2000, 293).

Berdyaev is also helpful in pointing out some of the negative practical consequences of the problematic theoretical features of classical theism. For example, although a system of divine rewards and punishments in the afterlife is not a necessary feature of classical theism, many classical theists outside of Judaism undeniably have defended a doctrine of eternal punishment for sinners, which Berdyaev sees as a type of sadism. In fact, he sees this doctrine as the most disgusting morality. This sadism is not unconnected to a concept of God who moves others, but who is unmoved by them; who is eternally active, but who does not respond to others and who is not influenced by them (Hartshorne 1937, 77; 1991, 653).

Service of God, on Berdyaev's view, consists not so much in conformity to rules regarding correct behavior as in the bringing into existence of creative new values, along with respect for old ones, that most closely approximate divine perfection. And immobility in the face of suffering is an imperfection indicative of the poverty of life, not its fullness. At the very least God suffers because we suffer; God is tragic because we are tragic and God loves us preeminently, but still on the analogy of a human love that we can understand. The contrasting classical theistic view provides very little stimulus to admiration, as countless atheists have rightly argued. Because God is immune to human influence in classical theism, many classical theists tend to assume that the whole point to human life is to maximize one's own interests in terms of an eternal reward in heaven, a transcendentalizing of self-interest that Berdyaev considered nothing less than odious and at odds with an ethics based on love (Hartshorne 1941, 229–230, 294; 1948, 43, 132; 1953, 105).

Once one confuses the absolute aspect of God (the idea that God's very existence is nonrelative in the sense that God does not require any particular others in order to continue to be) with God, as classical theists do, one will be faced with various contradictions. Classical theists are too willing to accept these contradictions without trying to escape from them by thinking through more carefully the logic of perfection. Absolutistic attenuation of sympathy, however, should not be pushed to the limit and then declared a divine attribute (Hartshorne 1953, 23, 189).

Not uncommonly philosophically inclined children ask the question, "but who made God?" The question is prescient in that it admits of no easy answer. In one sense, if God is everlasting then no one made God; in another sense, if God is capable of free choices then God is self-made; and in a still different sense, if God's actuality is enriched by the creatures then we help to make God. If creativity is in some way ultimate, then neither God's nor our own decisions are minor additions to forms of definiteness that exist eternally; rather, free beings, whether divine or creaturely, add something genuinely new to the universe. There is genuine creativity, he thinks, and not merely the actualizing of preexistent Platonic forms. The model for creativity here is dialogue, where one influences another, responds in a novel way to such influence, thereby providing an opportunity for one's dialogical partner to initiate new responses to such influence, and so on. All of this takes time. In the divine case one might even refer to super-time, given divine everlastingness, but this is a far cry from the classical theistic claim that God is outside of time altogether (Hartshorne 1967, 113, 123; 1970, 1, 65, 277, 291; 1991, 646).

We have seen that Berdyaev, like Whitehead and Hartshorne, is willing to use terms that are quite harsh in his assessment of classical theism. The view of unrelenting punishment in hell is sadistic, Berdyaev thinks, and the classical theistic God is something of a tyrant or a despot; furthermore, the last book of the Christian scriptures exhibits a barbarism that counteracts the agapic best in Christianity. The concept of God that we entertain has the potential to make us either better or worse, depending on the concept. But religion does not have to be a repository for hatred. If some of this language seems too harsh, it should be considered that one way to define a despot is in terms of someone who influences, but who seeks to avoid being influenced; who wants to be a cause, but not an effect; who seeks above all else to be independent. One is obviously reminded here of the divine attributes the great classical theists articulated. On the contrasting neoclassical or process view, the evils in the world are not the result of omnipotent divine fiat or divine neglect, the principal alternatives in classical theism to account for evil once divine omnipotence is emphasized. In neoclassical or process theism the evils of the world are due to either misused freedom or to conflict among multiple freedoms. But even if there is no misuse of freedom, good uses of freedom can conflict in a condition of pervasive pluralism of interests and multiple centers of power (Hartshorne 1972, 183–185).

Given the fact of multiple centers of power, there can be no complete coordination of the acts of various individuals, although universal divine inspiration and influence is nonetheless possible and, given the general harmony of natural laws and the flourishing of sentient processes, likely. The absence of pure chaos speaks in favor of the claim that there is divine inspiration and influence. Admittedly, however, because chance is real, so is suffering. In fact, if the Platonic claim that being *is* power makes sense, then the complete elimination of suffering and tragedy are metaphysically impossible. That is, the issue is not merely practical or logistical. Unfortunately, at times Berdyaev thinks that the concept of God that he affirms is defensible in spite of reason, but this language on his part has less to do with the rational inadequacy of the concept and more to do with the historical hegemony of classical theism regarding the concept of God. We simply do not have to accept as authoritative etiolatry (worship of Cause), ontolatry (worship of Being), or monolatry (worship of Unity), although causality, being, and unity are indeed defensible abstract aspects of the divine nature (Hartshorne 1972, 186–188).

Hartshorne says the following about the worldview he detects in Berdyaev: "The final words are process, relativity, or freedom just because these can (indeed, logically must) contain in themselves aspects of permanence, absoluteness, or necessity, whereas within the merely permanent nothing can change" (Hartshorne 1972, 189). This is another way of saying that the final concrete realities are experient occasions, not enduring individuals or substances.

Especially by loving others can we enrich the divine life; hence not all that God "suffers" is tragic. Thus the suffering God Berdyaev discusses does not lead to Patripassionism, the supposed heresy that suggests that the father (that is, God the Father) suffers, for two reasons. First,

God's existence does not suffer and is not in any way threatened by us or by anything else. And second, although God's actuality is affected by creaturely life, only some creaturely activities lead to divine suffering; some other creaturely activities (especially the loving ones) actually lead to divine enrichment, on Berdyaev's view. Because of such enrichment, something really significant is missing in classical theistic enslavement to being and in the resulting divine immunity to influence from others. Admittedly, however, the price to be paid for such enrichment is the possibility of tragedy in that love itself is a risky thing as the lover's actuality is affected by what happens to the beloved (Hartshorne 1983, 88, 191, 218, 231).

Berdyaev's version of the categorical imperative (as stated in chapters 3 and 4 of his *The Destiny of Man*) is to "Be creative and foster creativity in others." This imperative is a response to the question: What is the ethical ideal that fits best the self-creative and other-creative nature of human beings? Such creativity, assuming that it is loving, contributes something memorable to the divine life. Not only artists, but also politicians, teachers, and husbands and wives are involved in creating experiences in themselves and in helping others to do the same. Everyone is involved in the creation of new definiteness. In effect, Berdyaev's "creativity" is like a medieval transcendental in that it applies to God and the creatures alike as each personal line of inheritance is at each moment thrust into a future that requires decisions whereby some determinables are cut off such that some others are made determinate as they are chosen. Creativity, even divine creativity, requires a future yet to be determined (Hartshorne 1984a, 99, 248, 268, 279; 1991, 585, 680; 2011, 130, 153).

Either all that exists does so necessarily (as in the Stoics or Spinoza) or there is contingency. If there is contingency, then the transition from what could be to what is is either the result of creativity (related terms include freedom, spontaneity, self-motion, decision) or chance. But if the contingent is the result of pure chance, then no positive light is shed on such contingency: It just is. Perhaps the safest course is to say that the contingency that exists is a result of both creativity and chance and the interplay between the two. It can even be said that creativity and chance are ubiquitous. This course encourages a view of God not so much as an omnipotent tyrant but as a caring mother who has to both choose wisely for her child as well as deal with the surd elements that can affect her child due to forces outside of human control. The quintessential example of human love given by a mother's love for her child strongly encourages us to take Berdyaev's point seriously: If God is omnibenevolent love, then God not only suffers, God suffers preeminently. Once again, the cross is Christianity's sublime symbol for this insight (Hartshorne 1984c, 23, 58, 120–121; 1991, 38).

One of the most important differences between Berdyaev's neoclassical or process theism and classical theism concerns whether truths about specific historical events are timeless or temporal. By adopting the latter view he also adopts the stance that God, too, is changing and endlessly acquires new truths and values from the world. Our decisions in a way decide something for God as well in that we contribute to God actualities that were previously unactual. This is what it means to say that there is a divine time or a divine history. To know particular events in time is, in an honorific sense, to be finite and definite as opposed to being, in a less than honorific sense, infinite and indeterminate (Hartshorne 1984b, 67, 75, 100; 2011, 95, 117).

20
Mohammed Iqbal
(1877–1938)

This Muslim thinker from what is now Pakistan was heavily influenced by Whitehead's and especially by Bergson's thought, an influence that led him to a version of neoclassical or process theism. But his numerous and eloquent references to Muslim sources are also noteworthy. As before, despite what classical theists might think, classical theism has no proprietary lock on any of the major world religions. In fact, it is amazing just how influential classical theism has been in the Abrahamic religions considering it is most weak regarding the relationship between the concept of God and religious experience. That is, it is not paradoxical that there be a neoclassical or process Muslim; what is paradoxical are classical theistic versions of Islam (Hartshorne 2000, 294).

As Iqbal sees things, there is a multiplicity of "instants" in the divine life; indeed these instants are infinite in number. When these instants are seen as a whole or as a synthesis, we can then refer to God's life as an ultimate reality or as a duration. Furthermore, whereas human lives must distinguish between the self and the not-self, the divine life (as a result of properly understood omnibenevolence and omniscience) includes all. Iqbal alludes to the Koran in this regard in terms of Allah's ability to include everything in the divine: "What we call Nature or the not-self is only a fleeting moment in the life of God. [God's] 'I-amness' is independent, elemental, absolute." Here Iqbal is talking about God's very existence, but this divine existence must also have a character, a structure of events in the actual divine life. This structure is revealed to human beings in terms of Nature, which is a living, ever-growing organism. In a way, knowledge of Nature is knowledge of God (Iqbal 1934, 53–54).

Iqbal is like Bergson in seeing each moment in a temporal series as similar to a series of photos that when flipped quickly gives one a sense of motion; they no longer appear as photos but as a motion picture. However, none of the photos in this series symbolize future events because, due to the asymmetricality of time Iqbal affirms, there really are no future events, only the possibility or probability of such. Of course we can assume that there will be future events of some sort, but exactly which ones we cannot know in any great detail or with any great degree of assurance. These considerations have obvious implications for the concept of God and especially for divine omniscience. If one assumes that change is an imperfection, then classical theism follows quite easily. But Iqbal questions whether we need to make this assumption. Granted, beneath the surface of serial events in the divine life there is duration, where, in a certain sense, change does not occur. This changeless abstract aspect of deity is compatible with the idea that there is ceaseless creation in the divine life as actual (Iqbal 1934, 54–61).

Divine knowledge is always temporal in Iqbal's concept of God. That is, he criticizes the concept of God that involves a completely atemporal divine knowledge that captures in one glance the entire sweep of history: past, present, and future. He attributes this (Boethius-like) view to a Muslim classical theist named Jalaluddin Dawani. There is something psychologically appealing in this view in that it can give one who is skittish about the future the solace that comes from the realization that someone is overseeing the process of history and the course of one's life. Unfortunately, this eternal now version of divine omniscience presupposes what Iqbal calls "a closed universe, a fixed futurity, a predetermined unalterable order of specific events" (Iqbal 1934, 74, also 68–76). This prospect is truly frightening and outweighs any solace that might come from classical theistic omniscience. Certainly the future exists in some sense, but it exists as a set of possibilities, not as a fixed order of events with determinate outcomes. The classical theistic doctrine of predestination, especially prominent in Muslim fatalism, deliberately turns a blind eye to the obvious spontaneity of life, which is a pervasive fact of human experience.

Iqbal is especially insightful regarding the neoclassical or process critique of omnipotence (despite his flirtation with creation *ex nihilo*; see Ruzgar 2008), which is fortunate because, in my experience, this critique is most distressing to classical theists, who have a hard time conceiving of God without omnipotence. Iqbal is quite clear that "the word 'limitation' need not frighten us" (Iqbal 1934, 75–76). In fact, he thinks, the Koran (and, I might add, the Jewish and Christian scriptures) tends not to deal in abstract universals. Rather, it describes the concrete activities of God and all activity is a sort of limitation: God does this rather than that at such and such a time rather than earlier or later.

Although classifying Iqbal as a panpsychist or a panexperientialist would be inaccurate, we can legitimately say that he gestured in the direction of this position. Both "the body" and "the soul" (or "the mind") are systems of events and the common event character of these two features of human nature brings them together. Although the soul and mind characteristically exhibit spontaneity, and although the acts of bodies characteristically repeat themselves, this distinction is not rigid in that soul (or mind) has habits and bodies sometimes exhibit surprisingly abrupt changes. This leads Iqbal to speculate that matter itself may very well be composed of tiny centers of self-motion or units of becoming that are slightly spontaneous (Iqbal 1934, 100).

Iqbal does not, like Berdyaev, treat the idea that God suffers because God is omnibenevolent and is aware of all of the suffering of creatures. In this regard Hartshorne notes: "But scarcely any non-Christians and only a few Christians (among philosophers) seem to have dared to view the matter in this light. If there is any unique value in Christianity, this is surely close to the heart of it" (Hartshorne 2000, 297). Nor does Iqbal emphasize the idea that human beings contribute to the divine life, although this view seems to be close to the surface of his concept of God. However, he is clearly a dipolar theist, leading Hartshorne to say that: "The long reign of monopolarity and being-worship or etiolatry need not last forever" (Hartshorne 2000, 297; also 1984b, 67, 111). As a result of Iqbal's work Muslim thinkers have a model of a concept of God that will enable them to finally understand the opening lines of the Koran, which attest to the idea of God (Allah) as merciful and compassionate.

21

Martin Buber

(1878–1965)

We should note at the outset that Buber was not a metaphysician, but a phenomenologist of the religious life, and on this basis he can be seen as a neoclassical or process theist. That is, his contributions to neoclassical or process theism are especially welcome because they were unintended. Those who live a religious life have as an unmistakable datum of their experience the sense of relation. Indeed, the primary reality is that of relation. He views the world as existing in God, who is thus related to all things. Buber, as an Austrian-born Jew, would have been very familiar with classical theism, but his own version of theism can be seen as panentheistic, which once again refers to the belief that all is in God, say through divine knowledge and care. Furthermore, in that God derives value from the creatures who are known and loved, there is real becoming in God. This dynamic perfection is thus not at all eccentric, but is a modern or postmodern concept that brings out the best in the ancient wisdom found in Abrahamic religion (Hartshorne 2000, 302).

Those who take the concept of God seriously should never feel isolated, on the Buberian view. When we encounter God we also encounter the world as contributory to God. Or again, one does not find God by leaving the world, but by adopting a certain attitude toward it as holy, as a "Thou" to whom the "I" is related, or at least as contributory to the divine "Thou." Buber criticizes the view that it is only we who are dependent in the religious relation in part because it rests on the assumption that all sensitivity is a weakness and that all coercive power exerted from the superior to the inferior is good. This latter belief is at odds, however, with all that we hold dear in liberal democracies, where the ruled are permitted to influence the ruler. The point to this analogy is not to say that the ruler (God) is fallible and lacks all the answers. Rather, the point is to say that no one "has all the answers" in advance if the question is: What will self-determining beings do with their lives? The self-determining beings themselves provide their separate responses to this question. On this analogy the most powerful being is also the most sensitive being who awaits with preeminent attention and care the outcome to creaturely sufferings and volitions. This is in partial contrast to human rulers, who not only wield coercive power inadequately, but they also have very limited and biased powers of sensitivity (Hartshorne 2000, 302).

On Buber's view, because of the human power of self-determination we are able to not only participate along with God in the process of creation, but we are also able to contribute something to the divine life itself (in Hartshornian terms, to God's actuality). If God's appreciation of things is the measure of reality itself, then to decide anything is to register something in God's awareness. If we write anything at all in the book of life we write something in the divine life itself. And if we do not write anything at all we are not as much humble as inane. In different terms, if we do write something and what we write is not registered by God, then God is not the measure of all things. Buber helps us to avoid the pitfalls found in the classical theistic understanding of the concept of God, which is inimical to Buber's own understanding of the human-divine relationship as one between an "I" and a "Thou," rather than in classical theistic terms of an "I" and an "it" (Hartshorne 2000, 303; also see Davenport 2013).

Buber is most famous for his claim that "I" and "Thou" refer not so much to things as to a relation and this relationship is mutual. And he thinks that any relation an "I" would have with a nondivine "thou" gives us a glimpse into the life of the divine "Thou." He admits that the history of religion has had many instances of discourse about God in which the divine life is reduced to an "it," and hence one must always be alert to this danger. So whenever the word "God" or other words that have a family resemblance to "God" are used, we should be careful not to reduce the divine "Thou" to an objectified "it" status. He even goes so far as to say that when the divine "Thou" is reduced to an "it" status, there is an offense to the world (Buber 1937, 8, 75–80).

The weight of the present book rests heavily on the thesis that the concept of God in classical theism implies not a "Thou" but an "it" and that such a God is not capable of mutual relations with creatures. On Buber's contrasting view, however, God has relations with all of creation such that to enter into an "I-Thou" relationship with God is to be concerned with nothing isolated but with everything that is gathered into the divine relation: "For to step into the relation is not to disregard everything but to see everything in the *Thou*, not to renounce the world but to establish it on its true basis" (Buber 1937, 78–80). Pointing to the natural world "here" in contrast to a supernatural world "there" reduces God to an "it." This is true despite the fact that under the influence of classical theism, particularly in its influential Cartesian dualism version, this is the standard way to speak of religious matters in popular (and, unfortunately, academic) culture.

Buber helps us to understand the following irony: Understanding the concept of God as long as one remains "in the world" (in the sense of remaining in the grip of a compulsively consuming culture dominated by instrumental reason) is difficult, but understanding the concept of God if one tries to escape from the natural world by pole vaulting into a supernatural one (although there is a strong tendency in classical theism to do precisely this) is also difficult. Rather, an understanding of the concept of God is facilitated by viewing the natural world itself, including human beings in the natural world, differently, sacramentally, as populated by "thous" who enable one to participate in the divine "Thou." As Buber puts the point, "if you hallow this life you meet the living God" (Buber 1937, 78–80). On this account there is something misleading about talk concerning "seeking" God in that there is nothing in which God could not be found, given divine omnipresence. Here Buber is very much compatible with the Platonic World Soul, even if he does not explicitly endorse this doctrine.

Whether Buber has the same meaning as Hartshorne is not clear, although he does speak of the "I-Thou" relation as bipolar and mutual. He also suggests that in order to understand God we need to appeal to the *coindidentia oppositorum*, the coincidence of opposites. Here he seems to be very close to Hartshornian dipolar theism, such as when he says that not only do creatures depend on God, but in a certain sense God also depends on creatures (in the divine actuality if not the divine existence). Consider Buber's remarkable claim: "We know unshakably in our hearts that there is a becoming of the God that is" (Buber 1937, 82–83).

Because every abstraction is an "it," Buber tries to articulate the concept of God with as little appeal as possible to abstractions like being and becoming, although the above quotation from Buber makes clear that the latter is less objectionable than the former. That is, God is a person, for Buber, which is what it means to say that God is the supreme example of a "Thou" (Buber 1937, 84). Hartshorne is inclined to think that if there were no "Thou" there would be no "I," in contrast to Descartes's procedure in the *Meditations* wherein the attempt to argue for the existence of God presupposes the existence of the self. Hartshorne's view here is consonant with Buber's examination of *Ich und Du*, but this dependence of human beings on God is not at odds with the claim that in the divine actuality God is also dependent on us (Hartshorne 1953, 15; 1962, 133–134).

Our contingency in a way becomes God's contingency, on the Buberian view, without threatening in any way the necessity of the divine essence and existence. Granted, thought about God is schematic and at most gives us an outline; only personal encounter of a religious sort gives us concrete insight into God. But some outlines are far inferior to others, as in earlier maps of the world that omitted the Western Hemisphere altogether in contrast to those that depict all of the continents, however roughly. As Hartshorne emphasizes in Buber's wake, "to partake faithfully in dialogue, which is in principle the highest form of existence . . . one must accept influences coming from another, allow the other to determine part of the perceptual content of one's own experience." To leave this consideration regarding dialogue out of the picture in classical theistic fashion would be to offer a poor map of the terrain that underlies the logic of perfection (Hartshorne 1967, 123, 131; 1970, 232, 277).

Another great twentieth-century Jewish scholar, Abraham Heschel, viewed God (contra Aristotle and Maimonides) as the *most* moved mover, rather than as an Aristotelian unmoved mover. In fact, this is a major theme in his magisterial work on the Hebrew prophets. Likewise, Buber offers us hope that the grip of classical theism on the Abrahamic religions can be loosened. Indeed, it is axiomatic in neoclassical or process theism that God is the most *and best* moved mover (see Heschel 1962; also Hartshorne 1991, 41; and Artson 2013).

22

Pierre Teilhard de Chardin

(1881–1955)

This French Catholic paleontologist and theologian brings a certain sort of excitement to his defense of neoclassical or process theism. To cite just one example among many, he thinks that baptism is important not because it symbolizes cleansing, but rather because it symbolizes the plunge into the fire of purifying spiritual struggle. But human beings are not the only ones who have to struggle. Divine omnipresence, symbolized in Teilhard by cosmic Christ, becomes and grows; hence even God (in the sense of divine actuality) is in the fray. God is co-creator of an evolutionary world, according to Teilhard, which is another way of saying that creation is a process, not an isolated act accomplished once and for all (Teilhard 1971, 85; 1968b, 59).

Above all else, God is personal in Teilhard, but to be absorbed into the personal life of God does not mean that one's distinctiveness is lost. In fact, he thinks that the more we are absorbed into the personal life of God, the more we are distinguished in our individuality (in that as omniscient and omnibenevolent God would preeminently know and love our idiosyncracies). The elements of the world become more themselves, not less, as they are organically included in the divine life. Teilhard wavers regarding the "new God" he discusses: At times he is clear that God evolves, too, in the divine personal *inter*action with nondivine beings; whereas at other times he seems to be saying that the newness in question refers to the progressive awareness of the divine life on the part of human beings. But there need not be a contradiction between these two. When Teilhard refers to "God-Above" or the transcendent God, he is referring to what Hartshorne would call the essence or existence of God, rather than to the ever-changing actuality of God, which Teilhard sometimes calls "God-the-Evolver." Thus, the persons Teilhard describes, both divine and nondivine, are not the static substantial persons found in classical theism. Teilhard's meaning is more accurately portrayed when he speaks about the personal*izing* process of centration or becoming centered (Teilhard 1971, 241–242; 1970, 262; 1969, 91; 1975, 117).

A distinctive feature of Teilhard's neoclassical or process theism is his emphasis on progressive interiorization throughout evolutionary history, which is also called implosion, the opposite of explosion. This involves the process of developing an interior life or developing "centration," whereby human beings, in particular, more closely approximate a spiritual life as quotidian natural concerns are transubstantiated into love. But the spiritual life is always rooted in matter in hylomorphic fashion. A sort of spiritual power is latent in matter such that matter is the starting point of the process of spiritual ascent that has as its goal absorption into the dynamic life of God. "Neo-Christianity," as Teilhard uses this term, refers not as much to a new religion as to a renewed one that has fully come to terms with the reality of nature as evolutionary (Teilhard 1978, 80, 92).

Importantly, Teilhard's emphasis on interiorization, implosion, and centration is obviously not meant to work against the cliché that no person is an island. Rather, like Whitehead, he thinks that religion consists primarily in what one *does* with one's solitariness, which he hopes is to cultivate a sense of deeply social, evolutionary purpose wherein all of us together advance in wisdom, love, and justice (see Dombrowski 2015). His fear is that without a strong spiritual (centered) life one is more likely to be swept along unknowingly by the most superficial forces in society and that one would revert to the proto-interiorization found in prehuman nature. As Bergson notes, even Robinson Crusoe on his island remains in contact with other people as a result of the manufactured objects he saved from the wreck; Teilhard is well aware that we take our socialization with us when we retreat to an interior or centered life (see Whitehead [1926] 1996, 16–17; also see Bergson 1977, 16).

Admittedly, at certain points Teilhard seems to fall back into classical theistic modes of talking about the concept of God. But a charitable interpretation of his thought indicates otherwise. In at least four ways his apparent classical theism actually brings to light certain fascinating features of his neoclassical or process theism.

First, he speaks of an "Omega" or "Omega Point" to history, which could be interpreted to mean that the flux of history will come to an end in some sort of static divine state outside of, or beyond, time. Teilhard often gives advantage to this classical theistic interpretation. But we might be closer to Teilhard's meaning when we see him turn the word "Omega" into a verb form by speaking of the process wherein something is "omegalized" or progressively transfigured by becoming more centered or more interiorized. Something similar could be said about Teilhard's use of the term "pleroma," which refers to the natural world being brought to maturity. This might indicate a static telos to be reached in the endtime, but it might also indicate (and most likely does indicate) a dynamic "pleromization" of the universe. Or again, the second coming of Christ discussed in terms of the "Parousia" might refer (and most likely does refer) to human beings in any religious tradition becoming more Christlike (more interiorized, more centered) in the course of time (Teilhard 1970, 55–56, 84, 122; 1971, 177).

A second topic Teilhard discusses that could be interpreted as a retreat to the classical theistic concept of God concerns his use of the term "supernatural" to describe God. We have seen that on the classical theistic use of this term, especially in its Cartesian dualism version, there is a view of the universe as two-tiered, with a natural world governed by scientific laws and a supernatural world that can intervene into the natural world via miracles that violate these laws. However, Teilhard is instructive in the way he speaks of supernaturality in terms other than those popular among classical theists. That is, he distinguishes between the supernatural and the extranatural. The latter term plays into the hands of the classical theist. By "supernatural" Teilhard refers to something natural, but to the nth degree. The function of the supernatural is not to escape from the natural, but to leaven it or to transform it. On Teilhard's view, spiritual purity consists not in escaping from matter, but in entering into a deeper understanding of it. In matter is found the potential for love in the sense that matter contains within itself, at least in potency, the capacity for depth, inwardness, and care. We ourselves are examples of material beings who exhibit in rather complex ways these qualities. The supernatural is the aspect of nature in which the potential for spiritualization has already been, at least to a certain extent, actualized. On this view of the concept of God, divine stability consists in the constancy of this spiritualizing process (Teilhard 1971, 241–242; 1961, 64–65, 95; 1960, 136).

A third topic concerning which Teilhard might be interpreted as a classical theist, but concerning which Teilhard is ironically very insightful in a neoclassical or process theistic way, is his use of the concept of omnipotence to describe God or his use of the name "Pantocrator" to refer to God. As I understand him, however, Teilhard has in mind something somewhat different from the classical theistic concept of omnipotence. Here theodicy is crucial. In the tradition of ancient Greek tragedy, Teilhard recognizes evil as a natural fact. A plurality of at least partially free beings virtually insures that frustration or perhaps even tragedy will result as freedoms clash or get in each other's way. The structure of the world as evolutionary involves uncertainty, chance, and hence risk. In this context, no being, not even a divine one, can guarantee the absence of suffering and loss without destroying altogether the free beings in question. Evil is inevitable as a secondary effect of the evolutive universe we live in. That is, completely eliminating the possibility of evil would eliminate the evolutive world itself. Evil is the expression of a plurality of nonmechanical beings and, we should note, freedom, plurality, adventure, unpredictability, and risk are, in their own ways, good things. The panoramic screen of evolutive history forces us to reconceive divine "omnipotence," even if Teilhard himself continues to use this word. Perhaps he would have been better served to use Hartshornian designations such as "ideal power," "persuasive power," or "power compatible with dynamic perfection" (Teilhard 1960, 60; 1971, 82–85).

And fourth, Teilhard might initially seem to be something other than a neoclassical or process theist due to his frequent engagement with pantheism. The terminological issues here are complex in that he distinguishes among at least thirteen (!) meanings of the term "pantheism," but as I interpret his thought, his overall goal is merely to move away from the two-tiered classical theistic view of the universe. If I am correct in this interpretation, then he might have been better served to talk about divine "world-inclusiveness," rather than pantheism, in that pantheism (as in its Stoic or Spinozistic versions) is often assumed to be equated with both determinism and a complete lack of externality between God and the nondivine. In this regard Siôn Cowell is wise to see Teilhard as a (neoclassical, process) panentheist, rather than as a pantheist. In fact, relatively early in his career Teilhard identified positively with the Platonic World Soul, which is very much compatible with the panentheist position wherein the natural world is in God via divine omniscience (properly understood) and divine omnibenevolence: God knows and cares for all. But the natural world is not to be identified with God, as in certain versions of pantheism (see Cowell 2001, 141–145; also see Teilhard 1968b, 187).

Among the various uses of the word "pantheism" found in Teilhard is a distinction regarding a type of pantheism in which the unity of the whole involves a fusion of the various elements found in the whole such that the distinctiveness of each element disappears. This is not the view that Teilhard defends. Another sort of "pantheism," more properly called "panentheism," involves a divine whole in which the elements are not fused or annihilated but *fulfilled* by entering into a deeper and wider Center or supercenter. Here the elements are not confused but more fully differentiated because they are felt and known by an omniscient and omnibenevolent being. In this concept of God the divine is a Center of centers. Teilhard is driven to this view by his very strong sense of the organicity of a universe that contains all of the elements in flux, a view of God that he sees as very much compatible with St. Paul's *in quo omnia constant* (in whom all things hold together; Colossians 1: 17).

With these clarifications in mind, we can legitimately see Teilhard as a dipolar theist who is cognizant of both activity and passivity in God as well as being and becoming in God. God's being, on this interpretation, refers to the self-subsistency or self-sufficiency of God's essence as the greatest conceivable and to God's necessary existence; but it does not refer to the evolutionary flux of divine actuality from moment to moment. In Teilhardian terms, there is theogenesis (Teilhard 1960, 52; 1968a, 174; 1971, 177; 1975, 194).

Thinking that there is a contradiction between Teilhard saying that God is permanent being, on the one hand, and that God is forever in the process of formation, on the other, would be a mistake in that these contrasting (not contradictory) modes of discourse refer to different aspects of the divine nature. On the one hand, God is self-sufficient in existence and as the being who exhibits ideal knowledge, power, and love; on the other hand, the universe contributes something that is "vitally necessary" to the divine actuality. Unfortunately, Teilhard sometimes expresses guilt at defending such "contradictions," but this is perhaps because he was not sufficiently aware of Whitehead and

Hartshorne, especially the latter, who could have persuaded him of the cogency of the divine existence-actuality distinction. Teilhard is correct, however, to hope for a "higher metaphysics" than the classical theistic one that persistently opts for one pole only of dipolar contrasts. In different terms, although God is self-sufficient in existence, arguing for divine "omni-sufficiency." would be a mistake. He thinks that the most authentic versions of religious tradition and experience affirm that a "bilateral and complementary" relationship exists between God and the world and that these versions are not preserved well by traditional metaphysics. Christianity, in particular, he thinks, is given new life in the notion that a mutuality exists between the world and God that is needed in the pleromizing process (Teilhard 1978, 54; 1971, 177–179, 226–227).

Teilhard asserts as a fact in the phenomenology of religious experience that God is not present to us as all complete; rather, those who experience God do so as a discovery and as a growing process. The dynamism of religious experience actually enhances the apophatic dimension of the concept of God, rather than detracts from it. This is because the more we think we understand divine actuality, the more we realize that something is constantly added to divine experience and as a result escapes our grasp. The "inside of things," however, enables us to enhance our understanding, such as it is. Here Teilhard attempts to mediate between polytheistic and animistic religious traditions, which deified and personified every aspect of nature, and the modernist tendency to depersonify and disenchant everything that is most admired. David Ray Griffin, for example, is a contemporary theologian and the author of a magisterial book in which he labors along with Teilhard in the effort to "reenchant" a disenchanted and deracinated world. It is not only the great mystics who experience a Great Presence in nature, an extrahuman Energy more deeply infused into the nature of things than merely mechanical relations. Although not ubiquitous among human beings, a great number of people have experienced this Great Presence, although the labels for this presence vary greatly (Teilhard 1960, 119; 1999, 22, 183, 189, 209; also see D. Griffin 2001).

Teilhard takes quite seriously the ideas that something is born in the divine (actuality) when human beings love each other and that love constitutes the measure of progress in evolutionary history. God is elevated by our love, he thinks, although he does not indicate, like Berdyaev, whether he thinks that God is pained by our hatreds (Teilhard 1964, 5–76, 79, 120).

Of course God's essential nature and existence are not in need of our busy activity, but the emphasis Teilhard places on divine omnipresence (and on the related idea that God is not withdrawn from us and beyond the tangible sphere) means that such dependence is ensured regarding what Hartshorne would call divine actuality. Although we may nominally value activity over passivity, in that no self-respecting person wants to be run over, clearly our passive powers are just as crucial to a good life as the active ones. This Teilhardian insight is applied in neoclassical theism in a preeminent way to the divine case. In fact, the dynamism of life equally requires both activity and passivity. Bodily life, in particular, involves passive powers to absorb food and air, but mental life also requires the absorption of information, listening to others, and so on. Teilhard resists any facile bifurcation of mind and matter if such distinction distracts attention away from "holy matter" and the place of the material world, including our very bodies, in the spiritual life. God is revealed everywhere as the universal milieu in which the multiplicity of things in the world are indeed seen as parts of one immense world in movement that is constantly acquiring new qualities. The contrasts between activity and passivity and between mind or soul and matter involve the idea that these differing elements are in reality brought together, but not in such a manner that they are easily confused. The most important of our passive powers is the ability to receive divine influence in the midst of the material flux of events (Teilhard 1960, 15, 22, 33, 46, 67, 69–70, 73–74, 81, 91, 97, 99, 101, 103, 108, 110–111).

The vibrancy of the world that is apparent to Teilhard is due to the inwardness of all things (in vastly varying degrees) in a panpsychist or panexperientialist universe. We are so accustomed to viewing things from without, a view that is understandable enough in itself, that we might fail to consider that we are not the only beings in the universe who have insides, an impulse to react to previous stimuli and to advance. Likewise, religious traditions can be viewed from without, but Teilhard has a suspicion that relying exclusively on this sort of vision leaves something significant out of the picture. To be a religious believer is to be seized by the inwardness of the religious tradition in question. One of the features of Teilhard's thought that makes him distinctive is the way in which he weaves together the inward/outward distinction with the passivity/activity distinction; these two distinctions mutually enrich each other. The concept of God, on this interpretation, exhibits the highest expression of each of these four elements. "The basic mystical intuition issues in the discovery of a supra-real unity diffused throughout the immensity of the world" (Teilhard 1961, 91). Or again, "the world is a-building. This is the basic truth which must first be understood so thoroughly that it becomes an habitual and as it were natural springboard for our thinking. . . . A process is at work in the universe, an issue is at stake" (Teilhard 1961, 92–93). The issue at stake involves atoms as well as animals like ourselves. Evolution is holy and not even God (especially not God!) is finished (Teilhard 1961, 43, 83–84, 87, 91–93, 133).

Teilhard is chagrined to notice that the concept of creative trans-formation had no significant place in the thought of the great classical theists of the Middle Ages, and hence should be established without delay. Furthermore, the medieval scholastic thinkers emphasized too much the concept of God as creator, instead of emphasizing God as the creator of free beings who in a sense make themselves. He even goes so far as to say that it is contradictory to imagine God creating an isolated being who is nonetheless a participated being who depends on others; if any being exists, then a whole interrelational world of becoming must exist. The essential relationality of things means that world-in-clusiveness is part of what it would mean to be God. It is unfortunate, he thinks, that many who have been attracted to a religion of the whole have turned away from Christianity, presumably because of the Christian version of the classical theistic concept of God as supernat-ural in the sense of being outside of time and immune to change as a result of natural events. By contrast, Teilhard takes the Pauline view of the omnipresent, mystical body of cosmic Christ quite seriously. Unfortunately, classical theists did not consider the possibility that because our understanding of God obviously changes this progressive advance might be rooted in the divine history itself (Teilhard 1971, 24, 28, 31–33, 59, 64, 82).

Perhaps because of the influence of Roman jurisprudence on classical theists, discourse regarding the concept of God has often resembled a legal trial between God and the creatures or among the creatures themselves when discussing God, instead of emphasizing mutuality or at least a struggle that is not internecine. At the very least we need a dynamic version of theism, whether pacific or agonistic. To put the point in spatial terms, rather than the classical theistic God as *above* us, we might be better served to think neoclassically or processually in terms of God as *ahead* of us, not as a rigid telos toward whom we must advance, but as a Whiteheadian lure forward toward a better world (Teilhard 1971, 89, 133, 212, 239).

Part 4

Henri Bergson and
Alfred North Whitehead

As I see things, three neoclassical or process theists stand head and shoulders above the rest in the period that lasted until the mid-twentieth century where this book ends: Henri Bergson, Alfred North Whitehead, and Charles Hartshorne. As I have indicated, because the entire book has been written from a Hartshornian perspective, no separate chapter is dedicated to his thought in that it has been operative throughout the work in shaping the historical argument I offer. Hence, in this last part of the book I indicate why Bergson and Whitehead are major philosophical figures in the history of the concept of God.

In light of developments in the concept of God in late-twentieth- and early-twenty-first–century thinkers, there are at least two defects in the concept of God as we have seen it unfold thus far, even in the writings of neoclassical or process theists:

First, there has historically been an inadequate treatment of the concepts of sex and gender as they impact the concept of God, a defect that is perhaps not surprising given the fact that the concept of God has historically been male dominated. By contrast, the history of religious experience has not been so dominated, as is evidenced in the long line of classics in mystic literature, such as the Song of Deborah in the Hebrew scriptures, the writings of St. Teresa of Avila and St. Thérèse of Lisieux in Catholicism, the writings by and about Mary Baker Eddy and others in the Protestant tradition, and so on. The goal is to have the insights of these figures inform what is said philosophically and theologically about God. Classical theism has done a poor job in this regard due to the quintessentially male version of God found in a deity who is unmoved by the sufferings of others and who acts on others while being impervious to their supplications. On the classical theistic view, God has already from eternity "sponded" (rather than re-sponded) to such sufferings, which classical theists believe to be enough.

Second, there has historically also been an inadequate treatment of the relationship between the implications of the concept of God for environmental issues, to the extent that these were even noticed. Once again, classical theists have done a poor job in this regard as a result of their view of God as supernatural, not in the Teilhardian sense of a theistic naturalism in which God's natural reality is super or preeminent, but in the sense of being above or outside of time and nature because, it is alleged, God would be sullied or diminished if too strong a connection were made between divinity and nature.

Importantly, I do not think that Bergson and Whitehead say everything that needs to be said about these two issues. But I do think that they point us in the right direction and that they are vastly superior to classical theists regarding these two issues. Hence I show how Bergson and Whitehead prepare the way for various neoclassical or process theists in the late twentieth and early twenty-first centuries who articulate defensible versions of the concept of God that accommodate well both feminist and environmental concerns. In this regard I have the later writings of Hartshorne primarily in mind, but also the feminist versions of neoclassical or process theism (or views that are at least compatible with this position) found in the writings of Marjorie Suchocki, Catherine Keller, Carol Christ, Rosemary Radford Reuther, Anna Case-Winters, Sheila Greeve Davaney, and many others, as well as the environmental versions of neoclassical or process theism (or views that are at least compatible with this position) found in the works of John Cobb, Brian Henning, Donald Viney, George Shields, and numerous other scholars. Additionally, other scholars, such as Sallie McFague, treat the concept of God with both feminist and environmental concerns in mind. But a careful examination of these issues and these writers is beyond the historical scope of this book.

23
Henri Bergson
(1859–1941)

Bergson helps us to realize that the concept of God is rooted in social life, broadly conceived. But there are two sorts of social life, each of which is connected to a particular view of God. In "closed society," as Bergson uses the term, the concept of God is likely to have an imperative character that is supposedly inscribed from all eternity, as it were, on the transcendent tablets Moses acquired on Mt. Sinai. A breach of this social order appears as an anti-natural act. That is, closed society maintains tight bonds among three elements: alleged natural order, social order, and religious command. Nature, society, and religion live together as if they were cellular members of a living organism. To adopt a metaphor from Bergson himself in his great 1932 work *The Two Sources of Morality and Religion* (Bergson was a Nobel Prize winner in literature), just as in an aquatic plant whose leaves on the surface of the water are deeply rooted in what cannot be seen beneath the surface, so also the visible manifestations of natural and social order and religion are rooted in a concept of God that lies far beneath what is normally seen (Bergson 1977, 1–26).

The two sorts of society in Bergson, as well as the two concepts of God that are related to them, are also related to the two main lines of the evolution of animal life. The arthropods are typified by the instinct of insects, whereas the vertebrates culminate in human intelligence. Although the two interpenetrate (there is nascent intelligence in insects and human life is still largely influenced by instinct), the inventiveness of human intelligence has as its consequence the ability to partially transcend the reified characteristics of insect life. Human community is more variable in form and is much more open to progress than the rigidly communal lives of insects. What is natural in human beings is in great measure overlaid with what is acquired. Our societies, too, can be closed in the sense of being dominated by custom, habit, and instinct, but there is always at least the possibility of openness, intelligent choice, and progress. To be precise, human societies need instinct—surviving without it would be impossible—but this claim is nonetheless compatible with the idea that the difference between a closed society and an open one can be significant (Bergson 1977, 27–32).

Human beings have come to respect each other in degrees, gradually including those outside of one's clan, one's ethnic background, one's gender, and indeed outside of one's own species. These developments are often aided (or hindered) as a result of the concept of God dominant in a particular society. To the extent that this concept concentrates on a God of love, to this extent a society is able to progressively open itself. Great moral personalities are very often those who open us up to a more dynamic and defensible concept of God. And herein lies Bergson's contribution to a sound relationship between the concept of God and feminist as well as environmental concern: It is an ethics of love, integrally connected to a God of love, that facilitates an ever-expanding scope of concern to include not only all human beings, but also all sentient life, perhaps even all vegetative life and all natural processes (Bergson 1977, 33–41).

Of course the issue of whether society is primary and the concept of God derivative, or whether the concept of God is primary and society derivative, is a complicated one. But Bergson cautions us against a facile acceptance of the idea that the concept of God is pushed around by societal organization, especially in its material or economic aspects. For example, claiming that romantic love plagiarizes mysticism rather than the other way around is plausible, and hence those who criticize mystics for describing God in terms of passionate love are wrongheaded in their assumption that the mystics are borrowing from the raptures of two lovers. They may very well be reclaiming for mystic love of Preeminent Love what was originally its own. Romantic love has a definite history that started in the Middle Ages under the inspiration of the Song of Songs from the Hebrew scriptures. In this regard, that Bergson himself was a Jew who converted to Catholicism is noteworthy; he was, therefore, familiar with both of these great religions in both their closed and open varieties, making him something of an expert in four religions (Bergson 1977, 42; also see Levi 1959, chap. 3).

Emotion drives intelligence, despite all obstacles, in Bergson; it vivifies or vitalizes it. Hence there is the following sort of dynamism in his thought: Initially instinct drives things in closed religion; but as the intellectual abilities of human beings become enhanced, a concept of God develops that, in turn, affects moral discourse and the societal lives of human beings; yet despite the efficacy of the concept of God, in reality the morality of a group of religious people "wins souls" more than the concept of God or any other intellectual aspect of religion. This book has inserted into religious discourse a historical account of a version of the concept of God that is partially at odds with the classical theistic concept, but it has not questioned either the importance of instinct/intuition in the lives of religious believers or the importance of moral beliefs and structures on the concrete lives of individuals, whether or not they are religious believers. To take a familiar test case, the importance of love in Christianity has not been sufficiently supported (if supported at all) by the metaphysics of belief classical theism fosters; this lack of support has very practical (indeed negative) consequences (Bergson 1977, 43–50).

Neither closed nor open morality/religion can be found in a pure state, although a completely closed morality/religion can be closely approximated in some cases. An attitude of aspiration or the hope that there can be progress is one of the preconditions, it seems, for open religion to flourish. All of the great mystics in the Abrahamic (and other) religions aid the cause of open religion, albeit unwittingly in some cases, by saying, in effect, that by loving God we love all those made in the divine image (as qualified, however, by a prohibition of images in Islam). These mystics have a sense of a loving current passing from them to God and then back again through them to the rest of humanity and to the rest of nature. Bergson describes the effect of such a current (or lack thereof) in the following terms: "Between the first morality and the second, lies the whole distance between repose and movement. The first is supposed to be immutable. If it changes, it immediately forgets that it has changed" (Bergson 1977, 58). The second morality/religion is more complicated than the first because it does not have amnesia in this regard; it is both "neo" and "classical." And Bergson notes that both Socratic reason and the morality of the gospels implicitly point the way toward "openness," as Bergson uses the term, in that both Socrates and Jesus were open to divine influence in terms of either a mysterious *daemon* or a parental, caring force at work in the world, respectively (Bergson 1977, 51–64).

To note the failure of strictly intellectualist systems of morality/religion is perfectly compatible with noting the crucial role that rationality plays in the development of the open. Reason itself has a divine character, once again as Socrates's *daemon* and Jesus when seen as the *logos* indicate. Just as great political reforms at first seem impractical, so also great intellectual reforms, such as in reform of the concept of God. But an overflowing of love and rationality together is almost irresistible. Almost. Pure aspiration is a limit concept or an ideal in that there is always some closed or instinctual element in morality/religion, some formula or structure that endures and tends to resist change (Bergson 1977, 65–89).

But there is also the possibility of religious "mysticism," as Bergson uses this term, which consists in opening up to the oncoming wave of divine influence in the world. These mystics, who are at the forefront of open morality/religion, are not to be equated with those who have extraordinary visions and voices (although these are not unheard of), in that those who are open to divine influence, and who, in turn, influence the divine, are very often those who are efficacious actors in the world, such as St. Teresa of Avila, to take just one example, who was in effect responsible for the reform of the Catholic Church in Spain in the early modern period in the absence of any significant Protestant Reformation in that country. Bergson insightfully notes that those of us who are not mystics nonetheless often find an echo of what mystics say about their experiences in our own lives, which perhaps indicates that the capacity for religious experience at a high and nuanced level is dormant in each one of us (Bergson 1977, 90–101).

For neoclassical or process theists, thinking that the concept of God would be polished at an early stage of its articulation is implausible. Seen in this light, by the time of Philo in the first century and St. Thomas Aquinas in the thirteenth century half of the concept of God had been very carefully examined and illuminated (that is, God's permanence, if not God's change; God's activity, if not God's passivity; and so on). This is amazing in that fifty percent can be seen as a very high percentage. But by leaving the other half of the concept of God not carefully examined and not illuminated, classical theists have facilitated numerous theoretical and practical problems. As Bergson puts the point, "The spectacle of what religions have been in the past, of what certain religions still are today, is indeed humiliating for human intelligence. What a farrago of error and folly" (Bergson, 1977, 102)! For example, it is not unreasonable to think that the classical concept of God as active and not passive is not unrelated to the dismal history of religious intoleration and persecution. The proper response to this problem, however, is not to give up on religion (no more than we should give up on politics when political leaders make grave mistakes and no more than we should give up on art when talented people give themselves over to overly commercialized or exploitative creative projects), but to improve it by putting it on a more defensible abstract basis, including the effort to articulate a comprehensive yet consistent concept of God.

Despite all of the historical problems with the concept of God in particular and with religion in general, Bergson thinks it remarkable that neither the concept of God nor religion itself have died out. (Likewise, neither politics nor art have died out, despite a long history of political corruption and artistic "license" in the pejorative sense of the term.) As Bergson puts the point, "there is some demand for a forward movement, some remnant of an impulse, a vital impetus" to improve the concept of God and religion (Bergson 1977, 111). This impulse to improve means that in principle predicting what will happen in the future in any sort of detail regarding either the concept of God or religion is impossible. As we have unfortunately seen, the classical theistic version of omniscience would lead us to think otherwise (Bergson 1977, 115, 204–205).

Bergson defends the commonplace in process thought that an animal individual, including a human animal, is itself a society composed of cellular members, which are themselves micro-organisms. Although he is not explicit regarding the question of whether God is a World Soul whose divine society includes us as cellular members, such a view seems to be implied in his stance regarding the primacy of the social in nature. Indeed, he thinks that what it means to be a religious believer is to think that some sort of divine force is diffused throughout all of nature. But it need not be assumed that this diffused divine force is omnipotent; Bergson's biologized conception of philosophy requires him to think that chance plays a very real role in what happens in nature and in human culture (Bergson 1977, 117–119, 134, 147–148, 158).

Just as the neoclassical or process theistic critique of omnipotence makes it possible to better understand the chance elements in nature as detailed in evolutionary biology, so also neoclassical or process theism makes it possible to establish a significant difference between religious belief and magic. The latter involves a certain degree of selfishness, a desire to alter the laws of nature to conform to one's own wishes. Overconcentration on petitionary prayer to an omnipotent God who can at will alter any natural law, who can at will supernaturally contravene nature, can be seen as a glorified form of magic. By way of partial contrast, in neoclassical or process theism we are encouraged to see ourselves not as central to the cosmos, but nonetheless as significant parts of a mighty (but not omnipotent) Whole. The goal of a spiritual life on this basis is to understand and appreciate one's worth, but always within a larger Whole that involves tragedy for both us and God alike. It is to return to the best aspects of Platonic theism and to the insights of the Greek tragedians (Bergson 1977, 175, 201; also see Arnison 2012).

Although the dynamism of open religion might at times need the static and structured character of closed religion for its expression and diffusion, this is notably different from the idea that closed religion in itself is consistent and intelligible. The chief problem with closed religion, according to Bergson, is that it cannot come to terms with the concept of God as personal. Admittedly, static religion lives on in open religion to the extent that in neoclassical or process theism there is both a "neo" aspect as well as a "classical" aspect, with the latter indicating the importance, but not hegemony, of divine permanence. That is, equating God *simpliciter* with immutability is a huge mistake. Ancient Greek polytheists anticipated this point in their stories about Zeus and Dionysus, say, whose characters were never set in stone and exhibited significant changes. In this regard Bergson notes the relative poverty of Roman mythology to the Greek. The Roman gods tend to coincide with certain functions and tend to be immobilized by these functions; by partial contrast the Greek gods had more dynamic characters and histories. Or more precisely, to the extent that one can detect dynamism in the Roman gods it is with respect to those gods who are most derived from the Greeks (Bergson 1977, 178-179, 187-188, 194).

Furthermore, ancient polytheism anticipates in large measure the crucial Hartshornian distinction between existence and actuality. Whereas any particular god was contingent and could come or go, the gods as a whole had to exist, as Bergson argues in his analysis of ancient religion. This is similar to Hartshorne's idea, compatible with Bergson's treatment of ancient polytheism as an important bridge between closed and open theism, that God's actual experiences from moment to moment are contingent and can come and go, but God's everlasting existence is necessary (Bergson 1977, 200).

Thinking that a current of creative energy is at work in the world, a restless advance into the future at each moment is characteristic of a process worldview, which has profound implications for the concept of God. One of these implications is that if we talk about divine foreknowledge, then we have to qualify such talk by saying that such "foreknowledge" involves only possibilities or at best probabilities, even for the preeminent knower. The confidence that closed religion encourages needs to be transfigured, according to Bergson, in that there should always be a degree of inquietude regarding the future. It is true that at present—both Bergson's present in 1932 and our present in the early twenty-first century—people tend to turn to closed or static religion for support in time of trouble, but with mixed results. Bergson's metaphor is that of a ceremony wherein the participants go through the motions without really meaning them. But the situation is not hopeless. Even a listless and mechanical science teacher can occasionally awaken in a pupil the vocation to pursue research; likewise, even in closed, static religion, finding people who have been seized by the inwardness of a religious tradition and who start to wonder about how to articulate the concept of a God of love is not uncommon. Many of these despair of classical theism in this effort. In a strange way closed, static religion and open, dynamic religion are both antagonistic to each other and come together in a common pursuit. This is because neoclassical theism is, in part, inclusive of the best insights found in classical theism (Bergson 1977, 209–217).

Bergson correctly emphasizes that the sedimentation of the concept of God is in large measure the easily visible result of classical theism. But he is also astute to note that this sedimentation is due to seismic forces that are not on the surface easily seen. Primary among these is the dialectic among Plato, Aristotle, and Plotinus on the concept of God, as I argue in part 2. Whereas there is a prominent place for mysticism in Plotinus's philosophy, and hence for the possibility for open religion in his thought, there is as much or more Aristotle than Plato in his concept of God, which counteracts the tendency toward openness. The ultimate end of mysticism is contact with God; indeed, it is mutual influence between the mystic and God, as various giants in the history of religious experience in various traditions, including Plato's *homoiosis theoi* (becoming as much like God[s] as possible), reported. To establish such contact is to act in such a way to be able to passively receive divine influence, such as in working hard to pay attention to someone who says, "You have not been listening to me!" Once such contact with God occurs, it creates a wellspring of energy in the mystic, much like a lake filled to the brim with water that is held back by a dam; when the dam bursts, this energy flows back into the current of life and creates the open possibility for a richer understanding of both creaturely and divine dynamism (Bergson 1977, 219–220, 226–227).

Bergson not surprisingly speaks of "what a shock to the soul is the passing from the static to the dynamic, from the closed to the open, from everyday life to mystic life" (Bergson 1977, 229). But one can overcome this shock when we realize that we all have the potential for mystic experience, as I have mentioned. Mystic repose is the source of a sort of agitation to creatively change things, such as in a steam engine fully powered and ready to move forward. At the far side of the mystic dark night of the soul St. John of the Cross made famous is found an energetic movement into the light. As a result of *inter*action with God, the mystic comes out of contemplative repose ready to hurl himself or herself into vast enterprises. We can easily misunderstand the cliché in mystic literature regarding contemplative repose Plotinus made famous, alone with The Alone. Such aloneness (not loneliness) is but a moment in the systole/diastole movement of the spiritual life both mystics and neoclassical or process theists extoll. Granted, many of the great figures in the history of religious experience *claim* that they are orthodox (or classical) theists, but these mystics are always the first to point out the uneasy alliance between the religious experiences they report and what I have called the classical concept of God (Bergson 1977, 229–232). They often complain of "the God of the philosophers," without realizing that only some philosophers defend the concept of God that they see at odds with their personal experiences.

Human beings are, along with God, co-creators of the evolving universe. Such co-creation is especially dramatic when mystic open religion erupts within the confines of a particular closed religion; then all of the pieces of the closed religion have to be rethought. What personal religious experience pours red hot into human existence is then cooled under the rational analysis of philosophers and theologians, who engage in an abstract metadiscipline that tries to understand what happens at the more concrete level. Religious institutions are also the result of the cooling process, but not at an abstract level; rather, religious institutions serve the function of popularizing the insights and experiences of the great mystics, including Moses, Jesus, and Mohammed, among many others. The thesis of this book is that the influence of the God of Aristotle (which itself relies on one facet only of Plato's more complex concept of God) on the Abrahamic religions has had a distorting effect on the cool rational analysis of philosophers and theologians over the centuries. Distortion resulted because of an overly aggressive version of divine omniscience with respect to future contingencies, which runs afoul of a belief in human freedom, and an overly aggressive version of divine omnipotence, which runs afoul of the theodicy problem (Bergson 1977, 234–241).

Bergson legitimately wonders why Aristotle chose as his first principle a mover that remains motionless and a thought that can think only itself. He also understandably wonders why Aristotle identified this first principle with God, given the fact that the phenomenology of religious experience in various traditions indicates that God is a being who can hold communication with human beings. That is, Aristotle's immutable deity (or deities) has very little in common with either the ancient Greek gods or with the God in the Abrahamic religions. On Bergson's contrasting account, the real is mobile, or is rather movement itself. It would be a mistake, he thinks, to slow down the movement of life, even divine life, to the point where a particular frame was confused with the whole, such as when a motion picture is gradually slowed to a halt and all that can be viewed is an individual, static picture, as if in a frame. This is what occurs in the Aristotelian view of God. Immutability need not be seen as superior to mutability, as Aristotle thinks, nor should we assume that mutability itself indicates a deficiency. Rather than seeing time as a deprivation of eternity, we would be better served by viewing the everlasting as derivative from an endless series of temporal moments, which are primary (Bergson 1977, 241–244).

We do not find dynamic creativity unintelligible when we consider that the movement of life itself, activity, and freedom are commonplace.

When we think of God we should think of preeminent movement rather than of the complete absence of it. Philosophers need to intervene when thinkers distort the living world that we live in as a result of habits that tend to go unexamined. The Aristotelian tendency to view God as an unmoved, permanent, immutable being is one of the habits that deserves to be examined in detail, contra the classical theistic reflex (Bergson 1911, 196, 248, 322–325, 349, 351–352).

The indignant protests of those who see in mystic experience nothing but quackery and folly are contradicted by Bergson's (and William James's) observation that even those who have never had religious experiences nonetheless often resonate well when they hear them described by others; the religious experiences find an echo in the hearts of those who are not nominally religious. In different terms, the feeling that we are each parts of a mighty (if not omnipotent), meaningful beneficent Whole is widespread if not universal. Bergson even goes so far as to say that the chief contribution of mysticism is to attest to the claim that God is pervasive love. In fact, it is the inheritance of this mystical tradition that love is the essential feature of God (a view that is not handled well, if at all, in the monopolar terms of classical theism). Claims such as these lead to the conclusion that the mystic tradition is somewhat anti-intellectual. A more felicitous way to put the point is to say that those who have had religious experiences tend to tire easily of intellectual systems, including religious ones, which lose sight of these insights/experiences (Bergson 1977, 246, 251–254, 311): "As a matter of fact, the mystics unanimously bear witness that God needs us, just as we need God. Why should [God] need us unless it be to love us? And it is to this very conclusion that the philosopher who holds to the mystical experience must come. Creation will appear to [the philosopher] as God undertaking to create creators, that [God] may have . . . beings worthy of [divine] love" (Bergson 1977, 255). The Hartshornian distinction between divine existence and divine actuality is much needed here: To claim (legitimately) that divine existence is necessary and does not require any particular others is not to claim that there could be no others at all in that preeminent love requires some others to love. *How* God exists does partially depend on us if divine love is even remotely analogous to human love, which even the classical theist is willing to admit, albeit perhaps grudgingly.

One of the faults with classical theistic theodicy, in Bergson's estimation, is that by relying so heavily on divine omnipotence, divine omnibenevolence is threatened. Why is there so much evil in the world, or any evil at all, if God is omnipotent and could eliminate the evil? One standard response to this is that evil is the result of misused freedom on the part of human beings, but this leaves unexplained why nonhuman animals who do not have free will suffer intense pain. Even if one is not an animal rightist, as long as one's view is not the Cartesian one wherein nonhuman animals are machines and are hence incapable of suffering, one must account for how there could be nonhuman animal suffering. Bergson thinks that classical theists inevitably are led to something like Leibniz's theodicy wherein this is either the best of all possible worlds or the best way to reach it. But on this basis what are we to say to a parent who has just buried a child who died of an intensely painful illness? If evil is, as Bergson thinks, not merely a lesser good, then the Leibnizian view involves unwarranted optimism. Optimism of some sort may receive justificatory warrant, but not the hyperbolic Leibnizian kind of optimism that is the result of the classical theistic concept of God, especially the overly robust versions of omnipotence and omniscience with respect to future contingencies that are the hall-marks of classical theistic theodicy (Bergson 1977, 260–261; also see Dombrowski 2000).

Bergson is at his best, I think, when he criticizes the "a priorism" of classical theistic theodicy, in general, and its Leibnizian version, in particular. It is taken for granted that God must be omnipotent, on this view, and from there certain characteristics of the world are deduced, notably either that ultimately there is nothing that is evil or that what appears to be evil is instrumental in bringing about a greater good. Not surprisingly, then, as a result of this approach atheism and agnosticism look attractive. The neoclassical or process view needs to correct this triumphalist approach, which is almost the reverse. Start with the experience of pain and evil in the world and then see what this experience can tell us about the concept of God. What we are told is that it is not merely us, but God, too, who experiences tragic suffering if not death (Bergson 1977, 261–262).

The very substance of closed society/religion is its static nature. The fact that its obligatory character is embedded in many institutions accounts for its pervasive and long-lasting influence. But movement need not be seen as the diminution of the static in the manner that women were traditionally seen as lesser men. The metaphysical issue of finding the proper balance between permanence and change, between being and becoming, is not unrelated to the major problems in political philosophy. Closed societies tend to be undemocratic in the extreme in that they rely on the assumption that political authority is embedded in an immobile hierarchy. By contrast, the democratic virtues are dialogical rather than monological in character and involve hearing as well as speaking. As a result, the impassive classical theistic God is ill-suited to people who defend democratic political ideals; many classical theists opposed to democracy themselves have defended over the centuries the claim that I am making here (Bergson 1977, 270–271, 281–283).

It is becoming *and* being, change *and* permanence that must be accounted for in the concept of God. Bergson refers to the "law of twofold frenzy," which involves the idea that if two contrasting (not contradictory) ideas that are part of the same overall reality are severed and pursued separately, disastrous consequences will follow. Unbridled worship of being, say, would dry up the obvious indeterminacy of the future. If God is to be found (and here even agnostics could agree), it is in time. Bergson is well aware of the fact that he is calling for a thoroughgoing philosophical and spiritual reform concerning the concept of God, but, as the word literally implies, re-form does not mean that one has to start from scratch in an ahistorical manner. He is even willing to suggest that, if the universe has an essential function, it is this gradual reform in the effort to make gods, so to speak (Bergson 1977, 296–299, 313, 317).

Bowker and Capetz do not even mention Bergson in their treatments of the concept of God; Armstrong mentions him only briefly, both because he continues the Plotinian effort to philosophically articulate the importance of mysticism and because of his own influence on Iqbal, as mentioned in an earlier part of the book (Armstrong 1993, 101, 364; Hartshorne 2000, 294, 297). This relative neglect is unfortunate given Bergson's important contributions to the concept of God, not least of which is his realization that the idea that the future will be detailed is not equivalent to the idea that it is already detailed in any mind, even a divine one. It is time (albeit everlasting time) that leads us to God, not the fiction that there really is no time in the eternal divine mind. Although the present can influence the future, especially the near future, it cannot precisely necessitate it in that the world grows in determinations and concreteness. Earlier moments, even in the divine life, are abstract in the sense that they contain their futures only in outline (Hartshorne 1941, 14, 140, 269, 286–287).

When process is seen as the ultimate mode of reality, being does not vanish but is rather seen as an abstract aspect of that which becomes. The present contains within itself the necessity that some future will follow it, but how it will be superseded can be understood only within certain limits of variation rather than in terms of precise details, as Bergson realized (Hartshorne 1953, 20, 98). Due to the influence of Bergson and others: "Never again will it be possible for generation after generation of leaders of thought calmly to take it for granted that God must be conceived as motionless in pure perfection and self-sufficiency, incapable of receiving anything from [humans], or of being served by [humans] in any real sense, incapable of anything that ever has been meant by love" (Hartshorne 1953, 159).

Thinking that the progressiveness of open religion in Bergson is primarily due to a sort of Rotarian optimism on his part would be a mistake. It is, rather, principally due to a reasonable tenet of process thinking that reality is cumulative in character. Reality is enriched at each moment as new events come into being, but there is no necessity that previous phases have to pass out of existence. The more comes from the less. That is, reality is creative rather than destructive in character if, as Bergson along with St. Augustine think, memory is at base psychological in character in that in memory there is direct possession or grasping of past events by present ones (what Whitehead calls "prehension"). God as omniscient (properly conceived) and omnibenevolent insures that no achieved value is lost in that such would be preserved in the ideal Memory. In this regard we can even say that the past is immortal. Human freedom, in particular, exhibits a sort of creativity that has a very real effect on the divine actuality (Hartshorne 2000, 85, 95, 228, 469, 501, 509; 1962, 174, 185).

The very existence of time indicates that there is indetermination in things; time *is* that indetermination (Bergson 1946, 109–125). This enables many people to come to terms with both their finitude and their orientation toward infinitude, whatever their religious beliefs or lack thereof. After all, once we die we will be dead all the time. Furthermore, at least some events endure in later events and if there is a God then all of them so endure. But the fact that events endure in the memory of those who live on is not to be confused with the idea that the future was mapped out in detail beforehand in that inexorable purpose would be at odds with individuality, self-activity, and temporal reality itself. But these things do exist, which is good because it is in our free creations, our deciding of the otherwise undecided, the forming of the previously inchoate, that our dignity lies (Hartshorne 1962, 15, 18, 206, 232).

If reality, even divine reality, is essentially creative process, with an aspect of futurity or partial indeterminacy built into it, then objective necessity is what all possibilities have in common, their "no matter what" aspect. Experience, both human and nonhuman, is necessarily preservative and creative in that it inherits causal influence from its past and is thrust into new moments that require some sort of decision, whether conscious or not, some cutting off of some possibilities so that others are enacted. In a sense, to be is to create and what it means to be creative is to be incompletely determined in advance by causal conditions and laws; to be creative is to make additions to the definiteness of reality. Hence, reality, even divine reality, is predictable, but only to the extent that it is not creative and is habitual. Since Bergson is a major figure in the tendency to define being in terms of becoming, rather than the reverse, he is understandably comfortable with the claim that becoming is reality itself. Furthermore, the Bergsonian view holds that determinism attempts to abstract away from the creativity of experience and reductionistic materialism tries to abstract away from experience itself (Hartshorne 1965, 43; 1970, xv, 3–4, 13, 26, 29).

Neoclassical or process theists commonly think that modal distinctions in logic are ultimately coincident with temporal ones. The actual is the past and the possible is the future; the present consists in the process by which what is possible becomes actual. On this view, a future actuality is a contradiction in terms, despite what classical theists might claim in their defense of divine omniscience with respect to future contingencies (or, to be true to classical theism, "contingencies"). From a slightly different angle, the distinction between time and (classical theistic) eternity is itself a temporal one because eternity is a negation of temporality; temporality is not a negation of eternity. Time is a positive aspect of the real with which we are all, in a way, familiar, as not only Bergson holds, but also, in different ways, St. Augustine and Kant.

The centrality of time is in evidence when we notice that possibilities are determinables rather than determinates, contra classical theism and pantheism (Hartshorne 1970, 61–65).

The endurance of the past through causal influence, memory, or perception (of the immediate past), as Bergson and others defend, need not be as strange as it may initially sound:

> Past events do not exist, or are not present, *in the same sense* as they once did or were, but they may yet be, in a genuine sense, still real and still present. The new event cannot be in the old, but the old can be in the new. A novel whole can contain parts which are not novel. Novelty is inclusive, for the combination of old and new is always new, not old. . . . Becoming is the creation of novel wholes with non-novel elements. Bergson . . . and Whitehead are among the few who have seen this. Hence their "cumulative" theory of process, or of process as "creative synthesis." (Hartshorne 1970, 89, also 92)

On the basis of this view there is clearly room for some prediction of the future, but such prediction has to be abstract and incomplete if the details regarding the future are hidden from us. This hiddenness is not necessarily due to any defect on our part, but to the asymmetrical nature of time itself (Hartshorne 1970, 105, 109, 118, 192, 211).

Bergson's memorable phrase that captures the prime difficulty with the classical theistic version of divine omniscience is the "spatialization of time." According to the classical theistic view, God already knows our future actions. We have seen that the problem with this view is that it assumes that our future actions are already in existence for God to know. The classical theist, however, thinks that God can see these actions as a spectator from a great height. This involves the aforementioned effort to slow down the flux of history, which can be analogized to a film, to a single frame, which can be analogized to a photograph. This is precisely the spatialization of time wherein the new "totality" that comes into existence at each moment is fixed in a single, all-encompassing view. But there just is no fixed totality in the dynamic world within which we live. That is, the cliché that "truth is timeless" is a piece of baseless dogmatism; we can make sense of it only in terms of the constant features of an ever-changing reality. Reality is more filmlike than it is photographlike (Hartshorne 1970, 135).

The temporal structure of the real is evidenced in experience itself, where what is present epistemically is later than the datum experienced, given the time lag due to the speed of light or auditory waves. One of the reasons why classical theists might be skittish about attributing this temporal structure to God is the assumption that temporal succession involves loss or perishing of that which happened before. But God as the ideal knower would not allow the fading of immediacy as events cease to be present events. The order of succession involves not perishing but rather a distinct difference between retrospection and prospection. Later events grasp earlier ones, but the converse is not true. In fact, all of our experience of concrete actuality is retrospective, like a view from the back of a train whose objects are already past when seen (Hartshorne 1972, 5, 83–85; 1983, 342).

Except perhaps for truths in mathematics, logic, and the most abstract claims in metaphysics, truths come into existence at a certain time, but then they exist everlastingly due to divine memory. As before, becoming is creative, not destructive. Preservation-plus-creation characterizes all concrete singulars from subatomic particles/waves to God, who is the preeminent example of preservation-creation (Hartshorne 1984b, 68, 76, 102). As Hartshorne states: "As held by . . . Bergson, . . . to create with divine wisdom and power is to inspire decision making in all others in such a way that the chances of harmony and intensity will justify the risks of evil" (Hartshorne 1984a, 56). The creative advance that is reality itself finds its ideal in God. In one sense the past creates the present by supplying its necessary conditions, but in another sense the present occasion makes itself, even in the divine case. The former claim warrants saying that memory is the key to the temporal structure of the universe, but we have seen that even "present" perception is, in a peculiar way, a type of impersonal memory (Hartshorne 1984a, 107, 149, 178, 201).

Hartshorne offers some surprising support for Bergson's positive account of closed religion. On this view closed religion is something of a biological necessity even for members of a species who exist with a sufficiently high level of intelligence. Religious sanctions partially take the place of instinct as an antidote against destructive behavior, some of which is actually driven by intelligence. Hence creative advance is not the whole story in that religion itself can be seen as a natural defensive reaction against the dissolvent and destructive uses of intelligence.

Many societies have existed without science and philosophy, but none have flourished without religion. The creativity that characterizes open religion grows out of the best in closed religion. The best of religion in the past is embraced within the present without being determined by it; the past provides necessary but not sufficient condition for the present, even in the divine case (Hartshorne 1984c, 85, 105; Bergson 1977, 122, 131, 140, 205). Bergson more than makes up for what is sometimes claimed to be the paucity of logical rigor in his thought with original insight, such as in his subtle treatment of the relationship between closed and open religion and between closed and open concepts of God (Hartshorne 1990, 120, 393; 2011, 121).

Hartshorne is like Bergson in being a critic of static Platonic forms, including Whitehead's eternal objects, as we will see in the following chapters (Hartshorne 1991, 662). The problem here is to avoid a return to what Hartshorne calls old-style metaphysics based on the idea of substance and the primacy of being over becoming. In Bergson's new style of metaphysics, there is some self-motion, freedom, or creativity (assuming that there is a family resemblance among these three terms) at all levels of nature (Hartshorne 2011, 3). A prime example of such self-motion, and one concerning which Bergson's analysis is famous, is memory. Hartshorne says the following about Bergson's treatment of memory:

> Remembering is one's present (indistinct) prehending, feeling, of one's own past prehending or feeling. True, the body is involved in this, but as Bergson brilliantly points out, since what is not effectively, *distinctly* remembered at a given moment is always incomparably more than what is effectively remembered, the function of the brain is to largely filter out the irrelevant aspects of our past experiences; otherwise we would be utterly overwhelmed and confused by the plethora of mnemonic material. If memory is, at least in part, present feeling of one's own past feelings and sensation is feeling of some feelings of one's bodily constituents, then in either case it is prehending as involving an emotional duality. *No feeling is solipsistic*, a subject merely aware of itself. All feeling, all sentience, is social, and involves some degree of sympathy in a literal sense. (Hartshorne 2011, 15)

The concept of God is given needed nuance as a result of this quotation in that the points made apply to divine memory as well as to human memory. However, the filtering process mentioned in the quotation would not apply in the divine case, where even the fall of a sparrow is remembered, as we have seen.

Bergson's snowball metaphor is also instructive. The rolling ball acquires new layers while retaining old ones. Or again, an adult can remember his or her childhood, but no child has a comparable awareness of the adult life that individual might lead. This processual, asymmetrical, and cumulative set of circumstances typifies all of reality, including the divine case. Every actual occasion in this processual, asymmetrical, and cumulative scheme has a certain degree of power, which means that if God is aware of all actual occasions, each of these has a certain minimal power over God's actuality if not God's existence. This partial power of the creatures over God, however, does not play into the hands of classical theists who think that any concept of God that omits omnipotence leaves God in an utterly power*less* state (Hartshorne 2011, 71, 116). As Hartshorne points out in an allusion to the neoclassical or process version of the argument from design or order that does not require omnipotence:

> Either the instances of creative action throughout the universe merely happen to fit together sufficiently to maintain a viable world system or there is a supreme or eminent form of creative decision-making that, because of its unique intrinsic worth, is accepted by all lesser forms sufficiently to enable it to set tolerable limits to the conflicts, frustrations, and aspects of disorder inherent in the idea of a multiplicity of free or self-determining actualities. Order is either an affair of each entity adapting to the many others or it is an affair of each entity adapting, not only to the many others, but to one supreme entity, the same for all, and thus able to give guidance to all. (Hartshorne 2011, 135)

One of the most important tasks in the effort to find a defensible concept of God is to calibrate an idea of divine power that can be seen in equilibrium with all of the relevant factors that must be balanced: the order of nature, creaturely power, the presence of evil, and so on. Bergson himself refers to the need for "equilibrium on a higher level" in this regard. None of the nuanced problems involved here are solved by appeal to divine omnipotence. Bergson is correct to wonder what this word could possibly mean if every concrete singular has some power of its own. It is a pseudo-idea in that we can vocalize the word "omnipotence," but we cannot understand what it could possibly mean, given the multitude of dynamic centers of power in the universe. Furthermore, because belief in divine omnipotence has historically gone hand-in-glove with belief in creation *ex nihilo*, it is noteworthy that Bergson has offered one of the most detailed and insightful analyses of this concept, the conclusion of which is that the very idea of absolute nothingness makes no more sense than a square circle (Bergson 1977, 229, 251, 261).

Bergson is very much compatible with the comparable idea in Plato's *Sophist* that whereas relative nonbeing makes sense, absolute nonbeing does not. A basketball does not have the sort of existence that a baseball has and hence can be said to be "nothing like" a baseball. But each of these exists in some manner. Or again, when a creative action is taken one is bringing something into existence that did not exist before, but this is hardly creation out of absolutely nothing in that each of these absences is built on a certain sort of presence. The root of the difficulty lies in imagining the nonexistence of this or that thing, which leads to imagining the nonexistence of a whole class of things, which in turn leads to the erroneous conclusion that this imaginative process could go on indefinitely and that one could really imagine the nonexistence of everything. But to say that "it" (that is, everything) does not exist is, once again, to engage a sort of absence that is really a presence because the "absolute nothingness" in question would actually be something. To talk about "it" is to talk about somethingness rather than supposed absolute nothingness. The admirable classical theistic attempt to exalt God, which in itself is understandable, is not aided by attributing omnipotence to God in that such an effort both leads to logical contradictions and creates the nastiest version of the theodicy problem. However, given the general order of the world the overall problem is not easily solved by running to the other extreme by claiming that God is utterly powerless, or, what amounts to the same, claiming that there is no God (Bergson 1911, 273–298).

24
Alfred North Whitehead
(1861–1947)

Up to *Process and Reality*

This chapter explicates Whitehead's concept of God as it developed up until the time of his magnum opus, *Process and Reality*. The following chapter assesses his concept of God and explores how it developed in works after *Process and Reality*.

Whitehead was a world renowned mathematician at Cambridge University and the University of London before he wrote his famous philosophical works at Harvard in his sixties and seventies. But even before he came to Harvard he was clear that some of the more fantastic parts of Plato's philosophy were more valuable than Aristotle's patient scientific analyses. This judgment, along with Whitehead's observation that nothing in thought is completely new, gives a relatively early indication of where his concept of God might go. In his 1920 book *The Concept of Nature* Whitehead has conflicting views of metaphysics. On the one hand, he thinks that any importation of metaphysics into philosophy of science is illegitimate. But perhaps this view is not as negative as it sounds initially in that by "metaphysics" here he means any explanation that purports to go "beyond nature." This gives us a clue regarding Whitehead's later concept of God in that it will not be a supernatural deity in the classical theistic sense, but will have to be consistent with a naturalistic view of the world. On the other hand, Whitehead whimsically notes that the only crime that has never been imputed to the English Parliament is metaphysical subtlety. That is, there is an honorific place for metaphysics as long as it is not supernatural in character and as long as it is sufficiently nuanced. We will see that from a Whiteheadian viewpoint one of the biggest problems with classical theism is that it is too simple. Whitehead's motto, however, is indeed to seek simplicity, but then to mistrust it (Whitehead [1920] 2004, 18, 26, 28, 120, 163).

On Whitehead's view, the world is not composed of bits of stuff or substances, but rather processes and relations. Furthermore, a thoroughly relational view of reality (including divine reality) works against the bifurcation of nature into the material and the extra-material in that these two realms are either unrelated or insufficiently related to each other. In fact, Whitehead thinks of the bifurcation of nature as "vicious," presumably because it inevitably leads to the trivialization, marginalization, or elimination of that which the "extra-material" or "supernatural" is pointing toward: truth, goodness, and beauty. Nature is to be conceived as a relational whole, not as bifurcated into unrelated (or at least insufficiently related) parts. In addition, the relations that characterize nature cannot be wholly negative. Although the events that constitute nature do possess the quality of exclusion (that is, relative nonbeing), this quality cannot be absolutized without contradiction (that is, absolute nonbeing is impossible), a view that has the aforementioned consequences that work against creation *ex nihilo* and the concept of divine omnipotence that lies behind it (Whitehead [1920] 2004, 41, 168, 185–187, 194; 1922, 62).

Another relatively early indication of the later direction Whitehead would take regarding the concept of God comes in *The Aims of Education*, a collection of early essays. Here Whitehead makes clear that the essence of education is that it be religious in character, which for Whitehead means that it give to students some reticulative sense, both spatially and temporally, of how big things are such that an attitude of reverence is inculcated into students. An example he cites is that of a science teacher who sends a student to a telescope to look at the stars and the student ends up with an aperture into the glory of the heavens. In this example ordinary pedagogical experience is transfigured. I mention these passages to counteract in advance the objection that Whitehead's concept of God lacks "size" or "heft." Quite the contrary. Or again, to consider an example from the moral sphere, Whitehead thinks that moral education should avoid moral*ism* like the plague. The vitality of morality and religion, indeed the vitality of the concept of God, should survive the deadening influence of systems of morality and organized religious institutions. In Bersonian terms, moral and religious education should be more open than closed (Whitehead [1929] 1967, 14, 33, 39; also see Loomer 2013).

The first explicit version of Whitehead's concept of God is found in the chapter "God" in his 1925 classic *Science and the Modern World*. It is presented in direct contrast to Aristotle's Prime Mover. Despite his opposition to Aristotle's concept of God, Whitehead admires the fact that Aristotle was "entirely dispassionate" and was perhaps the last European philosopher to be so for many centuries. That is, Aristotle ends up with his Unmoved Mover deity solely as a result of his metaphysics of being over becoming, of actuality over potentiality, and so on, and not as a result of pressure from, or a reaction against, religious institutions. Later Jewish, Christian, and Muslim thinkers had a harder time of it. The irony is that Aristotle's influence on thinkers in the Abrahamic religions was so strong that it very often prevented them from taking seriously the data of religious experience from their own traditions that was not under the control of ecclesiastical authority. As we have seen, Aristotle's God (or gods) is not really available for religious purposes. But at least Aristotle was consistent in holding that deity did not know or care for creatures, was not affected by them, and so on (Whitehead [1925] 1967, 173–174).

In place of Aristotle's God as Prime Mover Whitehead introduces his concept of God as a principle of concretion. What does this mean? Whitehead's argument goes as follows: Either there is a structure to the process of the world or there is no such structure. However, our experience contradicts the thesis that there is no structure to the process of the world. Therefore, there is a structure to the process of the world. But there can be a structure to the process of the world only if someone or something provides a ground for this structure, some principle of limit applied to limitless possibility. And this is what Whitehead in *Science and the Modern World* calls "God" or the "principle of concretion" (Whitehead [1925] 1967, 174–179).

As a mathematician Whitehead has a robust sense of infinite possibilities that lie before us. The aforementioned structure to the process of the world refers to the fact that each actual occasion or experience or event that occurs imposes a limitation on the unfathomable possibilities regarding what could have happened. This occurs rather than that; and it occurs now rather than earlier or later. But there are no isolated occasions in that actual occasions or events are thoroughly social and together in a sort of unity as they interact with each other. The structure of the world in process includes the influence of the past on the present occasion, but never the complete determination of the present by the past. This is due to the fact that some sort of indetermination is inherently connected to futurity. The future determinables that are rendered determinate in the present of some actual occasion or event are so rendered abruptly when something happens. Furthermore, the structure to the world in process prohibits both anticipation of the past and memory of the future; one cannot undo what has been done. Or, in different terms, retrospection is quite different from prospection in the asymmetrically structured world in which we live. The above describes the ubiquitous metaphysical character to all actual occasions or events.

Whitehead thinks that the only way to understand the actual course of events is on the assumption of an antecedent limitation composed of certain conditions: the future as the realm of possibility, the past as the realm of actuality, the present as the process by which future determinables are made determinate, the asymmetrical character of time, the profound difference between retrospection and prospection, and so forth. These conditions are what Whitehead means by a principle of limitation or a principle of concretion. Ironically no reason can be given for this principle of limitation in that it is precisely this principle that makes possible the giving of reasons. However, although there is a metaphysical need for a principle of determination, there can be no metaphysical reason for what is determined. This comes very close to Hartshorne's distinction between divine existence and divine actuality; the former is necessary, but not the latter. We can know abstractly that there has to be a principle of limitation, but if we learn anything else about God it can only be as a result of particular experiences. The various religions of the world have interpreted these particular experiences in various ways.

Whitehead is skittish in *Science and the Modern World* about paying any more compliments to God other than saying that God is the principle of limitation, the provider of structure for the process of events. For example, if we said, a la classical theism, that God is also pure omnipotent activity, then God would become responsible for all of the evil in the world as well as for the good. Although how Whitehead's concept of God is any more personal than the Aristotle-influenced God of classical theism is still not clear at this stage in his career, it is clear that he is very much aware of the dangers involved in paying God metaphysical compliments of a classical theistic sort that eventually backfire (once again, see Whitehead [1925] 1967, 174–179).

God as a principle of limitation is related to Whitehead's desire to have science and religion reach some sort of rapprochement. Just as the use of large-scale maps has a tendency to diffuse tense situations among contending states, Whitehead thinks using a wide angle lens to view the relationship between science and religion is helpful. Confusing present conflicts with essential reality is a mistake. Although there has always been a tension between science and religion, both disciplines have always been in a state of continual development. Some religious believers have difficulty understanding the earliest Christians' general belief that the world was going to come to an end in their very lifetimes. But because science changes more quickly than religion, there is an unfortunate tendency to think that the latter is standing still, a static quality that plays into the hands of the classical theistic view of the divine nature itself as strictly static. Both disciplines need a way of fairly and rationally adjudicating disputes, such as when Newton's theory that a beam of light consists in a stream of minute particles and Huygens' theory that light consists in minute waves were synthesized. The contradiction between the two was only apparent in that one large group of phenomena can be explained only on the wave theory and another large group of phenomena can be explained only on the corpuscular theory (Whitehead [1925] 1967, 181–184).

A clash of doctrines, Whitehead notes, is not a disaster, but an opportunity, such as when divine fixity and divine change clash. A contradiction is, in fact, a sign of defeat, but a clash of contrasting doctrines can be the first step in intellectual progress. Given the gradual decline of religious influence, especially in Europe, but also in many other parts of the world, religion would be well served to find a way to higher ground and to ameliorate its most significant controversies. Here religious thinkers could learn from science in that Darwin's and Einstein's advances over their predecessors were not interpreted as signs of defeat for science, but as intellectual accomplishments. Whitehead puts the point succinctly: "Religion will not regain its old power until it can face change in the same spirit as does science" (Whitehead [1925] 1967, 189, also 185–188).

No longer can religion afford to express itself in misogynistic or environmentally rapacious terms that were better suited to bygone times. The difficulties here go right to the essence of the classical theistic concept of God, which strikes interpreters from many traditions, including Whitehead, as pointing toward a wrathful, male tyrant or toward an arbitrary tyrant who lies behind the unknown forces of nature. This view of God is obviously losing its hold on the imaginations of intelligent people. We can learn from science to meet apprehension with a critical analysis of the causes and conditions of the malady. This book attempts to do precisely this regarding the classical theistic view, which relies on a concept of coercive power. In one of his more moving and thought-provoking definitions of religion, and one that helps us understand what he means by God as a principle of limitation or concretion, Whitehead says the following: "Religion is the vision of something which stands beyond, behind, and within the passing flux of immediate things; something which is real, and yet waiting to be realized; something which is a remote possibility, and yet the greatest of present facts; something that gives meaning to all that passes, and yet eludes apprehension; something whose possession is the final good, and yet is beyond all reach; something which is the ultimate ideal, and the hopeless quest. The immediate reaction of human nature to the religious vision is worship" (Whitehead [1925] 1967, 192). Without a religious vision, without a concept of God, he thinks, human experience is boundless and amorphous, it is "a bagatelle of transient experience" (Whitehead [1925] 1967, 192). The power of God in this view is precisely the worship that such a God inspires in others; and the order found in the process of the world, on this view, is not so much imposed on the world as it is a persuasive and harmonious adjustment of the complex detail that is nature.

The classical theistic view in its Augustinian version (which informs Calvinist versions of Protestantism and Jansenist versions of Catholicism) leaves human beings helpless in the face of an expansive version of divine omniscience with respect to the future; this theological determinism is at least compatible with, and perhaps fuels, scientific determinism. Nothing as daring as determinism is intended in Whitehead's concept of God as providing the conditions for the enduring stability of nature, within which is a significant amount of room for creaturely freedom; indeed, the whole point to seeing God as a principle of limitation is to provide some very wide limits within which creaturely freedom can flourish, just as the banks of a river provide limits within which are infinite possibilities for each water molecule. The heavens do not lose the glory of God on this Whiteheadian view as they do in a bifurcated nature of the Cartesian variety, wherein water molecules, animals, and even human bodies are mechanized and subject to Augustinian/scientific determinism (White-head [1925] 1967, 75, 92, 195).

In Whitehead's 1926 book *Religion in the Making* we find another of his definitions of religion, this time in terms of religion as what one does with one's solitariness. Of course much depends on the word "does" in this definition. Whitehead makes clear that the highest reaches of religion involve a concept of God wherein one of the things one can do with one's solitariness is come to the realization that one is not alone, that God is always a "Companion," a word derived from the Latin for someone with whom one can eat bread. Here Whitehead clearly has an intimate, personal God in mind, in the event that this was in doubt as a result of his book from the previous year. Like Bergson, Whitehead traces the history of religion back to the very beginning of human beings on this planet, moving from a ritualistic stage of religion that involved certain emotions and beliefs and that eventually resulted in a more rational approach to religion that involved a concept of God that could be analyzed in terms of internal consistency, compatibility with other concepts that are required in some discipline or other, adequacy with respect to what we know about temporal asymmetry and the presence of evil in the world, and so on. A rationalized version of religion has flourished all over Europe and Asia for the past several thousand years, but especially in the past twenty-five centuries in Europe (Whitehead [1926] 1996, 13–30).

Whitehead's rational religion has a family resemblance to Bergson's open religion. In the former, rituals and beliefs have to be reorganized in that they have to conform not only to the experiences of life but also to the intellectual demands of metaphysical thinking where categories like being and becoming are contrasted. Religious rituals and beliefs can be gradually changed in light of an improved concept of God, on this view. The effort the ancient Greeks initiated, in particular, to partake in an intense struggle to rationalize closed religion continues to this very day. Once again reminiscent of Bergson, Whitehead characterizes religious history in the following terms: "History, down to the present day, is a melancholy record of the horrors which can attend religion: human sacrifice, and in particular the slaughter of children, cannibalism, sensual orgies, abject superstition, hatred as between races, the maintenance of degrading customs, hysteria, bigotry, can all be laid at its charge. Religion is the last refuge of human savagery. . . . [However,] religion can be, as has been, the main instrument for progress" (White-head [1926] 1996, 37–38, also 31–36).

And in the following remarkable quotation Whitehead indicates how the transition from ritual religion to rational religion (or from closed religion to open religion) also signals a shift from reliance on orthopraxy or orthodoxy to a concentration on perfect being philosophy of religion or perfect being theology: "The new . . . concept of the goodness of God replaces the older emphasis on the will of God. In a communal religion you study the will of God in order that [God] may preserve you; in a purified religion, rationalized under the influence of the world-concept, you study [God's] goodness in order to be like [God]. It is the difference between the enemy you conciliate and the companion whom you imitate" (Whitehead [1926] 1996, 41). Among the concepts of God that are debated in rational religion, Whitehead sees three as the most plausible candidates.

First, there is the concept of one God whose existence and every other aspect is absolute and underivative. This is the concept of an utterly transcendent God that underlies what I have labeled classical theism, although this God is also inconsistently alleged to be personal and decrees the derivative existence of what we call the actual world. Second, there is the extremely immanent concept of an impersonal cosmic order. This concept points not toward a world obeying an imposed rule, but a cosmic self-ordering of the world. And third, there is another concept of a personal God, which shares many of the features of the first concept, except that the actual world is part of the divine reality itself. Here the actual world is a phase within the complete divine reality (Whitehead [1926] 1996, 68–69).

Whitehead confuses matters a bit in his terminology. The least amount of confusion results, I think, if the second view is called "pantheism" and the third view is called "panentheism." The second and third views in a way invert each other in that in the second view when we speak about God we say something about the world, whereas in the third view when we speak about the world we say something about God. But the first and second views are those most opposed to each other, with the first view emphasizing divine transcendence and the second view emphasizing divine immanence. As Whitehead sees things, what is most problematic about classical theism is that it is completely outside of metaphysical rationalization; hence we should be wary of overly aggressive attempts at apophatic theology that are attempts to save it. That is, muscular versions of apophaticism actually disguise the defects in classical theism and ought to be replaced with a concept of God that does not rely to such a great extent on apophatic orgies. A God who is alleged to be wholly transcendent (outside of time altogether, pure being, pure activity with no passivity, and so forth) cannot be the conclusion to any intellectual effort that starts with features of the actual world such as time, motion, receptivity, and becoming. Such an effort would be doomed to failure from the start (Whitehead [1926] 1996, 69–71).

Whitehead is wise to note that Christianity (as well as the other Abrahamic religions) is not necessarily tied to what I call classical theism. The view of God as a loving parent and as a dynamic *logos*, which are crucial to the overall Christian message, are not captured well, if at all, in classical theism. Furthermore, we find a strong strand of divine immanence as well as of transcendence in the Christian scriptures. His hope is to move Christian and other thinkers away from the first two concepts and toward the third one. Contemporary individuals have largely lost God, who is not likely to be refound on a classical theistic basis. Also problematic is that the overall message of Christianity, based on love, was, due to the influence of classical theism, transformed into a message based on fear. This fear is accentuated due to a belief in divine omnipotence, which, as Whitehead sees things, shipwrecks classical theism on the rock of the theodicy problem (Whitehead [1926] 1996, 72–77).

Rational religion requires a metaphysical backing, with "metaphysics" here referring to the discipline that seeks to discover the general ideas that are indispensably relevant to all that happens. However, the universe is through and through interdependent such that, although metaphysics contributes something to religion, religious experience contributes something to philosophical theorizing about the concept of God. Or again, individuality or solitariness, on the one hand, and community, on the other, are both needed: "The world is a scene of solitariness in community. The individuality of entities is just as important as their community. The topic of religion is individuality in community" (Whitehead [1926] 1996, 88).

Among the individuals Whitehead has in mind is the divine individual and the community he has in mind is an all-inclusive universe that involves God. Hence he unfortunately at times refers to God in

Religion in the Making as a nontemporal actual entity, but a charitable (but by no means noncontroversial) interpretation of his view is that only God's existence (or, to use the later language of *Process and Reality*, God's primordial nature), in a way, escapes from the temporal flux in that if God always exists, God's existence can be seen as permanent and as exhibiting an unchanged consistency of character. But God's actuality (or, to use the language of *Process and Reality*, God's consequent nature) is eminently changing and subject to the vicissitudes of creaturely suffering (Whitehead [1926] 1996, 90–99, 112).

On Whitehead's (panpsychist or panexperientialist) view, every actual occasion has value of some sort and God's purpose is to enhance this value to the extent possible and to bring the various values in the world into as much harmony as possible. In fact, God can be seen as the ideal harmony of the world to the extent that such is realized. This project of valuation is thoroughly communal in the sense that no being is a substance on the traditional definition of "substance" as something that requires nothing else in order to exist. Not even God is a substance on this definition in that, although God does not need any particular creatures, some existents other than God are required in order for God to be omnibenevolent. The important thing for a philosopher of religion or a theologian is to bring the analytic force of one's concept of God into contact with religious experience. Both are needed. To paraphrase Kant, a concept of God without religious experience is empty, but religious experience without a concept of God is blind (Whitehead [1926] 1996, 100–120).

The concept of God is developed as a result of our ordinary capacities as human beings, but only when they operate at their highest pitch of discipline. That is, to take religious experience seriously is not to give a carte blanche to the dark recesses of abnormal psychology. Of course there is a wide range of capacities even within the normal human range such that some are more able than others to appreciate either love or the permanent aspect of the universe. These are the people who bring about progress in religion, a progress that is ultimately rooted in progress regarding the concept of God. Whitehead treads a fine line here: Although progress in religion via progress concerning the concept of God is brought about by people whose abilities are within the normal human range, this does not mean that their originality occurs by way of continuous and uniform development. Rather, a spark of insight, or a flash of intuition when a logical contradiction is noticed, occurs all at once and at the oddest moments. Although there is obviously no such thing as absolute solitariness, these sparks and flashes nonetheless occur to solitary individuals: Socrates in Athens, Whitehead in Ramsgate, Hartshorne in Pennsylvania. But what is learned in secret can only be verified and enjoyed in community (Whitehead [1926] 1996, 123–137).

As before, Whitehead wants to avoid two extremes regarding the concept of God: God as omnipotent and who creates the world *ex nihilo* (classical theism) and God as the impersonal order of the universe (properly called pantheism). It is not correct to claim (as in classical theism) that in all respects God is infinite in that, at the very least, God is limited by omnibenevolence. And when God decides something there is as a result some limitation in the divine nature. But these limitations do not detract from God's persuasive power to function as a mirror that discloses to every creature its own potential greatness in terms of the ideals to which it could or should aspire. In this regard God is the binding element that keeps the world in some sort of harmony (Whitehead [1926] 1996, 150–160).

Whitehead distinguishes between two sorts of reason, that of Plato and that of Ulysses (Odysseus). The latter sort is shared with the foxes and involves a sort of calculative endeavor—indeed it even involves cunning—and it is hence the reason of Plato that is involved in thinking through carefully the concept of God. As Whitehead puts the point metaphorically, "Ulysses has no use for Plato, and the bones of his companions are strewn on many a reef and many an isle" (Whitehead [1929] 1958, 12, also 10–11, 23). The point is for us to energetically keep working on the concept of God in a Platonic vein until we get things right; in this regard the real enemy of reason is not irrationality, but fatigue.

The most developed and magisterial expression of Whitehead's concept of God is found in his 1929 magnum opus *Process and Reality: An Essay in Cosmology*. Here the concept of God is developed within the context of a speculative philosophy that involves both rationalist elements, such as logicality and internal coherence, and empiricist elements, such as applicability and adequacy to practical experience. In both cases Whitehead thinks that in order to move forward there is a preliminary need to recur to pre-Kantian modes of thought, especially to the sort of cosmology found in Plato's *Timaeus* because of the

God who is found there. In a famous metaphor that can apply to his discovery of a defensible concept of God, Whitehead says the following: "The true method of discovery is like the flight of an aeroplane. It starts from the ground of particular observation; it makes a flight in the thin air of imaginative generalization; and it again lands for renewed observation rendered acute by rational interpretation" (Whitehead [1929] 1978, 5, also xi, xiv, 3). That is, the synoptic vision encouraged by a concept of God need not be at odds with the concrete "data" of practical experience, whether religious or otherwise. Furthermore, the thesis of this book is that classical theism is nothing short of incoherent, especially in its Cartesian formulation in terms of a bifurcated world wherein matter and mind never really meet.

The main error in philosophy is overstatement, according to Whitehead; hence regarding the concept of God we should be seeking a view that does not overstate the case for either divine permanence or divine change. If there is to be progress in philosophy of religion or theology, on this view, there has to be a transcendence of what is supposedly obvious regarding the classical theistic concept of God, while nonetheless preserving the important half-truths found in that tradition. In addition to the permanent primordial nature of God, however, there is the ever-changing consequent nature of God, which is introduced very early in *Process and Reality*, although this aspect of the concept of God is not treated in detail until the end of the book in part 5 (Whitehead [1929] 1978, 7–12).

Whitehead's concept of God as a principle of limitation has become clearer. Not all limitations on freedom are negative. In fact, "limit" can be seen as a positive word when used in a way that makes freedom possible. A scheme of limitation is needed so that among the infinite possibilities regarding the future some of them may be chosen concretely. A free agent can choose among alternatives, but he or she cannot establish the scheme of possibilities itself or the ordering of the possibilities into some sort of intelligible pattern. Once Whitehead started describing God in personal terms, and not merely as a principle, it became clearer that what he had in mind was a persuasive agency in the world that limits pure potentiality in such a way that concrete freedom becomes a very real possibility. "Limit" and "possibility" are correlative terms, as are "necessity" and "freedom," such that these pairs further articulate the dipolar logic of neoclassical or process theism. We are conditioned by the ordered structure of things, but we are not determined. Without some sort of limit or positive finitude (what the Greeks called *peras*) we would be confronted with a formless chaos (the Greek *apeiron*).

The ultimate metaphysical principle in Whitehead is the advance from disjunction to conjunction: The many influences on an actual occasion are prehended and then a creative addition is made to them, however slight. As Whitehead puts the point, the many become one and are then increased by one. Because of the consequent nature of God, the divine is not an exception to this metaphysical principle. For Whitehead, everything that exists has to be somewhere and here "somewhere" refers to some actuality. Regarding abstract objects like "threeness" and "goodness" (which Whitehead unfortunately calls "eternal objects" in that "everlasting objects" would have been more consistent with a thoroughly processual view of the world), these things exist in the mind of God as primordial. That is, the primordial nature of God is the everlasting aspect of God that is abstracted from God's commerce with particulars. Any instance of experience is dipolar in the sense that it has a physical pole and a mental pole. This is true in divine experience as well as in creaturely experience. In the divine case the mental pole refers to the primordial nature of God in the divine interaction with abstract possibilities, whereas the physical pole refers to the consequent nature of God in the divine interaction with concrete reality (Whitehead [1929] 1978, 21, 34, 36, 46).

Whitehead finds this sort of dipolarity in Plato, which is the occasion for what is perhaps the most famous quotation in Whitehead: "The safest general characterization of the European philosophical tradition is that it consists in a series of footnotes to Plato" (Whitehead [1929] 1978, 39). Furthermore, if we had to render Plato's general point of view intelligible, with the least changes added that are made necessary by 2,500 years of human history, it would be something like process philosophy (what Whitehead calls "philosophy of organism"), including the process or neoclassical concept of God. What is most enduring in Plato's cosmology, on Whitehead's view as informed by A. E. Taylor, is that over and above any human or divine law there is a factor of brute fact or the simply given, a surd or irrational element that Plato identifies with necessity (*anangke*). Because of this element Whitehead criticizes the idea of divine omnipotence, which, in turn, enables him to develop a theodicy that is believable, in contrast, say, to Leibniz's "audacious fudge" in terms of this allegedly being the best of all possible worlds. Nonetheless there is a *universe*, with God seen as that aspect of the universe that is its self-creative unity (Whitehead [1929] 1978, 42, 47).

Regarding Whitehead's critique of omnipotence, ridiculing this critique by saying that his God is limited in the pejorative sense of the term makes no sense in that this seems to presuppose that the concept of unlimited power is coherent. If to be *is* to have power, then no being, not even a divine one, could have unlimited power. Furthermore, if variety and multiple freedoms are good things, then the greater the variety and the more efficacious the freedom bring about a world in which intense discord is possible along with immense goodness. The avoidance of all possibility for discord would yield the evil of triviality.

Despite the plurality of agency in the world, with each agent exerting its own power, however slight, Whitehead clearly notices the solidarity of the world. Although Whitehead avoids the Platonic language of the World Soul with respect to God, he nonetheless affirms the idea that the entire actual world is a community of self-moving occasions of experience. There is a oneness to the universe, albeit a oneness that is always new because it is always in flux, and hence Whitehead's view is not "totalizing" in the pejorative sense of the term. Nonetheless many human beings (often called "mystics") experience themselves as having an individuality that merges into the whole of things. God is the agent of novelty in this community by providing ideals specific to each individual regarding how to maximize the scope and intensity of that individual's experience in its contribution to the beauty of the whole. To say that God is *primordial* is not to make God an exception to metaphysical principles, rather it is to suggest both that God's existence is everlasting and precedes the existence of any particular occasion of nondivine experience and that God always apprehends abstract objects. To say that God is *consequent* is to acknowledge that God grasps in time the nondivine occasions of experience found in the evolving world. And to say that God is *superject* is to claim that once God receives influence from the creatures in the consequent nature, that God's own reception and appraisal of this influence is then available, in turn, for creaturely reception and appraisal (Whitehead [1929] 1978, 56, 65–67, 71, 75, 87–88, 228, 231–232, 251; [1954] 2001, 160).

Whitehead is quite clear that of the two dominant statements of cosmological theory in the history of Western thought, Plato's *Timaeus* and Newton's *Scholium*, it is an updated version of the former that should be defended. This judgment is ironic for a few reasons. The scientific details of Plato's work now might seem foolish, but what it lacks in superficial detail it makes up for in terms of philosophic depth. That is, if it is read as an allegory, Plato's view delivers a profound truth. Whereas Newton's work is, in part, accurate regarding certain scientific details, it is philosophically inadequate. For Newton, nature is merely and completely there, externally designed and obedient to a supernatural agent. This is essentially a classical theistic worldview that, as Hume realized, could not withstand criticism. Even from a scientific perspective the Newtonian cosmology has problems. For example, Newton would have been shocked by contemporary quantum theory and by the dissolution of quanta into vibrations; Plato would have expected these. It is also in Plato's favor that the creation of the present cosmic epoch in the *Timaeus* is traced back to an aboriginal disorder that is persuaded into order by God; it is not the creation of matter itself, but of a certain type of order. This is in contrast to the Newtonian version of classical theism, wherein an omnipotent God creates the world out of absolute nothingness (Whitehead [1929] 1978, 93–96).

If the primordial aspect of God were viewed in isolation from the entirety of the divine life, it could be seen as unmoved; the everlasting existence of God in itself is not what is moved by the nondivine sufferings in the world, rather it is divine actuality that is so moved. This is the consequent aspect of God in which divine tenderness is directed toward each actual occasion as it arises. Because of the unintelligibility of unlimited power or divine omnipotence, absolute order in the world is impossible, but because of God's ideal power and love pure chaos is equally unintelligible and impossible. As in some of Whitehead's earlier works, it is as a result of God's activity in the world that there can be physical law. This book's focus on the concept of God is admittedly a narrow one in the sense that it is part of a more general category of religious feeling, most notably the feeling that each actual occasion has, whether explicitly or implicitly, of being lured forward in an intelligible way. Modifying agency is found throughout nature, but God is the supreme instance of such mentality (Whitehead [1929] 1978, 105, 111, 207, 283, 325).

Neoclassical or process theism is part of a tradition that goes back to Heraclitus in ancient Greece and to the Hebrew scriptures in trying to understand the cliché that all things flow. But there is also a rival notion going back to Parmenides that emphasizes permanence. White-head aims to do justice to both of these intuitions, which individually are incomplete. Although Plato is usually interpreted as a philosopher of permanence who denigrates becoming, an interpretation that has many texts in Plato in its favor, I have argued earlier that this is only part of the very complex Platonic story. Whitehead's own attempt to update Plato concentrates on two types of fluency in the world: the coming to be of an individual occasion of experience (which White-head called "concrescence") and the succession of one experience by another (called "transition"). These processes can be referred to as microscopic and macroscopic, respectively. The common line of inher-itance throughout the transitions among experiences is an important part of the story in Whitehead, making it possible to claim that an adequate response to the debate between Heraclitus and Parmenides can be forged (Whitehead [1929] 1978, 208–210, 214).

Reality, in general, is a creative advance into novelty, on White-head's view, which has as one of its results the idea that every actuality, including God but not only God, is characterized by a certain sort of transcendence of the past and of causal influence. The static morpho-logical universe of Newton, heavily informed by the tradition of classical theism, is at odds with this processual view. Although God supplies each occasion of experience with its subjective aim, thus making God the aboriginal and preeminent case of creativity, God's power is persuasive rather than coercive. This is why using the above language of partial transcendence is appropriate even in nondivine cases. This partial transcendence, however, involves cooperation with God in that without the ordering of, and presentation of, ideals by God, nothing significantly new would happen (Whitehead [1929] 1978, 222, 225, 247).

Thinking that abstract concepts or ideals are items in the divine psyche makes sense for Whitehead. This conflicts with the often-held view that Platonic forms are independent even of God (the extradeical view). However, we have seen that if "X is independent of Y" has a sharp logical meaning, it must be that X could exist even if Y did not, which implies that Y is contingent. If X stands for abstract concepts and Y for God, then the nonexistence of God is being taken as possible. But this "possibility" conflicts with the ontological argument and other argu-ments for the existence of God. In short, if abstract truths and God are both everlasting, then independence has no clear meaning between everlasting things. That is, God does not create ideals, but arranges them and lures us in the appropriate way toward them. Whitehead is a defender of the intradeical view that suggests that the most abstract ideals are items in divine psychical process (Whitehead [1929] 1978, 257).

Whitehead's concept of God receives its finest treatment in part 5 of *Process and Reality*. In a mere fourteen pages he gives quintessential expression to the neoclassical or process theistic view. Here he attempts to avoid what he takes to be the chief danger in philosophy: narrowness in the selection of evidence. Classical theists, in particular, fall victim to this danger in their adoption of divine permanence and activity, but at the expense of divine fluency and receptivity. Sheer contempt for classical theism, however, would indicate a certain sort of blindness in that permanence does characterize divine existence if not divine actuality. That is, the intellectual achievement of classical theism is immense as far as it goes. But there is also a heroic achievement found in those who try to replace the classical theistic view with something better. Philosophy does not have the luxury to ignore the multifariousness of the world (Whitehead [1929] 1978, 337–338).

"Permanence can be snatched only out of flux," however, such that we are required to avoid the classical theistic temptation to sever these two elements. In this regard Whitehead appeals to the Anglican hymn that encourages us to "Abide with me; / Fast falls the eventide." The second part points to the inevitable flux, whereas the former points to the fact that something permanent abides in the midst of the flux. Because God abides, and does so with perfect memory, time need not be seen as perpetual perishing (or at least perpetual perishing need not be seen as the last word), but as the moving image of that which endures. Being and becoming, as it were, are ideal contrasts. Another way to put the point is to say that progress regarding the concept of God will require both that order be preserved amid change and that change be permitted amid order. Although permanence is necessary, it is not sufficient; endurance entering upon novelty is required. A measure of the goodness of religious institutions is the degree to which they welcome in a friendly way the faint light of the dawn of a new age. Admittedly, the concept of God receives significantly from the past, but if it is to live, it can do so only in the present (Whitehead [1929] 1978, 209, 338–339).

A defensible concept of God has to deal adequately with the tension between the craving for novelty and the haunting terror of the loss of the past. For this reason I think that the label "neoclassical" theism is superior to the more popular label "process" theism in that the former encapsulates both poles in this tension. Whitehead even goes so far as to say that the ultimate evil in the temporal world is not any particular travesty, but the general problem that the past fades and that which is good might be lost. In particular, the fear that has driven the present book is that the best insights of Plato as they relate to the concept of God as dynamic might be either lost or reduced to triviality in contrast to the things he has to say that are positive regarding the importance of formal permanence (Whitehead [1929] 1978, 340–341).

We should not expect simple answers to very large questions. The question regarding which concept of God is the best one has received some simple answers that the present book has tried to render more complex and adequate to the subject matter in question. One simplification was the Aristotelian one whereby God was seen as an unmoved mover, instead of as the most and best moved mover. Another simplification was the modeling of God in the image of an imperial ruler, concerning which Whitehead observes that "the Church gave unto God the attributes which belonged exclusively to Caesar" (Whitehead [1929] 1978, 342). This attribution is nothing less than idolatrous on the Whiteheadian view. By contrast, Whitehead offers a concept of God that relies heavily on the Jewish and Galilean origin of Christianity found in the figure of Jesus. This alternative concept of God "dwells upon the tender elements of the world, which slowly and in quietness operate by love; and it finds purpose in the present immediacy of a kingdom not of this world. Love neither rules, nor is it unmoved" (Whitehead [1929] 1978, 343). However, thinking that this concept of God is part of an antimetaphysical project is a mistake. Rather, "God is not to be treated as an exception to all metaphysical principles, invoked to save their collapse. [God] is their chief exemplification" (Whitehead [1929] 1978, 343). Throughout, this book details the various ways in which the classical theistic God *is* an exception to metaphysical principles, rational discourse, and common uses of terms (such as "love" and "knowledge").

A source of debate among Whitehead scholars is how to deal with passages where he talks about God not as an everlasting series of actual occasions of experience, but as an atemporal actual entity reminiscent of a Boethian or Thomistic eternal now. One possible way to respond to this difficulty, and one that has formidable textual support, is that when Whitehead speaks in these ways he is not talking about God, but about an abstract aspect of God, specifically the primordial aspect of God. This is the aspect of God that classical theists have historically given a great deal of attention and nuanced analysis. But Whitehead is clear in many passages that this aspect of God is an abstraction away from the divine life itself. God as primordial refers to the everlasting existence of God and God's sempiternal consideration of the most abstract concepts and truths, such as in those found in logic and mathematics. Whitehead is also clear that God as primordial is not before or outside of the natural world, but with the created world. As an abstraction this aspect of God should not be confused with the actuality of the divine life as it plays out from momentary experience to momentary experience. The particularities of the world presuppose God as primordial, whereas God as primordial presupposes only the general metaphysical character of the creative advance of the world, not any particular creatures. This abstract aspect of God acts as a lure for creatures, as a standard on which creatures can model themselves along the lines of the everlasting (once again, Whitehead unfortunately says "eternal") ideal objects, like truth, beauty, and goodness (Whitehead [1929] 1978, 343–344).

There is another aspect of God that cannot be omitted, however, which means that Whitehead could not have intended the permanent aspect of God found in the primordial nature to be the whole story. This additional aspect is called the consequent nature of God. This aspect of God is in "unison of becoming" with every other actual occasion, and this aspect of God is affected by everything that exists. This aspect of God is derivative or consequent in the sense that everything that happens in the creative advance of the world has an effect on God. That is, in a manner analogous to all other actual occasions, God is dipolar. It is the consequent pole of the divine nature that is conscious of all that happens in the world and is affected by such happenings. Whereas the primordial nature of God is conceptual (by envisioning and ordering abstract objects), the consequent nature weaves together the feelings God has as a result of inheriting creaturely influence (Whitehead [1929] 1978, 344–345).

God is everlasting in the sense that God combines endless creative advance with retention of everything that has gone before. God exhibits "a tender care that nothing be lost" (Whitehead [1929] 1978, 346). This allows Whitehead to say, albeit as a figure of speech, that God "saves the world" as it passes moment by moment into the immediacy of the divine life. This requires patience on the part of God over an infinite amount of time. He speaks of God in the following moving terms: "God's role is not the combat of productive force with productive force, of destructive force with destructive force; it lies in the patient operation of the overpowering rationality of [divine] conceptual harmonization. [God] does not create the world, [God] saves it: or, more accurately, [God] is the poet of the world, with tender patience leading it by [God's] vision of truth, beauty, and goodness" (Whitehead [1929] 1978, 346). This view of God as the poet of the world (which is compatible with much that is instructive in later feminist theology), rather than as an omnipotent tyrant, provides the conditions under which a more worthy version of the concept of God can be developed (see Faber 2008; Keller 2003). By contrast, the classical theistic view involves a problematic separation of flux from permanence, leaving God in a purely static condition.

Whitehead's solution to "the final Platonic problem" is similar to that which Plato himself implied in those passages where the concept of dynamic perfection is depicted. Rather than adopting the notion of a strictly static God outside of time who (at best) condescends to interact with the world, and rather than abandoning the concept of God altogether, Whitehead sees the problem as dual and complex instead of singular and easy. God as primordial requires God as consequent. In the following passage Whitehead lists some antiphonal contrasts that should not be confused with contradictions:

> It is as true to say that God is permanent and the World is fluent, as that the World is permanent and God is fluent. It is as true to say that God is one and the World many, as that the World is one and God many. It is as true to say that, in comparison with the World, God is actual eminently, as that, in comparison with God, the World is actual eminently. It is as true to say that the World is immanent in God, as that God is immanent in the World. It is as true to say that God transcends the World, as that the World transcends God. It is as true to say that God creates the World, as that the World creates God (Whitehead [1929] 1978, 348).

I hope that at this point in the book this quotation is intelligible in that it presupposes an understanding of the neoclassical or process concept of dipolarity, the distinction between everlastingness and eternity, the prior intelligibility of some version of divine world-inclusiveness, and the unintelligibility of creation *ex nihilo*. And, of course, an understanding of this quotation presupposes an understanding of something like Hartshorne's distinction between divine existence and divine actuality.

On Whitehead's view neither God nor the world reaches static completion. They are both in the grip of the ultimate metaphysical principle that concerns the temporality of reality and its event-character: the creative advance into novelty. But God's primordial nature, characterized by divine conceptual realization of the most abstract truths, is "nonsense if thought of under the guise of a barren, eternal hypothesis" (Whitehead [1929] 1978, 349). God is a living being who requires as well the consequent nature, which is ever enlarged throughout evolutionary history. The practical import of this abstract commitment to a dipolar conception of God should be clear: When pain and sorrow are brought into the divine life via the consequent nature, they are, in a way, transformed in that they are then parts of a sublime, cosmic whole. This is what enables Whitehead to retain an element of triumph without succumbing to the sort of religious triumphalism that trivializes the tragic features of the world, in general, and of sentient life, in particular. There is, in fact, a sort of redemption through suffering that haunts the world, but only in the nontriumphalist sense where discordant elements can nonetheless contribute aesthetic value to a work of art as a whole (Whitehead [1929] 1978, 350).

The key to understanding how Whitehead avoids triumphalism and preserves a robust sense of the tragic is to work against the assumption that the "omnis" of classical theism stand or fall together. Rather, one can, along with Whitehead, affirm a commitment to divine omnibenevolence without affirming a commitment to divine omnipotence. The latter is at the root of (especially Christian) triumphalism and the trivialization of tragedy. A certain irony can be seen here when the symbol of the cross in Christianity is considered. Whereas in the hands of classical theists this symbol often conveyed the triumphalist sense that in its name Christians could conquer, in the hands of neoclassical or process theists who are Christian it symbolizes the tragic origins of this religion in the torture and murder of an innocent victim. And neoclassical or process theists who are Jews might be quick to notice that the classical theistic concept of omnipotence can be traced back to the Hebrew scriptures only with great difficulty. The English "almighty" and the Latin *omnipotentia* are problematic translations of the Hebrew *El Shaddai*, which refers to the God of the mountains or the Mountain One (see Arnison 2012; also Fretheim 1984).

Although at times Whitehead speaks as if God is a single atemporal actual entity, on my interpretation these passages are best seen as characterizing the stable identity of God in terms of the primordial nature. This interpretation is due, in part, to the passages where there is clearly a succession of divine experiences, with divine permanence referring to the continuity among the succession of divine experiences and the fact that no experience in this succession is ever lost. A human life is led concretely from moment to moment, such that my identity as "Dan" is a rather abstract way of identifying the line of inheritance that runs through these concrete experiences. God's life is also a succession of experiences, although presumably for God there is a "more complete unity of life in a chain of elements for which succession does not mean loss," to use Whitehead's phrase (Whitehead [1929] 1978, 350).

Whitehead clearly thinks that God loves the world and has providential concern for particular occasions of experience in the world. As these occur they are taken up into the divine life, at which point God's providential concern is then available for appropriation by creatures such that the process starts all over again. The relationship between human experience and divine experience is reciprocal. That is, love in the world passes into divine love, which then, in turn, floods back into the world. "In this sense, God is the great companion—the fellow-sufferer who understands" (Whitehead [1929] 1978, 351). This reciprocity gives zest to the religious life, wherein our immediate transitory actions in one sense perish, but in another sense "live for evermore."

The view of Whitehead's concept of God presented here is largely in agreement with the Hartshornian view of Burton Cooper, who criticizes the classical theistic perspective on God wherein change always flows away from God, but never toward divinity. The classical theistic God penetrates, but is impenetrable, as many contemporary feminist thinkers have emphasized. In addition, the Whiteheadian concept of God need not rely on an idealistic epistemology, wherein divine knowledge of outside things is attained by self-contemplation, as in Thomas Aquinas. To say, as Whitehead does, that creatures influence God is not to say that they influence God disproportionately or in the wrong direction, given the prominence of omnibenevolence in neoclassical or process theism (see Cooper 1974, 2–3, 21, 68).

25

Alfred North Whitehead

(1861–1947)

Appraisal and Works after *Process and Reality*

Whitehead goes so far as to say that the superstitious awe of infinity has been the bane of philosophy. The infinite deals with the very abstract realm of possibilities, not with any concrete situation in which something particularly good or beautiful can be found. Seen in this light, value itself is the gift of finitude; or better, both the infinite and the finite all alone are valueless. When some finite good is chosen out of an infinite range of possibilities, value comes into existence. Valorizing the infinite and denigrating the finite *simpliciter* was a mistake for classical theists. This made God into a mere abstract vacancy. On the dipolar logic of neoclassical or process theism, by contrast, God is infinite and finite in different aspects of the divine nature, to the extent that, and in the senses that, both infinity and finitude are exemplary. As one of the greatest twentieth-century mathematicians, Whitehead speaks with a certain degree of authority in the essay "Mathematics and the Good," when he claims that mathematics aids in the development of a better, more beautiful, world in that this discipline more than any other studies patterns of possibility in the infinite welter of opportunities regarding what could be. Finitude vivifies the infinite in terms of the choices made regarding these patterns (Whitehead 1941, 666–681).

The overall point here, however, is not to trash the infinite, but to place it in a context in which it helps us to make sense of the concept of God. Any finite perspective occurs against a background of infinite possibility that enables us to understand the finite perspective in question. Divine persuasion functions as a lure regarding a manifold of possibility: either as an incitement toward some ideal or as a deterrence away from some other ideal. This orientation toward ideal reality puts each actual occasion into relation with everything else that exists. Nothing whatsoever could have a completely independent existence; hence classical theists unfortunately depicted a God who was not interwoven with the rest of the universe. In the essay "Immortality" Whitehead makes clear that he defends a view of God that lies between the strictly permanent and independent God of classical theism and the strictly diffused God of pantheism. That is, the prime activity of Whitehead's God is persuasive coordination of the world (Whitehead 1941, 682–695).

One of the consistent themes in Whitehead's concept of God is the connection between the imposition of order on the world by the classical theistic God and the despotic character of such a God. The classical theistic God works on the world, not with it. In different terms, the God of classical theism cannot coordinate the world as a persuasive lure for such would mean that God would have to be affected by, be changed with respect to, the creatures. This means that the following two misconceptions mutually reinforce each other: that God is strictly independent and that God orders the world in a tyrannical way. In classical theism violence is the primary mode of sustaining large-scale social existence. From Whitehead's own perspective, this concept of God as the purveyor of arbitrary use of coercive power was a profanation (Whitehead 1941, 696–700).

The gloomy characteristics of the God found in the Hebrew scriptures do not necessarily embody the best in the biblical tradition, of which there two tendencies: One leans in the direction of gentleness and mercy, and the other leans in the direction of persecution and sadistic cruelty. Both of these tendencies occur in almost all historical religious sects. In this regard Whitehead both criticizes the violent tendency in religion as well as the debunking of this tendency when it is assumed to have brought down the concept of God or religion in general. As a result of these debunking projects, efforts at social reform or artistic endeavors have largely replaced religious beliefs in the contemporary world. These activities are certainly admirable in themselves, but they do not get us very far in dealing with the crucial problems with which the concept of God and religion are concerned: the proper link between the finite and infinite and the difficulty involved in talking about the latter in terms of a language that is finite. Whitehead thinks of most of theology as one of the great disasters in human history because it (classical theism) has focused almost exclusively on divine infinity rather than on divine finitude, on God as omnipotent rather than on God as persuasive, and so forth (Whitehead [1954] 2001, 28, 87, 100, 102, 131, 171; 1941, 14).

In the strongest terms possible, Whitehead is reported to have said that the ferocious, omnipotent God of classical theism can even be compared to Hitler. Even an incredibly admirable classical theist such as St. Francis of Assisi thought that divine love could be reconciled with the belief in eternal damnation (Whitehead [1954] 2001, 172–173). Admittedly, one can sense a gradual humanization not only of human beings, but also regarding what is said about God in the scriptures, but such discourse is rebarbarized in the last book of the Christian scriptures and in classical theists, generally, who do not do justice to the finer biblical elements. Whitehead notices the humorless character of much of the Bible, which is unfortunate given the fact that laughter may very well be a divine attribute (Whitehead [1954] 2001, 194–195, 352–353).

Whitehead is well aware of the fact that there is nothing necessarily commendatory about the appeal to Plato regarding the concept of God in that even St. Augustine borrowed from Plato, but with negative results. It is the Platonic God of the universe, rather than the reification of a formal world in a condition of separation (*chorismos*) from the universe, that needs to be appropriated for the purposes of contemporary philosophy, he thinks. Furthermore, Luther, Calvin, and the Puritans repeated the damage Augustine did. These thinkers botched the Reformation by jettisoning the very best in the Catholic tradition (its aesthetic appeal) and by retaining the very worst (the classical theistic version of an omnipotent tyrant). If Whitehead was forced to give a one word definition for the meaning of life, it would be "adventure." Successful adventurers must, indeed, know the past, but they must also show resolve by refusing to repeat past mistakes. In Bergsonian fashion, "static religion" and "death of thought" are rough equivalents in Whitehead (Whitehead [1954] 2001, 214, 232, 250–252, 273, 282, 286, 302, 306).

The problem with the religions that have been heavily influenced by classical theism is not that they are flat wrong, but rather that they have rested content with a simplistic, monopolar concept of God, a simple-mindedness that has made a mess of these religions regarding the theodicy problem, at the very least. Whitehead's snappy way to make the point is to say imagining anything more un-Christlike than Christian theology, that is, classical theism, is difficult. These criticisms of Christianity could not have come easily for Whitehead considering that his father was an Anglican clergyman (and an "Old Testament man"), although he also had ancestors who were Quakers and he admired the Unitarians, so he was not much afraid of being accused of heterodoxy. The death of his son, Eric, in World War I brought the theodicy problem home to him in a dramatic way such that he remained skeptical of any triumphalist use of the afterlife to erase the tragedy of human existence (Whitehead [1954] 2001, 1, 290, 292, 296, 303, 306, 353; 1941, 3, 9).

Armstrong's, Bowker's, and Capetz's engagements with Whitehead's thought indicate its importance in the overall sweep of the history of the concept of God. Capetz goes so far as to say that "process theology is the most original contribution to a philosophical approach to the question of God in the twentieth century" (Capetz 2003; 148). This is a remarkable claim. The contribution that he has in mind is at least threefold. First, he emphasizes the fact that, according to Whitehead, experience is our best clue as to the nature of reality as such. But the experience in question is not restricted to sense data. It includes the emotional, aesthetic, moral, *and* religious dimensions of experience. That is, the famous philosophical empiricists of the modern period (for example, Hume), who restricted experience to sense data, were defective because they were (quite ironically) not empirical enough. There are two forms of experience for Whitehead: sense data (which he refers to as experience in the mode of presentational immediacy) and a more primary, deeply felt experience (called experience in the mode of causal efficacy), such as in memory or the general feeling that there is an external world or that there are other minds in existence. God is responsible for ordering and then presenting the relevant possibilities among the infinite number of possibilities for each new moment of experience in the mode of causal efficacy.

Second, God's independence or aseity is clarified in process thought in that, although God's existence is everlasting and does not depend on any particular creatures for continuation, because the consequent nature of God is constituted by internal relations to the world, God is dependent on some creatures or other. Furthermore, God could not be an omnibenevolent being if there were no one to love. Neither God nor the world reach static completion in that both are in the grip of the creative advance into novelty and mutual influence.

And third, ideal power in process thought is persuasive rather than coercive, hence we are mistaken if we assume that God is omnipotent. Rather, Whitehead's God, as we have seen, resembles Plato's World Soul (even though Whitehead resists this precise label), including the mental functioning of the World Soul (the demiurgic function), who provides as much order and beauty and goodness as are possible given the recalcitrant nature of the subject matter to be persuaded. This view is congenial to contemporary science, Capetz thinks, with its concentration on generalized (but not universal) order, its use of scientific laws as statistical (but not as absolute, as in the Newtonian alternative), and its concern for predictability without a commitment to a rigid determinism.

The problem with classical theism is not that it relies on Greek philosophical concepts, as Capetz seems to suggest. Rather, it relies on a certain incomplete interpretation of Greek philosophy, specifically on its fascination with permanence and fixity. Both classical theism and neoclassical or process theism rely on the Greeks. Indeed, the differences between these two concepts of God largely rest on their different interpretations of Plato, with classical theists noticing only the ontolatry of Plato, while ignoring the Platonic emphasis on the dynamic perfection of soul, especially the World Soul (Capetz 2003, 148–152, 185).

Bowker calls attention to the commonplace in process thought that one of its advantages is that its God is available for the purposes of prayer and worship. Of course classical theists historically have said that their God is also available, but how a strictly permanent, immutable, and unmoved God could be available to re-spond to prayer and worship is unclear. Bowker is also instructive in calling attention to the role of Plato in Whitehead's concept of God, which has obviously been a major theme herein. The history of the concept of God is, if anything, complicated, requiring a significant amount of exegetical industry to figure out where the concept of God went wrong and how it could be put in a presentable fashion to jumpstart conversation in contemporary society and contemporary academe on questions regarding God's existence.

Bowker notices the general processual character of reality, such that if there is a God, this God would be in flux. The process God is pan*en*theistic, Bowker notes, thus offering a view of divine world inclusiveness that is not to be equated with pantheism. God works like an artist, say like a play director who allows the actors improvisational license, and who tries to bring as much beauty and goodness as possible out of the potentially tragic opportunities we all face. Bowker does not fail to notice the all-important Whiteheadian notion that God is the fellow-sufferer who understands (Bowker 2002, 154, 230, 317).

Armstrong also seems to be impressed with Whitehead's place in the history of the concept of God. She notes his influence on the thought of Iqbal, whom we have seen was a twentieth-century philosopher who took Bergson's and Whitehead's ideas to Islam and who appropriated the latter for the purpose of explicating the process concept of God. Armstrong also notices the significant influence of Whitehead's thought on the theologian Daniel Day Williams. God's unity with the world is most noteworthy in Whitehead, Armstrong thinks. This divine world inclusiveness entails the idea of divine suffering, wherein suffering in the world is transformed or transfigured into love when it is taken up into the sensitivity of the divine life. Toward the end of her book Armstrong seems to indicate that classical theists were mistaken in positing a supernatural order against the natural one that we experience. Seen in this light, she thinks that Whitehead's thought is, as Whitehead himself thought, simply an attempt to correct an imbalance created at either end by classical theistic strict transcendence and pantheistic strict immanence (Armstrong 1993, 364, 384–385).

Whitehead's overall hope is to overcome dualism in metaphysics, including the absolute separations of God and the world, mind and matter. This attempt to overcome dualism means that there is something a bit inaccurate in thinking of Whitehead as a pure process philosopher in that his concept of God involves both contrasting notions: flux and permanence. However, flux admittedly has the upper hand when one considers that in "process philosophy" being is seen as that which endures throughout becoming, which is given the last word. It is the religious aspect of Whitehead's writings about becoming that most haunts readers as they become aware of what the concept of God means as they ponder the endless succession of drops of time and experience passing into the everlasting memory of God, who fuels eros toward perfection over time (see Bixler 1941). This forward drive of the universe enables us to avoid a possible misinterpretation of Whitehead to the effect that if God is a principle of limitation, there might be some conceivable being who has what Whitehead's God lacks. But this objection presupposes the monopolar prejudice to the effect that infinitude is in all respects good (even when it implies a welter of possible goods, but no concrete, actual one) and that finitude is in all respects bad (even when it implies some determinately beautiful or good thing).

What is most noteworthy about Whitehead's concept of God from Hartshorne's perspective is the ability of Whitehead to avoid the fallacy of misplaced concreteness regarding God. To confuse God with the abstract, permanent aspect of God is to misunderstand the concrete character of God from moment to moment. Classical theists typically abstract away from the temporal character of all value and then identify such an abstraction as God. Or again, classical theists typically arrive at a concept of divine omnipotence by abstracting away from all of the concrete centers of power in the world and then identify God with all power. This commits the fallacy of misplaced concreteness by abstracting away from (or omitting) one pole of a conceptual contrast (Hartshorne 1972, 64).

The burden of proof, Hartshorne thinks, should be on the extremists who assert either the radical and complete independence of God or the complete identity of God with the world. To assert the more plausible dipolar view, however, is not to glory in contradictions, as does fifteenth-century thinker Nicholas of Cusa, in that the two poles of divine attributes refer to different aspects of the divine nature: primordial and consequent. God is "the unrivalled excellence of the activity-*and*-passivity, the unity-*and*-complexity, the being-*and*-becoming, yes the joy-*and*-suffering," which elevates God above all others (Hartshorne 1972, 69, also 65–70). The conceptual task is to praise God without talking nonsense by ensuring these contrasting terms are not turned into contradictions.

A criticism frequently leveled against Whitehead is that behind his God is a causal power that is more basic and that is the real deity in the Whiteheadian universe. But this would be to misunderstand the underlying process or creativity of the universe. This underlying process or creativity is not an actual entity or an agent or a person who does things; hence it is not a God behind Whitehead's God. Rather, "process" or "creativity" refer to the common property of all actual occasions or to a generic name for all of the doings in the universe, from the subatomic to the divine. There is a genuine division of labor and distribution of power in the universe, which helps us to better respond to the theodicy problem than the classical theistic attempt to do so as well as to better understand the tendency of the universe to be in tune, on the assumption that one power is greater than all others, albeit not omnipotently so (Hartshorne 1972, 72–73).

What is really unintelligible is the view of God as pure actuality found in classical theism. The complete denial of divine recipience unwittingly destroys the social nature of God, especially the vitally important concept of divine love. God as pure actuality, with no potentiality, is also at odds with divine omniscience, whether in its classical theistic or neoclassical theistic versions. "Knowledge of all things" means knowledge of each thing as it is: the actual as actual, the merely possible as merely possible, the past as past, and the future as future. Even for God there is a future, not because God is "ignorant" of what will happen, but because there literally are no "future events" or "future objects of knowledge." There are only relatively determinate outlines of probability. God's knowledge is always free from error and ignorance, yet it can be said legitimately that such knowledge perpetually improves upon itself in terms of richness of content and value. Thus, in one sense there is cognitive improvement in God, whereas in another sense there is no need for such improvement. But in the sense in which there is cognitive improvement, this does not so much indicate a lack in God as it indicates the preeminence of divine knowledge (Hartshorne 1972, 73–75).

On the interpretation I am offering, the primordial nature of God in Whitehead is somewhat of a misnomer in that it is not before or apart from all, but is with all process. Furthermore, possibility is either a property of existing reality or it is independent of all existence. Hence, if we assume the first alternative, that the general possibilities for the universe have to be somewhere (otherwise we would be left with the unintelligibility of the idea that there might have actually been absolutely nothing), then the nonexistence of the primordial aspect of God is not possible. This argument for the existence of God is implied in Whitehead, despite his distrust of such arguments. My purpose is not to assess this argument, but to notice that it helps us to better understand his concept of God, with the proviso that a being who is necessary in existence need not be necessary in all other aspects. God exists necessarily and all possibilities for the universe exist everlastingly in the divine mind, the intradeical view, rather than such possibilities existing absolutely nowhere, whatever this might mean, the extradeical view (Hartshorne 1972, 76–80).

God as temporally everlasting in Whitehead should not be confused with the classical theistic, eternal God outside of time who imposes laws of nature on dead matter. In one sense God has no past, but what this means is that nothing from the past entirely perishes or is ultimately lost if God is an ideal knower with ideal memory. God's life is fluent in that God is the personal order of the all-inclusive society of societies, which implies that the universe is God's body, a view that is easily deducible from what Whitehead says. The persuasion that God exerts on the subsocieties is, in a way, irresistible, but only up until a certain point at which the partially free creatures can decide on their own. If God thwarts the desires of creatures, then such thwarting is itself felt by God with a type of pain or sorrow. This is entailed by the claim that God is omnibenevolent. This point is crucial if only because there can never be a complete elimination of evil from the world if the opportunities for ever-new evil are always popping up in each new present, but these opportunities are also what make goodness possible (Hartshorne 1972, 82–95).

Admittedly, Whitehead's insight regarding the need for the general potentiality of the universe to be located somewhere, notably in a primordial mind, is captured infelicitously in the phrase "principle of limitation." But the insight remains. Imagining a multitude of agents selecting a common world and a common set of statistical laws that apply everywhere is difficult because they would have a tendency to nullify each other's efforts. In any event, Whitehead's concept of God is meant to respond to the question, who selects the general direction of, or at least the parameters for, local selections? His response to this question is in terms of an agent/patient with universal (albeit not omnipotent) influence. This influence is compatible with the idea of God as an everlasting linear sequence of occasions that are personally ordered. This is a series in which there is no lapse of memory and no loss of immediacy in the occasions already achieved. In fact, Whitehead is one of the first philosophers who can, with any degree of legitimacy, speak of divine personality, which includes a cluster of habits, purposes, and tendencies that are relatively stable in the midst of pervasive flux. This view is nonetheless compatible with the idea that God has defining characteristics, say omnibenevolence, that do not, however, determine in detail what will happen in the future (Hartshorne 2000, 273–274).

God's influence over us, on the Whiteheadian view, is largely the influence of thought over thought or feeling over feeling. Thus it would be a bit too much to say that God makes us to be who we are, rather we largely make ourselves by using divine beauty and goodness as inspiration. God influences us and we influence God. This communication back and forth indicates activity and passivity on both sides of the communication. This communication is such that we can depend on the same divine, personal sequence on the other side, but not necessarily the same particular divine actuality. If God exists necessarily then God would exist independently of any particular individuals who may or may not exist, although this is compatible with the view that God requires some other individuals to exist. All of this is quite different from the Unmoved Mover concept of God found in Aristotle and many classical theists; only the primordial aspect of God (not God as a whole) even remotely resembles this strictly permanent deity (Hartshorne 2000, 275–276).

Whitehead's idea that our sorrow and pain are transformed or transfigured when they are taken up into the divine life is his way of accounting for the not uncommon religious experience of redemption through suffering, a phenomenon that haunts the world and that resembles the aesthetic value of discord or dissonance in the construction of an overall work of art that is beautiful. This should not be confused with the claim some religious skeptics make that God sadistically exploits our sufferings in that God does not view our tragedy from the outside as a mere spectator or voyeur, but rather internalizes the suffering into the divine nature itself. That is, as we have seen in Berdyaev, God is not so much sadistic as tragic in the divine life itself. And there is no facile way to eliminate evil, say by eliminating freedom, in that this latter elimination would reduce rather than enhance the overall value of our lives and what we could contribute to the divine life. Both Whitehead and Hartshorne are quite clear that God is more important than we are such that in the midst of tragedy it is crucial to be reminded of the fact that our experiences live on as elements of divine actuality (Hartshorne 2000, 284–285).

Whitehead's concept of God is tailor-made to refer to a God of religion because it helps us to understand God as personal. One need not fit religious considerations and personal aspects of deity into his concept of God with a shoehorn. They fit. Personhood refers to the defining characteristics of the divine society of occasions in a linear, temporal order. Because the consequent nature of God consists in a sequence of supremely sensitive experiences that contain prehensions (that is, graspings) of the content of the world, Whitehead's concept of God includes much of what religious believers have generally meant by "God." The least emergent features of Whitehead's cosmos are its general determinables, which he calls "eternal objects." But these are abstractions in that what is determinate is that which has been made so in the asymmetrical process that is decision making. That is, with the possible exception of eternal objects (like threeness itself or the concept of being itself, and so forth), all of the concrete occasions in the Whiteheadian universe are emergent and subject to a temporal asymmetry wherein memory of the past concerns details, whereas anticipation of the future, especially the distant future, involves generalities at best (Hartshorne 1972, 13–14, 32, 51–52).

The world is a unified individual—that is an empirical fact; our speaking of "physics" or "chemistry" rather than of "Peruvian physics" or "Jewish chemistry" attests to this fact. The postulation of God's existence helps to (and, on Whiteheadian grounds, is necessary to) explain this fact. God's memory is the standard regarding the past, just as God's knowledge provides the standard regarding the truth in genetics, say. These exalted functions performed by God help to counteract the charge that, because of his critique of omnipotence, Whitehead's God lacks "size." Whitehead does not "limit" God in contrast to some supposedly more powerful being; rather, he is pointing out that there is a social element in the very idea of power. Creativity, in general, is not a power; it just *is* power. The neoclassical or process God is the greatest conceivable being at least in part because only in this being (as a result of divine world inclusiveness) do altruism and self-interest coincide. This consideration also helps us to respond to the charge that religious belief de-individualizes us. My present happiness is, once again via divine world inclusiveness, a contribution to divine happiness, but it is still my happiness that is contributed, in contrast to yours. In fact, the more individually differentiated we are, the greater the aesthetic worth of our contributions to the beauty of the cosmic whole (Hartshorne 1972, 60–61, 100, 103, 106–107).

Classical theists did a fine job of interpreting God as the Absolute of absolutes (that is, in one sense God is the least relative to others due to divine everlastingness), but they did not, like Whitehead, also consider carefully the claim that God is also the most Relative of relatives (that is, that God is the most related to others). Nor did they even think of the possibility that the consequent nature of God really *is* God, with divine absoluteness referring to the abstract idea that God always changes. This ubiquity of change is what it means to say that Whitehead's use of the word "primordial" to refer to divine steadfastness is a bit misleading. Likewise, Whitehead's language regarding the perpetual perishing of actual occasions from moment to moment is a bit misleading in that the steadfastness of divine memory is such that, although the occasion's own experience perishes, it is nonetheless preserved forever as it is taken up into the divine life. To cite just one more example, Whitehead's language regarding God as a single actual entity, rather than as a series of actual occasions, also causes confusion in some circles. Once again, the permanence of God refers to what is common in all of the occasions in the consequent nature of God; and such permanence (the primordial nature) is an aspect of God, but it is not to be confused with God. Unfortunately, although Christian doctrines such as the Incarnation and the Trinity seem to point toward a consequent nature of God, these theological positions were not given appropriate philosophical or rational articulation by classical theists in their concept of God as unmoved, impassible, and strictly permanent (Hartshorne 1972, 116, 145, 165, 168, 177, 179).

On a processual view of the world, anything that exists exerts some power (however minimal) to act on others and to receive influence from others, which means that reality is thoroughly social. Our own existences consist in feeling of feeling wherein there is a society of interlocked experiences; or better, wherein there is a society of societies of interlocked experiences. God is that in the cosmos whereby it *is* a cosmos or a community of things such that the individuals who compose it are not closed into ineffable privacy and hence are irrelevant to everything else. God is the cosmic individual and the most inclusive society of societies. Seen in this light, deity is not an exception to the social principle, but its chief exemplification. The distance between this concept of God and the classical theistic one could be minimized, but only if classical theists were willing to say that what they really mean by God is God in one aspect, not God as a whole. However, if this admission is not granted, then the gap between neoclassical and classical theism is quite wide in that the latter leads to the view of God as tyrant who coerces the world to be what it is rather than persuades it in ways that are respectful of creaturely freedom. We need not worship brute power (Hartshorne 1941, 50–51, 239; 1948, 29, 44, 142, 155).

Whitehead's view is a higher synthesis that rises above both classical theism and pantheism. By saying that he deviates from the thought of the Scholastics or Calvin, however, is not to say that he has deviated from the best elements found in the Hebrew prophets, Jesus, or Mohammed. In fact, the concept of God in Whitehead is more congenial to a personal God than the concept found in classical theism. Furthermore, there is no reason to fear the view of God as possessing a developmental character in that divine omnibenevolence endures even if particular expressions of God's goodness are subject to change. Whitehead challenges the assumption that God as absolute or as independent of the world is superior to God as related to the world. On the neoclassical or process view, God is not degraded by being related to the world by way of knowledge and love. Far from being a mere superfluous condescension of deity, creation is part of the divine life itself. Each one of us is a significant addition to the universe as mystics throughout the centuries in various religious traditions have noted (Hartshorne 1953, 18, 31, 196–212; 1962, 144).

Like several Buddhist thinkers, Whitehead takes events or momentary states to be the ultimate units of concrete reality, hence enduring individuals are to be conceived as somewhat abstract sequences of events. For Whitehead, if not for the Buddhist thinkers, this applies to the divine individual as well. This means that an individual's life can be determined only retrospectively in that a partially new individual arises at each moment. To be precise, the identity of an individual is not to be located in its members, but in the defining characteristic of an event sequence, in the qualities that are shared among them. And part of what is shared is creativity, which is a transcendental in process philosophy in that it is a universal category rather than one that is applicable to God alone. God is to be distinguished from creatures in terms of ideal creativity in contrast to lesser forms of creativity. Each level has an actualization of certain potentials within limits, say due to the fact that a certain value is incompatible with another value, so both cannot be chosen simultaneously (Hartshorne 1965, 51, 217–218, 291; 1967, 22–23, 26, 74; 1970, 73, 188, 198, 200, 204).

To be is to create on the Whiteheadian view. But one of the impediments to appreciating the neoclassical or process concept of God is the assumption that mind or experience is necessarily inextended. Overcoming this assumption is crucial in the effort to avoid the strictly immaterial, atemporal, and ultimately uncreative concept of God found in classical theism. If space is seen as the pattern of causal inheritance among events, however, then mind or experience is extended across the whole world of causal interaction. Real creativity involves experiences that are not mere repetitions of what has always existed in eternity; new experiences can and do occur. In one sense this is obvious, but in another sense the public, including the intellectual public, seems unprepared to appreciate a concept of God that involves dynamic perfection. It is to be hoped that this public itself will grow into this concept (Hartshorne 1970, 1, 8, 65, 87–88).

Reality perpetually perishes not in the sense that the vital actuality of the present turns into a corpse, but rather in the sense that the vital actuality of the present is also an object for other subjects, especially the divine one. It can even be said that memory, especially divine memory, is the paradigm case of experiencing and provides the avenue by which to best understand why perpetual perishing is not the last word. God is not a mere spectator, but a participant in the process of the world with ideal memory. God changes us by changing the divine nature itself in response to our previous responses to God. This self-surpassing deity thus exhibits a divine time that involves a settled past and at least a partially open future. This reality of a settled past that is then capable of being prehended by knowing subjects indicates that, in a sense, change is not the only thing to account for in a world of becoming. That is, becoming is addition to, not subtraction from, what is real (Hartshorne 1970, 118, 218, 263, 277, 291; 1981, 7).

Whitehead's concept of God provides a moderate position between the extremes that fueled the rise of certain existentialist views, especially Jean-Paul Sartre's, in the mid-twentieth century. There is a false dichotomy between the classical theistic view, which Sartre and others interpreted (perhaps legitimately) as saying that omnipotent divine power settles everything and hence there really is no human freedom, and the Sartrean view that there is no God and therefore we have absolute freedom. It is Sartre's understandable (given the hegemony of the classical theistic view) misunderstanding of the concept of God that leads to this false dichotomy. That is, classical theists are in many ways the greatest obstacles to theism itself. Thus, the nonexistence of the God of classical theism need not cause grief. In that contrast is essential for beauty to exist, a beautiful world would require some measure of freedom or creativity at both the divine and nondivine levels (Hartshorne 1981, 15–18, 23).

Some version of what Whitehead calls the primordial nature of God is needed in any defensible theism, but one ought not to identify this abstract aspect of God with concrete divine actuality. This abstract aspect is not the God who knows us here and now. The consequent nature of God, however, has preeminent prehensive power, with "prehension" referring to both perception and memory or the ability to grasp the experiences of others and one's own prior experiences. In a way, memory is more basic than perception because whereas memory explicitly involves a grasping of one's prior experiences, perception is implicit about this. But on reflection one can realize that there is always a time lag, however short, between the time the perceptual information is given and our experience of it. Furthermore, there is always a time lag, however short, between the cellular reception of perceptual information (say in nerve cells in the eye) and our experience as sentient individuals. And God is not an exception to the temporal structure of memory and perception. Without some sort of participation on the part of present experience in other experiences, speaking of any rational or even sentient individual would be meaningless (Hartshorne 1983, 77, 164, 180, 287, 291, 300).

Religious feeling consists in an awareness of the concrete cosmic whole, but this whole is not "totalizing" in the pejorative, static sense of the term in that at each moment there is a partially new cosmic whole in that God's consequent nature is constantly being enriched. At every turn the dipolarity of neoclassical or process theism counteracts the monopolarity of classical theism. The classical theist contends that God is distinguished from everything else as cause is different from effect, as unity is different from plurality, as infinity is different from finitude, as the unmovable is different from the movable, and as the immutable is different from the mutable. This one-sided view distorts not only our concept of God, but also our concept of nondivine beings who are seen by classical theists as possessing only the latter element in each of these contrasting pairs. It makes sense for Hartshorne to claim that the sort of dipolar theism found in Whitehead can easily be seen as a sort of dual transcendence: "God is exalted above other realities not as cause surpasses effect, or unity, plurality, or being, becoming; but rather as eminent cause surpasses ordinary causes, and eminent effect, ordinary effects; similarly, as eminent being *and* becoming surpass ordinary being and becoming, or eminent unity *and* plurality surpass ordinary unity and plurality" (Hartshorne 1983, 314–315, also 308, 316). Furthermore, this dual transcendence can be mapped rather easily on to Plato's view where there is a strong analogy between the primordial nature of God and the Demiurge and between the consequent nature of God and the World Soul.

If God infallibly knows all that can be known, then it can be said that God prehends all. But in addition to claiming that God is the universally prehending reality, one can also claim that God is universally prehended in the sense that each concrete occasion has some vague feeling of its being part of a whole. That is, God can be universally prehended without being universally known. It does not follow from the idea that all subjects inchoately feel God that they all think about or know God (Hartshorne 1984a, 112). Perhaps some will object that divine prehensions seem to imply physical feelings on the part of God. The proper response to this objection is to grant the objection but to deny its significance. Once physical and mental feelings are distinguished, God can be said to have both, albeit preeminently. "Mentality is sense of the future, of possibility; physical feeling is sense of the past, of concrete actuality" (Hartshorne 1984b, 39; 1984c, 27–28, 93). Whitehead's primordial and consequent natures of God, respectively, are intended to highlight both of these aspects of divine feeling, which are also exhibited by all singulars who causally inherit from the past and anticipate, however vaguely, the future. God differs from us not in the mere having of physical and mental feelings, but in having them ideally or preeminently.

Because Whitehead is free from the classical theistic (especially Leibnizian) doctrine of sufficient reason, a doctrine that depends on a concept of God that centers on the attribute of omnipotence, he is able to avoid the theodicy problem in its worst form. There is no need to discover a precise reason why particular misfortunes occur because they are the result of partly chance intersections of multiple freedoms: human and subhuman. Theologically speaking, only the risk of evil needs explaining and such explanation comes in the form of the opportunities that are inseparable from the risks (Hartshorne 1990, 385).

There are several internecine disputes among neoclassical or process theists, and two are noteworthy. First, at times Whitehead speaks as if God is a single actual entity rather than an everlasting series of actual occasions that are linked together through divine prehension, where previous divine occasions from the past are grasped and literally included in God's present. The problem with the former way of speaking, from my Hartshornian point of view, is that it is too close for comfort to the problematic, static, classical theistic way of speaking about God. Whitehead can be rescued from this difficulty, I have alleged, by interpreting his view of divine permanence in terms of the primordial nature of God if not God as a whole. This interpretation is part of a general tendency to move away from the idea that God is merely creator and is not partially created by the creatures (in divine actuality if not in divine existence). Whitehead's own view regarding the consequent nature of God best enables us to see this. And second, Whitehead tends to emphasize abstract objects as eternal, a tendency that is not problematic if it refers only to the most abstract objects in mathematics or metaphysics in that some abstract objects are emergent and are themselves subject to the general process of the universe. For example, it makes a big difference if the abstract object in question is "threeness" as opposed to "the greatest poet after Shakespeare." In any event, the difference of opinion among process thinkers regarding Whitehead's eternal objects need not be exaggerated in that both Whitehead and Hartshorne defend an intradeical view wherein abstract objects are housed in the omniscient divine mind, in contrast to an extradeical (ultra-Platonic) view wherein abstract objects or Platonic forms are free-floating and hence are quite mysterious in the pejorative sense of the term "mystery" (see Hartshorne 1991, 642, 645).

Whitehead's development of the concept of God continues after *Process and Reality*. In *Adventures of Ideas* ([1933] 1967) he claims that progress in religion is defined in terms of the denunciation of the prevalent gods who are worshipped idolatrously. In this regard the God of classical theism is really an idol. There is a long history of such denunciation, such as when Plato banished the gods of the poets (and, unfortunately, the poets themselves) from the Republic. Plato's own religion is based on what he thought a God could be. In the history of

Christianity Whitehead thinks that it was unfortunate that the Protestant reformers did not really reform the concept of God, but accepted the same idolatrous God of classical theism. Plato's great innovation, on this account, is to say in the *Timaeus* that the creation of the world (including the world of civilized order) signals the victory of persuasion over force. Continued progress in religion requires both the intellectual generality and rigor philosophy provides as well as the moral energy religious believers themselves provide. The religion that will succeed in the contemporary world is one that can render clearly in popular terms some everlasting greatness found incarnated in the passage of temporal events (Whitehead [1933] 1967, 11–12, 18, 25–26, 33).

History can be viewed as a series of oscillations between worldliness and otherworldliness, according to Whitehead. The current aggressive opposition to otherworldliness is in large measure a reaction against the exaggerated eternalism and otherworldliness of classical theism. It is also largely a reaction against the omnipotence of the classical theistic God, who is quite legitimately tagged with responsibility for the theodicy problem. The historical influence of ancient despotisms on Christianity has left it with certain scars that have been slow to heal. Granted, some degree of dominion over human beings is necessary in order for social coordination to occur, but it is crucial that this dominion not be exaggerated and it is equally crucial that we not divinize tyrannical government. Tradition itself can be a sort of compulsion and religious tradition is, in general, clearly losing its force. This perhaps makes it more likely that neoclassical theism would get a fair hearing, but such a hearing is likely only if a reverential vision of the world itself survives and flourishes (Whitehead [1933] 1967, 43, 85, 99).

The concept of God Whitehead defends is an alternative to the classical theistic God who externally imposes law on the natural world and on human beings. It is also an alternative to viewing God as strictly immanent, as in pantheism. The problem with this latter view is that it provides no reason why the universe should not be steadily relapsing into lawless chaos. Whitehead's third alternative to imposition and immanence is divine persuasion of a Platonic sort. The first extreme view, imposition, presupposes an essential transcendence to God and only an accidental immanence, whereas pantheism presupposes an essential divine immanence with no real transcendence. We would be mistaken to think that these two alternatives exhaust the possible concepts of God. In a way, Whitehead's Platonic alternative is a fusion of the doctrines of imposition and immanence, although the word "imposition" is a bit too strong, given the fact that the Platonic-Whiteheadian God must persuade or cajole the sentient and intelligent activities of indwelling souls. The important thing is to avoid any divinity with the frigid title of First Cause or Unmoved Mover. As before, if being *is* power, then divine power would have to be relational in character and capable of adjustment in light of the various powers of nondivine beings. Whitehead's view is very much at odds with the imposition of order from outside of the world found in classical theism, which, in Christianity, at least, is combined with a myth regarding an omnipotent God intentionally sending his only son into the world to suffer torture and a hideous death, a view that Whitehead sees as nothing less than outrageous (Whitehead [1933] 1967, 115, 121–123, 129; [1954] 2001, 366).

Leibniz's preestablished harmony is an extreme version of the classical theistic doctrine of divine imposition. This view is significantly different from Plato's divine craftsperson who elicits as much order out of disorder as is possible given the recalcitrant material God has to deal with. There is sufficient order in the world to call it a *universe*, however. Whitehead even goes so far as to say that the ancient Greek *physis*, which is usually translated as "nature," could more accurately be translated as "the process of growth in nature" or more simply as "process" because the ever-advancing history of the world constitutes a cosmic community in motion. The chief advantage of the concept of divine persuasion is that it enables us to understand both the general order of the world and the fact that this order is not absolute. Brute forces at work in the world resist all attempts at measure and harmonization. And at the human level we can notice both positive responses to the divine lure and resistance to divine persuasive ideals. One needs to account for both (Whitehead [1933] 1967, 133, 147–148, 150, 160, 168, 190; [1954] 2001, 159).

The hope is that a "New Reformation" is in progress wherein the very concept of God is being re-formed. As in the word "neo-classical," both parts of "re-form" are necessary. The first Reformation was, despite its successes in other areas, a complete failure regarding the concept of God, Whitehead thinks, except perhaps for some contributions made by Quakers to the idea of God as persuasive. These contributions are added to the base built by Plato, who can be seen as the great discoverer of the superiority of persuasive divine agency to coercive divine agency. In contrast to the classical theist's God, who omnipotently disposes of a wholly derivative world, Whitehead's God interacts with the world on its own terms in the gentle effort to move it to a better, more beautiful, place. Classical theists, including Christian classical theists, despite appearances, do not give Jesus' persuasive message of love and peace a friendly reception. The classical theistic notion of God as absolute despot has stood in the way of both progress regarding the concept of God and the understanding of the tenderness of life Jesus emphasized. There is no reason to despair, however, as Whitehead notes: "The history of religion is the history of the countless generations required for interest to attach itself to profound ideas" (Whitehead [1933] 1967, 171, also 161, 166–170).

Importantly, we must recognize that Whitehead is at home with both notions: In one sense God is temporal and in another sense God is nontemporal. The latter refers to the primordial nature of God, which everlastingly maintains the identity of God through myriad changes. Classical theists ably treated the permanent aspect of God, and we are in their debt because of their efforts. But we need to add to their achievements if we are to more closely approximate an adequate concept of God. Despite the permanence of the primordial nature, this aspect of God functions as a lure forward toward the aforementioned ideals of truth, beauty, and goodness. In this regard Whitehead actually refers to God, in general, and to the primordial aspect of God, in particular, as the eros of the universe, as that which goads us onward toward our best selves and that helps us to satisfy our craving for happiness. No static maintenance of perfection is possible, either for God or for us, to the limited degree to which we are able to perfect ourselves. In this light, "eros" refers to the inarticulate desire to advance creatively. Without eros we would stagnate. This is precisely why Aristotle's glorification of static perfection, and the undue pervasive influence this notion has had on the history of classical theism, is such a dangerous doctrine in that it has the tendency to convince us, as if this were possible, that in some fashion everything is right and acceptable in the world right now (Whitehead [1933] 1967, 235, 253, 274–276).

One of the reasons living beings must advance is that they are constantly confronted with incompossible possibilities. To put this important point trivially, should I have toast or a bagel for breakfast? Assuming that I am not hungry enough to eat both, a decision has to be made. Even in the divine life there is the ongoing actualization of some possibilities but not others and one cannot opt out of the decision-making process altogether. That is, peace is not to be understood in terms of an absence of decision making or as an escape from the rigors of life. Rather, Whitehead sees it as the partial repose that comes from an understanding of tragedy (Whitehead [1933] 1967, 277, 286). In one of his most memorable passages, he puts the matter as follows: "At the heart of the nature of things, there are always the dream of youth and the harvest of tragedy. The Adventure of the Universe starts with the dream and reaps tragic Beauty. This is the secret of the union of Zest with Peace:—That the suffering attains its end in a Harmony of Harmonies. The immediate experience of this Final Fact, with its union of Youth and Tragedy, is the sense of Peace. In this way the World receives its persuasion towards such perfections as are possible for its diverse individual occasions" (Whitehead [1933] 1967, 296). The tragedy mentioned in this quotation is, in part, a result of finitude, but we should remembered that finitude also makes possible any determinate achievement, whether aesthetic or moral.

The development of Whitehead's concept of God continued until his last book, *Modes of Thought* ([1938] 1968). In it he is clear that one function of great philosophers (and literary writers) is to evoke a vivid feeling of what lies beyond words. This is somewhat different from an aggressive sort of apophaticism that merely points out that God is beyond words. Period. Granted, there is always a vague "beyond" that characterizes even the most articulate versions of the concept of God, but it is nonetheless crucial both to take language as far as it can go regarding the concept of God and to evoke a vivid feeling of what lies beyond. Both the inner lives of the minutest actual occasions of experience and the inner life of the very unity of the Universe (divine actuality) constitute this "beyond." Connectedness is the key to understanding the latter, such that abstraction away from connectedness always involves omission of some sort (Whitehead [1938] 1968, 5–9).

The checkered history of religion is the main reason many people want to put it aside, but Whitehead thinks that this makes no more sense than putting politics aside due to the checkered history of corruption in that field of human interest or putting aside music because most of what is heard on the radio is repetitious, exploitative, or insipid. The question regarding the proper relationship between the finite and the infinite will not go away merely because classical theists have problematically divinized the latter if not the former. Complete understanding, if such were possible, would involve a perfect grasp of both the finite and the infinite aspects of the dipolar divine life. In reality understanding is never characterized by a completed, static frame of mind. Instead it bears the character of an always incomplete process of grasping or prehending. In this regard it is important to notice both that any understanding of the finite includes implicit reference to the background of infinite possibility against which the finite appears, contra religious skepticism, and that any understanding of the infinite includes implicit reference to the finite, contra classical theism (Whitehead [1938] 1968, 19, 42–44).

Neoclassical or process theism involves a new (or a revitalized version of an old Platonic) view of divine perfection wherein the patterns of relationship between God and the world are quite different from those found in classical theism. Perfection is a concept that haunts human imagination; hence the concept cannot easily be put aside due to previous mischaracterizations of perfection as strictly permanent, unchanging, and unmoved by the world. Life and motion themselves can be perfect, as Whitehead sees things. Because of an unbalanced emphasis on infinity and permanence, in contrast to the positive values found in finitude and adaptability, classical theists have offered us a view of perfection in which God has less value than a squirrel. At least the mother squirrel can care for her young and respond to their plight. These baby squirrels, here and now, deserve the attention that only a being capable of finite goodness can give. God's importance, on the neoclassical or process view, is made manifest in the way that, among an infinite array of possibilities, some particular values are chosen over others (Whitehead [1938] 1968, 77–80, also 57, 69).

Although philosophers have long distinguished different modalities or ways of being real (expressed with phrases such as "what might be," "what must be," and "what must not be") they have tended to avoid the claim that these modalities coincide with temporal distinctions. Aristotle and Peirce are exceptions in this regard. The actual coincides with the past, the possible with the future, the necessary with the real at all times, and the impossible with the real at no times. Furthermore, the distinction between the physical and the mental also coincides with temporal distinctions. The former is the reception of the many crystallized feelings from the past, whereas the mental is a feeling of coming-to-be in response to this reception and in anticipation of the future (see Gilroy 2005).

Given the realization that in some sense human existence is transitory, the fact that classical theists have been dazzled by a view of timeless eternity is quite understandable. But there are other ways to be dazzled, in the absence of which we have not really thought through carefully enough the logic of perfection. How exactly to derive the present world of change from the utterly changeless world of classical theistic ultimate reality? The switch from classical theism to neoclassical theism is made easier as a result of the realization that the same philosopher (Plato) who emphasized the changeless, abstract world of mathematical, formal reality also emphasized the divine character of life and motion. Other great philosophers (for example, Descartes) counterintuitively held a concept of God as static that doomed his defense of the ontological argument from the start. His overconcentration on mathematics constituted a citadel for an indefensible concept of God. Purposefulness, hope, and energy all require a view of divine perfection as dynamic (Whitehead [1938] 1968, 81–83, 86–87, 97, 100–101).

God provides value for the world in addition to the value provided by us, but the divine value is ideal such that it also provides an aim for us when we are driven by the better angels of our nature. On a Whiteheadian view three values attach to each singular experience: (1) intrinsic value or value for self; (2) value for others; and (3) value for the Whole. That is, each occasion of experience has significance both for itself and for others, including for God. The dynamism involved in this generation of value is an indication of the fact that the conception of ultimate reality as a static fact makes no sense. At each moment we are deposited into a future that has never yet existed such that the idea of an isolated instant of time is an abstraction rather than anything anyone has ever actually experienced (Whitehead [1938] 1968, 102, 110, 119, 152).

The epilogue to Whitehead's *Modes of Thought* ([1938] 1968, 171–174) deals with the aims of philosophy, which are integrally connected to the subject matter of this book. If "philosophy" refers to the love of (in the sense of the dynamic search for) wisdom, then philosophy is an avocation that is denied to God as omniscient (as omniscience is understood in neoclassical or process theism). For a human being to be content with existing wisdom is to cease being a philosopher. In this regard, the very aims of philosophy are not unrelated to the aims of "mysticism," which Whitehead defines as direct insight into depths yet unspoken. The vector characters of both mysticism and philosophy (both of these involve movement toward that which is known only partially in the effort to asymptotically know even more) enable us to claim that philosophy is the attempt to rationalize mysticism, to intellectually coordinate the insights of the great mystics, and to develop novel verbal characterizations (for example, panentheism) and new conceptual schemes (for example, dipolar theism) so as to better articulate mystical prehension of divine actuality. Seen in this light, philosophy *is* mystical.

Bibliography

Adams, R. M. 1994. *Leibniz*. New York: Oxford University Press.

Al-Ghazzali. 1912. *Die Dogmatik al-Ghazzali's Nach dem II Buch seines Hauptwerkes*. Edited by Hans Bauer. Halle, Germany: Buchdruckerei des Waisenhauses.

Allen, E. L. 1951. *Freedom in God: A Guide to the Thought of Nicholas Berdyaev*. New York: Philosophical Library.

An-Na'im, Abdullahi Ahmed. 1990. *Toward an Islamic Reformation*. Syracuse, NY: Syracuse University Press.

Anselm, St. 1962. *Basic Writings*. Translated by S. N. Deane. LaSalle, IL: Open Court.

Aristotle. 1984. *The Complete Works of Aristotle*. 2 vols. Edited by Jonathan Barnes. Princeton, NJ: Princeton University Press.

Armstrong, Karen. 1993. *A History of God: The 4,000 Year Quest of Judaism, Christianity, and Islam*. New York: Ballantine Books.

———. 2006. *The Great Transformation: The Beginning of Our Religious Traditions*. New York: Knopf.

———. 2009. *The Case for God*. New York: Knopf.

Arnison, Nancy. 2012. "A Tragic Vision for Christianity: Aeschylus and Whitehead." Ph.D. dissertation. University of Chicago.

Artson, Bradley. 2013. *God of Becoming and Relationship*. Woodstock, VT: Jewish Lights Publishing.

Augustine, St. 1998. *Confessions*. Translated by Henry Chadwick. New York: Oxford University Press.

———. 2010. *On the Free Choice of the Will*. Translated by Peter King. New York: Cambridge University Press.

Barbour, Ian. 1990. *Religion in an Age of Science*. San Francisco: Harper and Row.

Barnes, Jonathan, ed. 1995. *The Cambridge Companion to Aristotle*. New York: Cambridge University Press.

———. 2000. *Aristotle*. New York: Oxford University Press.

Barthelemy-Madaule, Madeleine. 1963. *Bergson et Teilhard de Chardin*. Paris: Editions du Seuil.

Berdyaev, Nicholas. 1936. *The Meaning of History*. Translated by George Reavey. London: Centenary Press.

———. 1937. *The Destiny of Man*. Translated by Natalie Duddington. New York: Scribner's.

———. 1953. *Truth and Revelation*. Translated by R. M. French. London: Geoffrey Bles.

Bergson, Henri. 1911. *Creative Evolution*. Translated by Arthur Mitchell. New York: Henry Holt.

———. 1932. *Les Deux Sources de la Morale et de la Religion*. Paris: Presses Universitaires de France.

———. 1946. *The Creative Mind*. Translated by Mabelle Andison. New York: Philosophical Library.

———. 1977. *The Two Sources of Morality and Religion*. Translated by R. Ashley Audra and Cloudesley Brereton. Notre Dame, IN: University of Notre Dame Press.

Bixler, Julius. 1941. "Whitehead's Philosophy of Religion." In *The Philosophy of Alfred North Whitehead*. Edited by Paul Schilpp. LaSalle, IL: Open Court.

Boler, John. 1963. *Charles Peirce and Scholastic Realism*. Seattle: University of Washington Press.

Bowker, John. 2002. *God: A Brief History*. London: DK Publishing.

Bracken, Joseph. 2000. *Christianity and Process Thought*. Philadelphia, PA: Templeton Foundation Press.

Brown, Peter. 1967. *Augustine of Hippo*. Berkeley: University of California Press.

Buber, Martin. 1937. *I and Thou*. Translated by R. G. Smith. Edinburgh, UK: T. and T. Clark.

Burrell, David. 1986. *Knowing the Unknowable God: Ibn Sina, Maimonides, Aquinas*. Notre Dame, IN: University of Notre Dame Press.

Byrne, Peter. 2007. *Kant on God*. Burlington, VT: Ashgate.

Capetz, Paul. 2003. *God: A Brief History*. Minneapolis, MN: Fortress Press.

Case-Winters, Anna. 1990. *God's Power*. Louisville: Westminster John Knox Press.

Christ, Carol. 2003. *She Who Changes: Re-Imagining the Divine in the World*. New York: Palgrave Macmillan.

Clarke, Norris. 2009. *The Creative Retrieval of St. Thomas Aquinas*. New York: Fordham University Press.

Cobb, John. 1991. "Hartshorne's Importance for Theology." In *The Philosophy of Charles Hartshorne*. Edited by Lewis Hahn. LaSalle, IL: Open Court.

———. 1999. *Transforming Christianity and the World*. Maryknoll, NY: Orbis.

———. 2007. *A Christian Natural Theology: Based on the Thought of Alfred North Whitehead*. 2nd ed. Louisville, KY: Westminster John Knox Press.

Cobb, John, and Charles Birch. 1981. *The Liberation of Life*. New York: Cambridge University Press.

Cobb, John, and Herman Daly. 1994. *For the Common Good*. Boston: Beacon Press.

Cooper, Burton. 1974. *The Idea of God: A Whiteheadian Critique of St. Thomas Aquinas' Concept of God*. The Hague, Netherlands: Martinus Nijhoff.

Cory, David. 1932. *Faustus Socinus*. Boston: Beacon Press.

Cottingham, John. 1986. *Descartes*. New York: Blackwell.

Cottingham, John, ed. 1992. *The Cambridge Companion to Descartes*. New York: Cambridge University Press.

Cowell, Siôn. 2001. *The Teilhard Lexicon*. Brighton, UK: Sussex Academic Press.

Cunning, David. 2013. "Descartes on God and the Products of His Will." In *Models of God and Alternative Ultimate Realities*, edited by Jeanine Diller and Asa Kasher. New York: Springer.

Davaney, Sheila Greeve, ed. 1990. *Feminism and Process Thought*. New York: Edwin Mellen.

Davenport, John. 2013. "A New Existential Model of God: A Synthesis of Themes in Kierkegaard, Buber, Levinas, and Open Theism." In *Models of God and Alternative Ultimate Realities*, edited by Jeanine Diller and Asa Kasher. New York: Springer.

Davidson, Herbert. 2005. *Moses Maimonides*. New York: Oxford University Press.

Davies, Brian. 2011. *Thomas Aquinas on God and Evil*. New York: Oxford University Press.

Davies, Brian, and Brian Leftow, eds. 2004. *The Cambridge Companion to Anselm*. New York: Cambridge University Press.

Davies, Daniel. 2011. *Method and Metaphysics in Maimonides' Guide for the Perplexed*. New York: Oxford University Press.

Descartes, Rene. 1988. *Selected Philosophical Writings*. Translated by John Cottingham et al. New York: Cambridge University Press.

Despland, Michel. 1973. *Kant on History and Religion*. Montreal: McGill-Queen's University Press.

DiCenso, James. 2011. *Kant, Religion, and Politics*. New York: Cambridge University Press.

Diller, Jeanine, and Asa Kasher, eds. 2013. *Models of God and Alternative Ultimate Realities*. New York: Springer.

Dombrowski, Daniel. 1992. *St. John of the Cross*. Albany: State University of New York Press.

———. 1996. *Analytic Theism, Hartshorne, and the Concept of God*. Albany: State University of New York Press.

———. 2000. *Not Even a Sparrow Falls: The Philosophy of Stephen R. L. Clark*. East Lansing: Michigan State University Press.

———. 2004. *Divine Beauty: The Aesthetics of Charles Hartshorne*. Nashville, TN: Vanderbilt University Press.

——. 2005. *A Platonic Philosophy of Religion: A Process Perspective*. Albany: State University of New York Press.

——. 2006. *Rethinking the Ontological Argument: A Neoclassical Theistic Response*. New York: Cambridge University Press.

——. 2009. *Contemporary Athletics and Ancient Greek Ideals*. Chicago: University of Chicago Press.

——. 2011. *Rawlsian Explorations in Religion and Applied Philosophy*. University Park: Pennsylvania State University Press.

——. 2015. "Religion, Solitariness, and the Bloodlands." *American Journal of Theology & Philosophy* 36: 226–239.

——. Forthcoming. *From Mechanism to Organism: From Force to Persuasion*.

Dorff, Elliot. 2013. "Jewish Images of God." In *Models of God and Alternative Ultimate Realities*, edited by Jeanine Diller and Asa Kasher. New York: Springer.

Eisen, Robert. 1995. *Gersonides on Providence, Covenant, and the Chosen People*. Albany: State University of New York Press.

Emery, Gilles. 2010. *The Trinitarian Theology of St. Thomas Aquinas*. New York: Oxford University Press.

Enxing, Julia, and Klaus Muller, eds. 2012. *Perfect Changes: Die Religionsphilosophie Charles Hartshorne*. Regensburg, Germany: Verlag Friedrich Pustet.

Eslick, Leonard. 1953. "The Dyadic Character of Being in Plato." *Modern Schoolman* 31: 11–18.

Faber, Roland. 2008. *God as Poet of the World: Exploring Process Theologies*. Louisville, KY: Westminster John Knox Press.

Fechner, Gustav. 1922. *Zend Avesta*. Leipzig, Germany: Leopold Voss.

Field, Claud. 1909. *The Confessions of Al-Ghazzali*. London: J. Murray.

Fock, Otto. 1847. *Der Socinianismus*. Kiel, Germany: Carl Schroder.

Ford, Lewis, ed. 1973. *Two Process Philosophers: Hartshorne's Encounter with Whitehead*. Tallahassee, FL: American Academy of Religion.

Fretheim, Terrence. 1984. *The Suffering of God: An Old Testament Perspective*. Philadelphia, PA: Fortress Press.

Friedlander, Paul. 1958. *Plato*. Translated by Hans Meyerhoff. New York: Pantheon.

Gamwell, Franklin. 1990. *The Divine Good*. San Francisco, CA: Harper Collins.

Gelpi, Donald. 2001. *Peirce and Theology*. Lanham, MD: University Press of America.

Gerson, Lloyd, ed. 1996. *The Cambridge Companion to Plotinus*. New York: Cambridge University Press.

Gilroy, John. 2005. "Neuro Wine in Old Vessels: A Critique of D'Aquili and Newberg." *Process Studies Supplements* 8: 1–42.

Godlove, Terry. 2014. *Kant and the Meaning of Religion*. New York: Columbia University Press.

Grene, Marjorie. 1985. *Descartes*. Minneapolis: University of Minnesota Press.

——. 1991. *Descartes among the Scholastics*. Milwaukee, WI: Marquette University Press.

Griffel, Frank. 2009. *Al-Ghazzali's Philosophical Theology*. New York: Oxford University Press.

Griffin, David Ray. 1976. *God, Power, and Evil: A Process Theodicy*. Philadelphia, PA: Westminster Press.

——. 1991. *Evil Revisited*. Albany: State University of New York Press.

——. 2001. *Reenchantment without Supernaturalism: A Process Philosophy of Religion*. Ithaca, NY: Cornell University Press.

Griffin, Michael. 2012. *Leibniz, God, and Necessity*. New York: Cambridge University Press.

Guyer, Paul, ed. 1992. *The Cambridge Companion to Kant*. New York: Cambridge University Press.

Hadas-Lebel, Mireille. 2012. *Philo of Alexandria*. Leiden, The Netherlands: Brill.

Hartshorne, Charles. 1934. *The Philosophy and Psychology of Sensation*. Chicago: University of Chicago Press.

——. 1937. *Beyond Humanism*. Chicago: Willet, Clark.

——. 1941. *Man's Vision of God*. New York: Harper.

——. 1948. *The Divine Relativity*. New Haven, CT: Yale University Press.

——. 1953. *Reality as Social Process*. Boston: Beacon Press.

——. 1962. *The Logic of Perfection*. LaSalle, IL: Open Court.

——. 1965. *Anselm's Discovery*. LaSalle, IL: Open Court.

——. 1967. *A Natural Theology for Our Time*. LaSalle, IL: Open Court.

——. 1970. *Creative Synthesis and Philosophic Method*. LaSalle, IL: Open Court.

——. 1972. *Whitehead's Philosophy*. Lincoln: University of Nebraska Press.

——. 1976. *Aquinas to Whitehead*. Milwaukee, WI: Marquette University Press.

——. 1981. *Whitehead's View of Reality*. New York: Pilgrim Press.

——. 1983. *Insights and Oversights of Great Thinkers*. Albany: State University of New York Press.

——. 1984a. *Creativity in American Philosophy*. Albany: State University of New York Press.

——. 1984b. *Existence and Actuality*. Edited by John Cobb and Franklin Gamwell. Chicago: University of Chicago Press.

——. 1984c. *Omnipotence and Other Theological Mistakes*. Albany: State University of New York Press.

——. 1987. *Wisdom as Moderation*. Albany: State University of New York Press.

——. 1990. *The Darkness and the Light*. Albany: State University of New York Press.

———. 1991. *The Philosophy of Charles Hartshorne*. Edited by Lewis Hahn. LaSalle, IL: Open Court.

———. 2000. *Philosophers Speak of God*. Edited by William Reese. Amherst, NY: Humanity Books.

———. 2001. *Hartshorne and Brightman on God, Process, and Persons: The Correspondence, 1922–1945*. Edited by Randall Auxier and Mark Davies. Nashville, TN: Vanderbilt University Press.

———. 2011. *Creative Experiencing*. Edited by Donald Viney and Jincheol O. Albany: State University of New York Press.

Hasan, Ali. 2013. "Al-Ghazali and Ibn Rushd (Averroes) on Creation and the Divine Attributes." In *Models of God and Alternative Ultimate Realities*, edited by Jeanine Diller and Asa Kasher. New York: Springer.

Haught, John. 2000. *God after Darwin: A Theology of Evolution*. Boulder, CO: Westview Press.

Heidelberger, Michael. 2004. *Nature from Within: Georg Theodor Fechner and His Psychophysical Worldview*. Pittsburgh, PA: University of Pittsburgh Press.

Henning, Brian. 2005. *The Ethics of Creativity*. Pittsburgh, PA: University of Pittsburgh Press.

Heschel, Abraham. 1962. *The Prophets*. New York: Harper and Row.

Hume, David. 1980. *Dialogues Concerning Natural Religion*. Indianapolis, IN: Hackett.

Iqbal, Mohammed. 1934. *The Reconstruction of Religious Thought in Islam*. London: Oxford University Press.

———. 2013. *The Reconstruction of Religious Thought in Islam*. Translated by M. Saeed Sheikh. Stanford, CA: Stanford University Press.

Jalabert, Jacques. 1960. *Le Dieu de Leibniz*. Paris: Presses Universitaires de France.

John of the Cross, St. 1973. *The Collected Works of St. John of the Cross*. Translated by Kieran Kavanaugh and Otilio Rodriguez. Washington, DC: Institute of Carmelite Studies.

Jolley, Nicholas, ed. 1995. *The Cambridge Companion to Leibniz*. New York: Cambridge University Press.

Kant, Immanuel. 1921. *Zur Logik und Metaphysik*. Band 46. Leipzig, Germany: Verlag von Felix Meiner.

———. 1930. *Kritik der Reinen Vernunft nach der ersten und zweiten Original-Ausgabe*. Band 37a. Leipzig, Germany: Verlag von Felix Meiner.

———. 1933. *Prolegomena to Any Future Metaphysics*. Translated by Paul Carus. Chicago: Open Court.

———. 1960. *Religion within the Limits of Reason Alone*. Translated by Theodore Greene and Hoyt Hudson. New York: Harper.

———. 1978. *Lectures on Philosophical Theology*. Translated by Allen Wood and Gertrude Clark. Ithaca, NY: Cornell University Press.

———. 1996. *Kant's Critique of Practical Reason*. Translated by T. K. Abbott. Amherst, NY: Prometheus Books.

Kasser, Jeffrey. 2013. "Peirce on God, Reality, and Personality." In *Models of God and Alternative Ultimate Realities*, edited by Jeanine Diller and Asa Kasher. New York: Springer.

Keller, Catherine. 2003. *Face of the Deep: A Theology of Becoming*. New York: Routledge.

Kennedy, Robert. 2013. "Thomas Aquinas: Model of God." In *Models of God and Alternative Ultimate Realities*, edited by Jeanine Diller and Asa Kasher. New York: Springer.

Kenney, John. 2013a. "Augustine and Classical Theism." In *Models of God and Alternative Ultimate Realities*, edited by Jeanine Diller and Asa Kasher. New York: Springer.

———. 2013b. "The Platonic Monotheism of Plotinus." In *Models of God and Alternative Ultimate Realities*, edited by Jeanine Diller and Asa Kasher. New York: Springer.

Kerr, Fergus. 2009. *Thomas Aquinas*. New York: Oxford University Press.

Kolakowski, Leszek. 1985. *Bergson*. New York: Oxford University Press.

Kraut, Richard, ed. 1992. *The Cambridge Companion to Plato*. New York: Cambridge University Press.

Kretzmann, Norman, and Eleonore Stump, eds. 1993. *The Cambridge Companion to Aquinas*. New York: Cambridge University Press.

Lacey, A. R. 1989. *Bergson*. New York: Routledge.

Leibniz, Gottfried. 1931. *Discourse on Metaphysics, Correspondence with Arnauld, and Monadology*. Translated by George Montgomery. Chicago: Open Court.

———. 1949. *New Essays Concerning Human Understanding*. Translated by A. G. Langley. LaSalle, IL: Open Court.

———. 1952. *Theodicy*. Translated by E. M. Huggard. New Haven, CT: Yale University Press.

Levenson, Jon. 1988. *Creation and the Persistence of Evil: The Jewish Drama of Divine Omnipotence*. San Francisco, CA: Harper and Row.

Levi, Albert William. 1959. *Philosophy and the Modern World*. Bloomington: Indiana University Press.

Loomer, Bernard. 1976. "Two Conceptions of Power." *Process Studies* 6: 5–32.

———. 2013. "The Size of the Everlasting God." *Process Studies Supplements* 18: 1–45.

Lucas, George, ed. 1986. *Hegel and Whitehead*. Albany: State University of New York Press.

Maimonides. 1885. *The Guide of the Perplexed*. Translated by M. Friedlander. London: Ludgate Hill.

Malik, Hafeez. 1971. *Iqbal*. New York: Columbia University Press.

Malone-France, Derek. 2007. *Deep Empiricism: Kant, Whitehead, and the Necessity of Philosophical Theism*. Lanham, MD: Lexington.

Marion, Jean-Luc. 2007. *On the Ego and God: Further Cartesian Questions*. New York: Fordham University Press.

Maritain, Jacques. 1955. *Bergsonian Philosophy and Thomism*. Translated by Mabelle Andison. New York: Philosophical Library.

Mavrodes, George. 1970. *The Rationality of Belief in God*. Englewood Cliffs, NJ: Prentice-Hall.

May, Gerhard. 1994. *Creatio ex nihilo: The Doctrine of "Creation out of Nothing" in Early Christian Thought*. Translated by A. S. Worrall. Edinburgh, UK: Clark.

McFague, Sallie. 2008. *A New Climate for Theology*. Minneapolis, MN: Fortress Press.

Misak, C. J., ed. 2004. *The Cambridge Companion to Peirce*. New York: Cambridge University Press.

Mohr, Richard. 1985. *The Platonic Cosmology*. Leiden, The Netherlands: Brill.

———. 2005. *Gods and Forms in Plato*. Las Vegas, NV: Parmenides.

Moltmann, Jürgen. 1985. *God in Creation*. San Francisco, CA: Harper and Row.

More, P. E. 1921. *The Religion of Plato*. Princeton, NJ: Princeton University Press.

Mortley, Raoul. 2013. *Plotinus, Self, and World*. New York: Cambridge University Press.

Mullarkey, John. 2000. *Bergson and Philosophy*. Notre Dame, IN: Notre Dame University Press.

Neville, Robert. 1993. *Eternity and Time's Flow*. Albany: State University of New York Press.

Nuland, Sherwin. 2005. *Maimonides*. New York: Schocken.

Ochs, Peter. 1998. *Peirce, Pragmatism, and the Logic of Scripture*. New York: Cambridge University Press.

O'Connell, Robert. 1986. *Imagination and Metaphysics in St. Augustine*. Milwaukee, WI: Marquette University Press.

Olson, R. Michael. 2013. "Aristotle on God: Divine *Nous* as Unmoved." In *Models of God and Alternative Ultimate Realities*, edited by Jeanine Diller and Asa Kasher. New York: Springer.

Orange, Donna. 1984. *Peirce's Concept of God*. Lubbock, TX: Institute for Studies in Pragmatism.

Origen. 1929. *Origen: Selections from the Commentaries and Homilies*. Translated by R. B. Tollinton. New York: Macmillan.

Ottmann, Klaus. 2013. "Schelling's Fragile God." In *Models of God and Alternative Ultimate Realities*, edited by Jeanine Diller and Asa Kasher. New York: Springer.

Palmer, G. E. H., et al., eds. 1979–1995. *Philokalia*. 4 vols. London: Faber and Faber.

Palmquist, Stephen. 2013. "Kant's Moral Panentheism." In *Models of God and Alternative Ultimate Realities*, edited by Jeanine Diller and Asa Kasher. New York: Springer.

Peirce, Charles Sanders. 1935. *The Collected Papers of Charles Sanders Peirce.* 6 vols. Edited by Charles Hartshorne and Paul Weiss. Cambridge, MA: Harvard University Press.

Pfleiderer, Otto. 1886. *The Philosophy of Religion on the Basis of Its History.* 2 vols. Translated by A. Menzies. London: Williams and Norgate.

———. 1888. *Grundriss der Christlichen Glaubens und Sittenlehre.* Berlin: Druck and Verlag von Georg Reimer.

———. 1909. *The Development of Theology in Germany since Kant and Its Progress in Great Britain since 1825.* 3rd ed. Translated by J. Frederick Smith. London: Swan Sonnenschein.

Philo. 1929–1962. *Philo.* 10 vols. Translated by F. H. Colson, G. H. Whitaker, et al. Cambridge, MA: Harvard University Press.

Plantinga, Alvin. 1965. *The Ontological Argument from St. Anselm to Contemporary Philosophers.* Garden City, NY: Anchor Books.

Plato. 1901–1976. *Platonis Opera.* 5 vols. Edited by John Burnet. Oxford, UK: Clarendon Press.

———. 1989. *The Collected Dialogues of Plato.* Edited by Edith Hamilton and Huntington Cairns. Princeton, NJ: Princeton University Press.

Plotinus. 1966–1988. *The Enneads.* 6 vols. Translated by A. H. Armstrong. Cambridge, MA: Harvard University Press.

Plutarch. 1870. *Plutarch's Morals.* Translated by William Goodwin. Boston: Little, Brown.

Popper, Karl. 1972. *Objective Knowledge: An Evolutionary Approach.* Oxford, UK: Clarendon Press.

Pundt, Hermann. 1989. "A Prefatory Essay." In K. F. Schinkel. *Collection of Architectural Designs.* New York: Princeton Architectural Press.

Raposa, Michael. 1989. *Peirce's Philosophy of Religion.* Bloomington: Indiana University Press.

Raschid, M. S. 1981. *Iqbal's Concept of God.* Boston: Kegan Paul.

Rescher, Nicholas. 1979. *Leibniz.* Totowa, NJ: Rowman and Littlefield.

Reuther, Rosemary Radford. 1983. *Sexism and God-talk.* Boston: Beacon Press.

Rogers, Katherin. 2000. *Perfect Being Theology.* Edinburgh, UK: Edinburgh University Press.

———. 2013. "Anselm's Perfect God." In *Models of God and Alternative Ultimate Realities,* edited by Jeanine Diller and Asa Kasher. New York: Springer.

Royce, Josiah. 1908. *The Philosophy of Loyalty.* New York: Macmillan.

Russell, Bertrand. 1945. *A History of Western Philosophy.* New York: Simon and Schuster.

Ruzgar, Mustafa. 2008. "Islam and Process Theology." In *Handbook of Whiteheadian Process Thought,* edited by Michel Weber and Will Desmond, vol. 1. Frankfurt, Germany: Ontos Verlag.

Sandmel, Samuel. 1979. *Philo of Alexandria*. New York: Oxford University Press.

Schelling, Friedrich von. 1942. *The Ages of the World*. Translated by F. de Wolfe Bolman. New York: Columbia University Press.

———. 1978. *System of Transcendental Idealism*. Translated by Peter Heath. Charlottesville: University of Virginia Press.

———. 2000. *The Ages of the World*. Translated by Jason Wirth. Albany: State University of New York Press.

———. 2010. *Philosophy and Religion*. Translated by Klaus Ottmann. Putnam, CT: Spring Books.

Schenck, Kenneth. 2005. *A Brief Guide to Philo*. Louisville, KY: Westminster John Knox Press.

Schilpp, P. A., ed. 1967. *The Philosophy of Martin Buber*. LaSalle, IL: Open Court.

Schimmel, Annemarie. 1963. *Gabriel's Way: A Study into the Religious Ideas of Sir Mohammed Iqbal*. Leiden, The Netherlands: Brill.

Seeskin, Kenneth, ed. 2005. *The Cambridge Companion to Maimonides*. New York: Cambridge University Press.

———. 2013. "Strolling with Maimonides on the *Via Negativa*." In *Models of God and Alternative Ultimate Realities*, edited by Jeanine Diller and Asa Kasher. New York: Springer.

Sevilla, Pedro. 1970. *God as Person in the Writings of Martin Buber*. Manila, Philippines: Ateneo de Manila University.

Shields, George, ed. 2003. *Process and Analysis: Whitehead, Hartshorne, and the Analytic Tradition*. Albany: State University of New York Press.

Sia, Santiago, ed. 1990. *Charles Hartshorne's Concept of God*. Boston: Kluwer Academic.

Silverman, Eric. 2013. "Impassibility and Divine Love." In *Models of God and Alternative Ultimate Realities*, edited by Jeanine Diller and Asa Kasher. New York: Springer.

Singh, Iqbal. 1997. *The Ardent Pilgrim: An Introduction to the Life and Work of Mohammed Iqbal*. New York: Oxford University Press.

Solmsen, Friedrich. 1942. *Plato's Theology*. Ithaca, NY: Cornell University Press.

———. 1961. "Greek Philosophy and the Discovery of Nerves." *Museum Helveticum* 18: 150-167, 169-197.

Stern, Josef. 2013. *The Matter and Form of Maimonides' Guide*. Cambridge, MA: Harvard University Press.

Stump, Eleonore. 2005. *Aquinas*. New York: Routledge.

Stump, Eleonore, and Norman Kretzmann, eds. 2001. *The Cambridge Companion to Augustine*. New York: Cambridge University Press.

Suchocki, Marjorie. 2003. *Divinity and Diversity*. Nashville, TN: Abington Press.

Taylor, A. E. 1928. *A Commentary on Plato's Timaeus*. Oxford, UK: Clarendon Press.

Teilhard de Chardin, Pierre. 1960. *The Divine Milieu*. Translated by Bernard Wall. New York: Harper and Row.

——. 1961. *Hymn of the Universe*. Translated by Simon Bartholomew. New York: Harper and Row.

——. 1964. *The Future of Man*. Translated by Norman Denny. New York: Harper and Row.

——. 1968a. *Science and Christ*. Translated by Rene Hague. New York: Harper and Row.

——. 1968b. *Writings in Time of War*. Translated by Rene Hague. New York: Harper and Row.

——. 1969. *Human Energy*. Translated by J. M. Cohen. New York: Harcourt, Brace, and Jovanovich.

——. 1970. *Activation of Energy*. Translated by Rene Hague. New York: Harcourt, Brace, and Jovanovich.

——. 1971. *Christianity and Evolution*. Translated by Rene Hague. New York: Harcourt, Brace, and Jovanovich.

——. 1975. *Toward the Future*. Translated by Rene Hague. New York: Harcourt, Brace, and Jovanovich.

——. 1978. *The Heart of Matter*. Translated by Rene Hague. New York: Harcourt, Brace, and Jovanovich.

——. 1999. *The Human Phenomenon*. Translated by Sarah Appleton-Weber. Brighton, UK: Sussex Academic Press.

——. 2004. *The Divine Milieu*. Translated by Siôn Cowell. Brighton, UK: Sussex Academic Press.

Teresa of Avila, St. 1976. *The Collected Works of St. Teresa of Avila*. Translated by Kieran Kavanaugh and Otilio Rodriguez. Washington, DC: Institute for Carmelite Studies.

Thomas Aquinas, St. 1972. *Summa Theologiae*. Blackfriars ed. New York: McGraw-Hill.

Timpe, Kevin. 2013. "Introduction to Neo-Classical Theism." In *Models of God and Alternative Ultimate Realities*, edited by Jeanine Diller and Asa Kasher. New York: Springer.

Topping, Ryan. 2010. *St. Augustine*. New York: Continuum.

Torchia, N. J. 1999. *Creation ex nihilo and the Theology of St. Augustine*. New York: Lang.

Van Nieuwenhove, Rik. 2012. *An Introduction to Medieval Theology*. New York: Cambridge University Press.

Van Riel, Gerd. 2013. *Plato's Gods*. Burlington, VT: Ashgate.

Viney, Donald. 1985. *Charles Hartshorne and the Existence of God*. Albany: State University of New York Press.

——. 2013a. "Hartshorne's Dipolar Theism and the Mystery of God." In

Models of God and Alternative Ultimate Realities, edited by Jeanine Diller and Asa Kasher. New York: Springer.

———. 2013b. "Relativizing the Classical Tradition: Hartshorne's History of God." In *Models of God and Alternative Ultimate Realities*, edited by Jeanine Diller and Asa Kasher. New York: Springer.

Whitehead, Alfred North. [1920] 2004. *The Concept of Nature*. Mineola, NY: Dover.

———. 1922. *The Principle of Relativity*. Cambridge, U.K.: Cambridge University Press.

———. [1925] 1967. *Science and the Modern World*. New York: Free Press.

———. [1926] 1996. *Religion in the Making*. New York: Fordham University Press.

———. [1929] 1958. *The Function of Reason*. Boston: Beacon Press.

———. [1929] 1967. *The Aims of Education*. New York: Free Press.

———. [1929] 1978. *Process and Reality*. Corrected ed. Edited by David Ray Griffin and Donald Sherburne. New York: Free Press.

———. [1933] 1967. *Adventures of Ideas*. New York: Free Press.

———. [1938] 1968. *Modes of Thought*. New York: Free Press.

———. 1941. *The Philosophy of Alfred North Whitehead*. Edited by P. A. Schilpp. LaSalle, IL: Open Court.

———. [1954] 2001. *Dialogues of Alfred North Whitehead* Edited by Lucien Price. Jaffrey, NH: Nonpareil Books.

Whittemore, Robert. 1966. "Panentheism in Neo-Platonism." *Tulane Studies in Philosophy* 15: 47–70.

Wildman, Wesley. 2013. "Introduction to Negative Theology." In *Models of God and Alternative Ultimate Realities*, edited by Jeanine Diller and Asa Kasher. New York: Springer.

Williams, Daniel Day. 1968. *The Spirit and the Forms of Love*. New York: Harper and Row.

Williamson, Ronald. 1989. *Jews in the Hellenistic World*. New York: Cambridge University Press.

Wilson, Walter. 2010. *Philo of Alexandria*. Leiden, The Netherlands: Brill.

Wirth, Jason, ed. 2005. *Schelling Now*. Bloomington: Indiana University Press.

Wirth, Jason, and Patrick Burke, eds. 2013. *The Barbarian Principle: Merleau-Ponty, Schelling, and the Question of Nature*. Albany: State University of New York Press.

Wolfson, Harry. 1948. *Philo: Foundations of Religious Philosophy in Judaism, Christianity, and Islam*. Cambridge, MA: Harvard University Press.

Wood, Allen. 1978. *Kant's Rational Theology*. Ithaca, NY: Cornell University Press.

Wood, Robert. 1969. *Martin Buber's Ontology*. Evanston, IL: Northwestern University Press.

Wright, Robert. 2009. *The Evolution of God*. New York: Little, Brown.

Index

Made in the USA
Middletown, DE
03 November 2021

51610155R00168